A Stone Bridge North

Also by Kate Maloy

Birth or Abortion: Private Struggles in a Political World

A Stone Bridge North

Reflections in a New Life

Kate Maloy

COUNTERPOINT

WASHINGTON, D.C.

AUTHOR'S NOTE
I have used fictitious names for a few of the people mentioned in this book,
either because the circumstances I recount are sensitive or because the people
themselves prefer not to see their real names in print.

Library of Congress Cataloging-in-Publication Data
Maloy, Kate, 1944–
A stone bridge North : reflections in a new life / Kate Maloy.
p. cm.
ISBN 1-58243-145-0 (alk. paper)
1. Maloy, Kate, 1944– . 2. Country life—Vermont.
3. Quakers—Vermont—Biography. 4. Vermont—Biography. I. Title.
CT275.M4528 A3 2002
974.3'043'092—dc21   2001047228

Jacket and text design by David Bullen

Printed in the United States of America on acid-free paper that
meets the American National Standards Institute z39-48 Standard.

COUNTERPOINT
P.O. Box 65793
Washington, D.C. 20035-5793

Counterpoint is a member of the Perseus Books Group

10 9 8 7 6 5 4 3 2 1

This book is for Alan and Adam

Nothing is sudden. . . . Just as the earth invisibly prepares its cataclysms, so history is the gradual instant.

Anne Michaels, Fugitive Pieces

Prologue

For many years before the events in this book began to unfold, I lived a straight-edged life, a cubist arrangement of familiar rectangles — office, computer screen, paycheck, city blocks, mortgage coupons, calendar pages, television screen. These confined me more than I knew. Most confining of all, for most of those years, was the four-square house I occupied like a resentful ghost through half my marriage.

Then came a series of unforeseen changes, and now I live amid the meandering, irregular shapes of nature — rivers, woods, mountains, and the back roads that follow their contours. My house has more odd angles than right ones, and I share it with my surprising soul mate and my teenage son. The center of the nearest village has no blocks at all, just a town hall, fire station, store, post office, and church. The state capital, six miles south of us, has only two major downtown streets. I have no mortgage and no nine-to-five schedule. I am no longer a ghost in my life.

My personal history, like anyone's, and like the grander course of human generation and planetary time, has brought many of the moments that the Canadian writer Ann Michaels calls "gradual instants" — changes and turning points that may seem sudden but are long in the making and variable in effect. Some such instants in my life have been deliberate, others seemingly haphazard; some indelible, others readily forgotten. I have paid attention to them the way most of us do, trying to sort out right actions from wrong ones, trying to understand my nature and use my strengths to good purpose. I knew the kind of person I was — open but with areas of inviolate privacy; fond of company if I could bank sociability with solitude; capable of great love and joy but susceptible to the blues; and always in search of expression — my own through writing, gardening, drawing, cooking, conversation, and contemplation, and others' through reading, watching, and listening.

What I didn't know were two things I have learned in writing this book — how fearful I was and how near at hand was the antidote to fear.

A few people have told me that my actions in recent years have been hazardous and ill-considered, yet it is the life I left behind that looks dangerous to me — my careful, right-angled, urban existence. For reasons that will become clear, my fear was legitimate; it was simply misplaced. I feared divorce when I should have feared the spiritual and emotional void of a marriage beyond saving. I feared financial insecurity when I should have feared the dehumanizing atmosphere of the job I endured for a decade. I feared the disapproval of some old friends when I should have feared assumptions that framed the friendships.

I failed to recognize the real hazards in my life because I had dressed them up in garments of responsibility, necessity, and caring. Then came miracles, both subtle and dramatic, in a ragged, joyous parade. I can see now that I recognized and embraced each miracle out of faith, yet it was a faith I had always doubted, a faith whose depths I did not suspect. As it has grown stronger through the events I have chronicled, faith — which looks to me like love's identical twin — has proved to be the antifear serum that was there all along. It has pushed out all the edges of my life, giving me a much more expansive territory to explore.

A Stone Bridge North tells of miracles found and fears allayed. It is a record of my reconfigured family's first year in the woods of central Vermont, an account of our move, our challenges, and the joys of being in this steep, wild, rocky place — a new state and a new state of being. Because gradual instants come only out of everything that has gone before them, the book is also a search for the first beginnings of my life's wholesale transformation. I did not understand this when I started writing. I thought I was just keeping track. Instead I learned that all the elements connect; my life makes sense; it has all along had pattern and purpose. The accidents, coincidences, random events, and haphazard moments contribute as much to the overall design as the deliberate choices I've made — sometimes more.

As I wrote *A Stone Bridge North*, I ranged over whatever subjects arose in my mind: love, God, friendship, family, motherhood, nature, politics, diversity, risk, violence, power, language, silence, imagination. For a while, I could not see the defining connection in this big array — I did not see that my doubting faith was what drew the most important strands together. I considered my faith weak because I questioned it, because it fled when I tried to see it straight on, because I simply forgot about it as often as I searched for it. I did not realize that doubt is inevitable in faith because faith, by its nature, is elusive. It grows strong through repeated cycles of knowing and not knowing, experiencing mysteries directly and then questioning the experience. I knew this book would be about miracles, but I did not know that writing it would enrich my knowledge and experience of faith. I simply set down what I thought, remembered, and did. I was often startled by what I wrote. I did not fully realize what I believe, or why I believe it, until I saw words, phrases, and the spaces between them appear before me as if from some place below or beyond my mind.

The more I wrote, answering whatever was uppermost, the more frequently the exercise felt like looking through a book of Magic Eye images — those prismatic, seemingly abstract patterns of shapes and colors that you *know* will resolve into readable pictures if only you can relax your eyes, if only you can focus for distance while studying the close-up page. Now and then, as I peered at my past and present experience, I caught sudden, revelatory sight of sense. The glimpses came most often when I could look far and near at once, when I could see myself and my personal concerns afloat with all humanity on a deep, historic sea of enterprise and seeking.

It took time for my eyes to find that dual focus. It still does. Every time it happens, though, the shift from an abstract to a readable form is instantaneous—a sudden recognition, gradually achieved. No matter how long the transformation takes, once it happens, it is total. It is also elusive, like faith itself. If I look away for a moment, the hard-won clarity can dissolve, no matter how sharp it might remain in memory.

Writing this book thus formed and informed my faith again and again. Questions that had dogged me—questions about myself as well as bigger ones about good and evil, life, spirit—opened up, becoming clear if only for a moment. This did not happen every time I sat down to work on this book, just now and then, amid anecdotes and descriptions, during occasional digressions, and after lengthy speculation. The ordinary events described are the stuff of life, and life goes on even as we are trying to understand it. The lofty and mundane, the celebratory and dispirited all prepare us for the gradual instant, ready us for the revelations that evolve from our small, daily acts.

When, by degrees, the act of writing revealed sense and purpose where I had been mystified, the moment of clarity came with seismic surprise; it shook me like the voice of God or a view through God's eye. It certainly *felt* like sudden, direct contact with some other plane, some zone in which all fear is permanently displaced by love and liberation— and it seems to me that each intuition of this realm coincided with moments when my personal fears were displaced by thankfulness and joy. These feelings and insights came suddenly and blessedly, like a swooping rescue, a helicopter dangling a lifeline at the lip of the falls.

This is how the changes in my life have felt—like a rescue, but one that brings a message from the rescuer. Picture not brandy but some ancient text inside the cask of the life-saving St. Bernard. This text explains that gifts can arrive like manna, unlooked for and unearned; but then they need to be honored.

A Stone Bridge North is my effort to honor the abundant gifts that have brought me a new partner, a new home, and a new view of both my own life and the human saga of which it is a small but inseparable part. By necessity, the book explores very personal questions. I have sometimes felt uneasy about putting these before the eyes of strangers, and even more before the eyes of friends and family. But the personal is where we discover our relationship to eternal forces, and this process of discovery is the heart of the story I am impelled to tell. Just as the smallest details of our lives prepare the gradual instant that can show us our purpose or enlighten our minds, I think an individual life—a tiny detail of the grander scheme—can offer glimpses of the overall design to any who care to look.

The separateness of human lives now feels illusory to me at nearly every level from the cellular to the cosmic. We all share the same DNA structure and, given the growing body of evidence indicating a single common ancestor, some of the same ancient genes. We are all particles of the original light and strands in the history of being. Every single one of our lives weaves tightly into the pattern of this history—this real history, this complete human story played out in kitchens, bedrooms, gutters, trenches, barns, fields, schools, factories, hospitals, and playgrounds—not the selective, didactic history interpreted by scholars and later revised by their own students.

The specific and minute can illuminate the larger humanity that we all share, and I offer this account in the hope that certain particulars of my commonplace life, especially those that have resolved into Magic Eye clarity, will become for others like small windows on the human condition, narrow peepholes through which a larger vista can be seen. Any life could offer the same to any other. We can all recognize ourselves in each other if we get close enough.

None of this is to say that I have everything figured out. To the contrary, I succumb to anxiety, doubt my perceptions, feel faith slip away, and fall into slumps, confusion, and fear—still. My eyes can hold the readable image only for a moment. But I presume, in my own muddled humanity, to believe my life can connect with other lives, if only because I myself have been most profoundly moved and taught by the words of strangers who have written down their stories, ideas, and intimate struggles. All writing is personal, all lessons universal. The lesson I cherish most is that faith works; it transforms a life that gives it even the smallest bit of room in which to move things around.

AUTUMN

Without our effort, grace moved us forward.

Una Spenser, in the novel *Ahab's Wife*, by Sena Jeter Naslund

September

Home

This story opens sometime after the beginning, because I can't pinpoint its beginning. I choose to start it at the autumnal equinox, on the day in which one fleeting, annual instant hangs in perfect balance between waning light and gathering darkness. Today is the first day of autumn, and I am back in northern New England, where the summer days are longer and the nights cooler than elsewhere, and this season produces reds, golds, yellows, purples, russets, and oranges that pulse against the dark evergreens among them. The foliage is just now catching fire across the upper hillsides; the molten colors flow slowly down into the valleys, distracting us from the cold to come and brightening our slide into the darkest time of the year. The light, which somehow never shows itself in postcards of New England in the fall, is an element unto itself, the essential source of brilliance and clarity — which are qualities of sound as well as color, and this light vibrates the air like a bell struck just out of earshot.

This is not where I was born, nor even where I have lived except for a dozen formative years in my youth. It is simply where I belong, where I first felt the sense of place that I never found elsewhere in the twenty-eight years I was away. I lived in San Francisco, Palo Alto, and Pittsburgh in that time. Two marriages bracket those years. The end of the first one—begun at nineteen, in ruins by twenty-five—drove me from the North Country late in 1970. The end of the second, by miraculous indirection, has brought me back. I have held numerous jobs, had a few small publishing successes, and been involved with various communities in various ways, but I have never settled until now. Now I am at home in the Green Mountains, on ten rocky, wooded acres north of Montpelier, Vermont. The exile years are a long story, the journey back a better one, the being here a completely satisfying denouement.

The members of my northwoods household, in the order they entered my life, are—at the time of this writing—Adam, my thirteen-year-old son; Topper, our black and white (Holstein) cat; Alan, my soul mate; Emmylou, the scrappy little calico Alan found under the deck he built on our house in Pittsburgh; and Annie and Hank, two retriever-mix puppies, brother and sister. At night I take the dogs out to the clearing in front of our house. I look away from the lights for a while and wait for my pupils to grow large enough to perceive the stars. The Milky Way, which arcs like a shining fog right over the rise where I stand, runs more or less north and south, like our numerous rock ledges, the edges of our woods, and the river far below. So many stars. You forget, living in cities, that they are even there.

I call to Annie and Hank and sit down on a rock outcropping at a right angle to the house. I look back into the light, into our rooms, with my starry-eyed perspective still fresh. I see Adam and Alan moving about, one or the other sitting on the couch, opening cupboards, answering the phone, or getting a drink of water. Alan, whom I married a few weeks ago, has lived with us for sixteen months. He and Adam are still forging their relationship, and I see their movements inside as part of a dance— formal as a minuet, clownish as a hoe-down, and sometimes wary, like boxers circling. Except for far-away friends and family, that house, this clearing, those stars, and the state of Vermont contain everything I ever wanted. I am all the more fortunate because I have come to realize this in such a fundamental way.

The puppies like it that I am on the ground, at their level, and they bound over to slurp my face and muddy me with their paws. They have been wading in the narrow drainage ditch that winds to the bottom of the clearing. The pups are untrained, unmanageable, irresistible — and growing by the minute. I have bought a book by the Monks of New Skete — brothers in a monastery in upstate New York who raise and train German shepherds — that is full of compassionate principles for turning our rowdy dogs into happy, obedient members of a pack, with the three of us humans as interchangeable alphas. The book tells us how to make our dogs confident, eager to please, sociable, and polite, all by working with their nature and seeing the world through their ancient, infant, wolfish eyes.

If my parents and teachers and that whole World War II generation of adults had shared the perspective of the Monks of New Skete, even more than that of Benjamin Spock, my commonplace tale might contain less sound and long-spent fury. But that is neither here nor there. If I had not had my particular parents and teachers, I never would have come to this part in my tale at all, for my tale would have been altogether different and I someone else. I am as much my parents, and their parents, as my dogs, deep down, are wolves. To imagine my parents different is to imagine myself out of existence.

The same is true of my son, Adam. Though my overlong marriage to his father was in the end a painful mismatch, Adam is Adam, the specific child of his parents, and I cannot imagine him otherwise. All his life I have told him he is just the right kid for me.

We all are, and we all produce, the outcomes of a thousand thousand generations — we descend from primitive organisms, early primates, and the first humans through millions of others with whom we most likely share an ancient forebear. That alone should cause us to regard ourselves and others with awe. Instead, we tend to look at one or two generations' sins and errors, and we nitpick. We miss the big picture — the possibility of a purpose to each minuscule, momentary life within these eons — and with it our chance for joy, a deep eternal current that runs far beneath the surface calms or eddies we call happiness or sorrow.

Loss and Gain

The cold is coming. Our first frost will descend any night now. That will put an end to the cluster flies and mosquitoes, at least for a while. We had a couple of warm, muggy days last week, which hatched a pestilence of flies — we killed hundreds with the torn pink flyswatter left by Harriet and Sandra, the former owners of our house. According to my oldest friend, Sarah, who lives in town, these last swarms of flies help you resign yourself to winter, even making you wish acutely for a killing frost. Winter itself, for Sarah's husband, Joe, "is what keeps the flat-landers out." Imagine Vermont without its severe six-month winter, and you can imagine the whole small state packed end to end with develop-ment and urban sprawl — which even so is spreading like an oil slick at the edges of Burlington, the state's largest city, whose population is only about 40,000. Areas of great natural beauty tend to attract hordes who then destroy the very thing that brought them. A harsh climate is no guarantee that that won't happen, but it does help.

The cold may be a boon, but its onset also represents a loss, of free-dom if nothing else: The freedom to walk outside without layering on more clothes. The freedom to send the puppies out for hours, to run off their seemingly limitless energy. The freedom from wood — stacking it, bringing it in, and setting it afire in the heat-seeking rituals we have already begun to observe on these chilly mornings. The freedom of space — the three of us are going to be crowded indoors this winter. This house is too small by one bathroom, a proper office, many square feet of boy-room, and a bigger living space. We can't begin adding on until the cold spends itself and the weather turns warm again, and so the three of us and our four animals face at least seven months of intimate physical confinement.

The seasons change, life changes, and we are always dealing with loss, even as we welcome gains and surprises. Accepting them all can boost our powers in ways we could never deliberately design. This is one of life's best ironies. Even better is how little we control the process — how we gain more by trying less.

Writing is a good example. It has always exacted a price from me, a steep entrance fee made up of struggle and insecurity. I have often had to force it or give up — and surrender has usually proved the wiser of those two courses. I meant to write from the moment we arrived in Vermont, in mid-June, to embark upon a life I would never have thought possible just two years ago. I wanted to keep a steady record from the beginning, and I chafed at my failure to do so. I made a few lame journal entries from time to time, none of which captured in the least this remarkable relocation or the cycles of change that have led to it.

Alan and I did accomplish a lot in our first months here. He built himself a carpentry workshop at the far end of the rise in our clearing. I unpacked and organized as best I could in our new, smaller space. Together we bought another house, in Montpelier, and spent all of August painting, papering, repairing, and carpeting so we could rent it by the first of September. We took care of countless not-so-small details — a water filtration system and new wiring at our own house; vehicle registrations, insurance, and driver's licenses; health insurance; voter registration; and the endless clearing of brush and weeds, including the denuding of a big rocky hillside now covered with rotting straw and black plastic sheeting. The object is to kill undesirable vegetation — wild blackberry, bindweed, comfrey, and a hundred other invasive, tenacious plants I can't identify — in preparation for landscaping in the spring. I took on a freelance writing assignment, too, but I did not count that as "real" writing.

The only writing that counted, in my mind, was the kind that could help me understand the changes in my life. I found this an elusive enterprise, and I grew frustrated. I began taking long morning walks over dramatic terrain, willing myself to exhale impatience, to focus on the sweeping views and the sounds of rushing streams and rivers, to greet the horses, sheep, and dogs I encountered, to name the wildflowers beside the road. I needed to trust that something in me would stir when the time was right. I needed to relax, get to know my new condition and surroundings, and accept the priorities that asserted themselves.

Loss led to unforeseen gain, as it often does. We had to have Alan's failing basset hound, Lucy, put down in August. Thirteen-year-old Lucy — a charming sneak, a friend to all warm-blooded creatures, a vocal wizard who could sound like geese, donkeys, rusty hinges, or dying swans — was finally the victim of dementia, cataracts, cancer, and arthritis. She was incontinent. She had open sores on her body that would not heal. She had a malignant mass near her ribs, and her frequent cough indicated that her lungs were affected. Alan and I made the sad decision, took her to the vet, and sobbed as she put her head down on her paws and gave us murderers her last adoring look.

I thought it would be months before Alan could even consider having another dog around, but within a week he had circled an ad in the paper for retriever puppies — they turned out to be mostly yellow Lab but with hints of Chesapeake Bay retriever in their narrow muzzles and the coarse curls on their backs and shoulders. We figured on one and ended up with two, unable to decide between the female and the male. (One of the many things I love about Alan is an apparent slowness in his style that somehow disguises how quickly he thinks and acts. He doesn't talk much, and when he does his speech is slow, his voice low and rumbling. He never moves faster than a relaxed amble, but if he were a boat he would leave a high, whitewater wake. He accomplishes more, faster, than anyone I have ever known, but you can never quite catch him doing it. It feels as if you just turn around and find it done and marvel at the skill and artistry in the finished thing, which invariably has an organic quality, as if he had not built it so much as helped it to grow.)

Anyway, it was Annie and Hank who opened the gate for me. Taking them out at night, looking at the near and distant lights of the house and stars, feeling part of that big picture while safely ensconced in my small family, house, and personal concerns, I have found my way back to expression, which must always, if it is going to teach you anything new, be about much more than yourself and your own small life. It is the more-than-self part that comes from recognizing instead of insisting on the right moment, the one you are somehow led to through a necessary fallowness and frustration, the one that is sparked by the distant lights as much as the ones close by.

Not Home—Yet

This house, though it enfolds the life I have wanted for so long, doesn't yet feel like our own. We bought it from two women in their thirties who, during their five years here, cleared away some trees and built a two-story addition onto the original small cottage, an A-frame box about fourteen by sixteen feet with a loft above and a second room stuck on at a downstairs corner. They also erected a tiny one-room cabin about two hundred feet from the house, and they made a sketchy start on a perennial garden. We haven't yet put our mark on the house. It remains exactly as Harriet and Sandra left it, right down to the kitchen shelves that Sandra, the builder, never properly affixed to the walls.

I discovered Sandra's lapse when I was unpacking boxes in the kitchen and, in reaching for a high corner shelf by the sink, held onto a lower one for a little extra lift. The lower one tilted forward, spilling a glass that shattered at my feet. The shelves in the laundry room are similarly tilty—more evidence that Sandra and Harriet took off with the place undone, eager to be in Maine, where the ocean and their best friends are. The not-quite-finished addition holds a kitchen, bath, laundry area, and tiny living room downstairs and our large bedroom upstairs. All of these rooms lack major or minor touches, like cupboard and closet doors, drawers in the kitchen, trim around some of the windows. We knew the house was incomplete, though. It was one reason we bought it, so we could build onto the work Sandra had begun—beautiful work, in spite of missing details.

We found the house in March, closed on it in May, and moved here from Pittsburgh in mid-June, just before the summer solstice. Adam stayed behind with his father and joined us a short time later.

In one sense, that move made itself, after events that had led to it had made themselves. It all happened as if orchestrated. Losses and gains in my life, and others in Alan's life, somehow brought us together as if that had been their sole purpose. That same smooth flow carried us lightly through all the preliminaries to moving. On our one and only house-scouting trip, as we crossed into Vermont from New York State, a full moon emerged from the clouds just as the Stan Getz CD on the truck's player started in on "Moonlight in Vermont." That stagy prologue set us up perfectly, and within the next two days we had found this place and put our earnest money down on the spot.

Still, the physical work of the move was exhausting. We packed everything ourselves, hired a truck and some hefty professionals to load it, and then made two trips to Vermont from Pittsburgh. On the first one, we drove the rattlebang rental truck, stuffed so tight you couldn't have slid a ticket stub into the load. It overheated on hills and set up a clangor of warning bells as it labored along. It did only slightly better empty, on the trip back to Pittsburgh. Once there, we turned the truck in, went back to our echoing house, and stayed for two nights and a day so we could load our own truck with the last items and leave for good, towing our car, which held Lucy on a blanket and the two cats in cages.

As Alan and I pulled away from the neat, tree-lined block on which we had lived for our first year together, I waved a private good-bye to Regent Square, the quiet section of Pittsburgh where that block was located. It is an area bounded on two sides by the woods and green meadows of Frick Park and on the other two by an eight-lane highway and a small commercial area with a bakery, dry cleaner, jeweler, florist, and our favorite tavern — an easy walk from home when no one wanted to cook.

I also said a silent farewell to the rest of the pretty American city in which I had lived for eighteen years. Pittsburgh has long since outlived its sooty reputation. It is clean, safe — as cities go — generally friendly, and more midwestern than eastern in its atmosphere and values. I had made numerous friends there, had declared myself a Quaker there after years of attending meetings around the country, had grown as a writer even in an unpleasant job, had ridden the pitching waves of a long marital struggle — and most of all had borne my son and experienced the greatest joy of my life. I knew it was time to leave, but the leaving was hard.

Together, Alan and I waved good-bye to our immaculate Arts and Crafts house, with its box beams, oak floors, leaded-glass windows, deep front porch, and brand-new kitchen. Alan had done a lot of work on that house in the year he lived there with me. He added a deck in the back and a guest room and bath in the basement. He built that new kitchen after gutting and enlarging the space where the old one had been. That job made a god-awful mess. He had never worked on a brick house before, let alone one in an industrial city, and although he could predict dust and rubble, he wasn't prepared for the clouds of coal dust that choked the whole first floor when he knocked out a section of exterior wall. When he was done, though, the new room sat quietly next to the old ones as if it had always been there. The simple wallpaper and white routed cupboards did not scream "update" but instead issued a mellow invitation.

When we left that house, I mourned especially its ninety-year-old, well-tended charm and all that it had meant to me. It was the first house I had ever bought by myself, a house I had chosen because you could see from the front bay windows all the way out through the tall dining room windows to the backyard. That house stood for my liberation from a sad marriage past saving. From the street, the house glowed at night, looking Old Worldish and warm. I loved having friends come for dinner, especially when the weather was mild and we could sit on the porch swing, well above the sidewalk in front, surrounded by the dark-green sea that was the top of the broad yew hedge. I loved how quickly the furnishings, lighting, prints, drawings, and plants came together after I moved in with Adam. People said it looked as if we had been there forever, after just a few weeks. Although Adam and I lived in that house together for only a year before Alan unexpectedly came along, it witnessed the full measure of my joy in my release. Eventually, in everything Alan brought and built there, it also reflected the surprise and deeper joy of finding a true love at fifty-two.

After leaving that house, I wasn't sure, during our first few days in Vermont, that I could bear the contrast. Sarah had hired some wiry teenagers to unload the rental truck, and they had to bring everything in through the rain. No choice — the truck had to be emptied that day, and that day it rained nonstop. All the furniture and boxes, no matter how big, heavy, fragile, or precious, had to be wrestled out of the truck bed, over a muddy hump, down a narrow wooden staircase, across a few feet of grass and mud, up four more wooden steps, and in through the mud-room door, which has only a thirty-inch opening. Muddy footprints spread like a fast brown mold over all the floors. Wooden furniture needed a wipe-down as soon as it came through the too-small entrance. The piano, Adam's pretty walnut spinet, survived against my expectations, but it still bears a watery pockmark here and there. It was horribly out of tune.

We were confined for several days to the old cottage room and what is now Adam's room, the grittiest, dampest, roughest parts of the house, an odd mix of tolerable inside and tarpaper shack outside — more than half of this unfinished house has no siding. Enormous spiders resented our intrusion. I still imagine their bodies as mouse-sized, their legs two inches long. They moved fast. They appeared from nowhere, hairy and menacing, and then they stood there, defiant. Or so it seemed to me. Alan is not plagued by overreaction. His imagination is not hair-trigger, like mine, and I have never seen him panic. When I became squeamish and wrought up about the spiders, he said, exasperated, "Just step on them." I broke down and cried, from fatigue and a bottomless aversion to guts over the entire sole of my shoe, and said, "I can't, you have to." So he did, rolling his eyes, oblivious to the yellow, puddingy mess he made. What was one more mess, when we already had so many of them?

All I could see for days were cobwebs, dust, mud, grit, and insects, the latter in such variety it seemed we had entered a horror-movie set. Sarah said the spiders would move out as soon as they realized we were there to stay. She was pretty much right. Only one or two hung on, like old folks refusing to budge from a bungalow smack in the way of freeway construction. I grudgingly respected the spiders' tenacity, and then, feeling stupidly dainty — not to mention guilty for pronouncing the death sentence — called Alan to stomp them.

Little by little, with a slowness less deceptive than Alan's, things came together, not the way they had in the Pittsburgh house, but without much order or proportion. Our overflow was stashed every which way in a rented storage shed on the other side of town — table saws, band saws, and tools amid bicycles, sleds, lamps, and boxes of books and winter clothing. The loft was piled high with more boxes, extra furniture, futon mattresses, and luggage. Computer towers, keyboards, monitors, and file cabinets filled up the cottage room, now our temporary office. There was no place to sit except the couch, surrounded by leaning towers of boxes.

The water from our well was as hard and rusty as an old nail. It stained the toilet bowl and within a month had killed the two-year-old washing machine we had bought with the house, finally packing its hoses so full of particulate matter that it could never be cleaned. Its last couple of loads came out dirtier than they went in. We had a filtration system put in after testing confirmed how desperately we needed one. It was sold to us by a certain kind of typical Vermonter, an actor-musician with a day job. We knew, before we came here, that Vermont has more artists, writers, crafters, and performers per capita than any other state. This performer fixed the water problem, and now we have soft, sweet water in abundance, as long as the power doesn't go out, taking the pump with it.

Eventually, we had the services we needed and a place to put everything we had to lay our hands on. Adam arrived from his father's house a week or two after we had moved in, and he assured me that he liked "our secluded little house." The animals, Topper, Emmylou, and Lucy, were blissed out. Alan, who had been living in the rural Northwest, just outside Cave Junction, Oregon, when we met, was in his element. He had escaped from his year of city life as if from ten years in prison. He couldn't leave Pittsburgh fast enough.

I finally looked up from the rough, unfinished, cobwebby areas of our new life and saw the mountains and sky and remembered why I had longed to be here, ever since I had first left New England. The North Country has always felt like home — it has always spoken to me directly of wildness and stunning beauty, of human lives that move with the cycles of nature and come to terms with the elements. I could envision our hilly clearing with perennials, flowering shrubs, and fruit trees planted and thriving. I could see the view we will have once a local logger opens a line of sight to the west-southwest. I could picture Alan's shop, just then marked out with posts and string, completed at the end of the rise. I could imagine the new spaces he will build onto Sandra's excellent beginning, everything growing and branching from what is already here.

One day, a few weeks after we had moved in, I looked at Alan in surprise and said, "I don't miss the house in Pittsburgh. I haven't missed it even once."

"There were a few days there when I wasn't sure," he said, putting his arm around me, looking relieved.

Alan had nothing against Pittsburgh in particular. In fact he loved its hills and parks, its varied architecture, and especially its funky, ungentrified market district, with produce stands, bakeries, coffee roasters, two marvelous fish stores, and "Penn Mac"—the Pennsylvania Macaroni Company—where you could buy bulk cheeses, dense and flavorful peasant breads, olives, nuts, pasta, and every kind of Italian seasoning or ingredient in a frantic but invariably cheerful atmosphere. Still, Alan just doesn't like cities. He prefers a human scale and a human touch in all his comings and goings, not just in trips to Penn Mac.

What's more, he had come to Pittsburgh from Oregon, a place he truly loved, in order for us to be together. From the beginning, we agreed we would move away from the city as soon as we could. We chose Vermont after exploring other areas, from western North Carolina to Virginia and Maine. Among many other factors was the need for Adam to live only a short flight away from his father. That necessity served my personal preference. I wanted to stay in the East, wanted to be on the same side of the Mississippi as my extended family and most of my friends, wanted to come back to New England.

I had meant to return to New England almost from the time I first left, in 1970, after the breakup of my first marriage, to a man named Ned, whom I had met in college. Instead, after an aimless winter in Boston, I accepted a friend's offer of a ride to California, and I stayed out West for eight restless years. When I left California, itching for change, it was to join the man who became my second husband, who was teaching in the

Humanities and Social Sciences Program at Carnegie Mellon University in Pittsburgh. I thought Pittsburgh would be a temporary sojourn on the way back to New England, but I was off the mark about that. One thing led to another and I stayed, developing a certain affection for the city, a fondness that never turned to love but had the strength of long association.

The one physical piece of Pittsburgh that I really did love was my house, but I could not hitch it to the rental truck and bring it along. That house wouldn't look right in Vermont, anyway. Vermont is filled with houses in transition or disguise — old ones being renovated; new ones going for years without siding or finished roofs; houses that have grown like Topsy over the decades and through the generations; houses that have sprung up out of whatever is at hand; houses that were meant to be barns, sheds, or lean-tos; houses gently subsiding into the earth. Granted, there are more immaculate and expensive new homes all the time. Long-time Vermonters call them starter castles, or McMansions. And there are well-kept old homes around, especially right in town or fronting on the narrow back roads. But a great many houses have a seat-of-the-pants look about them. And this house, in this clearing, is where Alan and I want to be. Zoning in our area is lax, if it exists at all, so we can give our house whatever shape we want it to have. Alan has said to me, "I always thought you should be able to build a house like a sculpture."

And we will. First, though, we have to weather the winter.

Grace

Sometimes I wonder about the relationship between serendipity and faith. Of all the pathways there are to faith, I have, to my great surprise, found myself on one that has opened up by happenstance, with no planning or forethought from me. The recent turns in my life seem unearned blessings, which have dropped from heaven upon my life beneath. But why? What has led me here, to Alan and Vermont? What has made me ready?

Faith, or my need for faith?

If good fortune is insistent enough, does it breed belief and trust, perhaps by opening our eyes to our blessings? Or does a strong-enough faith, even one we are not quite sure we have, bring us what we halfway trust will come?

Alan lives his life trusting and giving thanks for what he envisions, and sure enough his imaginings come true, often in startling or dramatic ways. This creative energy works in lean times and fat. He has always thanked God for abundance, even when he has been down to a single sack of potatoes in his larder. One deep winter, in the northwest woods, a buck volunteered himself to go with those potatoes. He stepped right out of the cover of trees and looked Alan in the eye and as much as nodded. Alan, with mouths to feed at home and one round left in his rifle, accepted the deer's offer with gratitude.

My habits of skepticism in these matters run deeper than Alan's, while his, about politics, run deeper than mine. My spiritual skepticism somehow corresponds with my insecurities. I am uneasy about admitting faith or honestly articulating a sense of cosmic grace at work in my life, especially after spending decades among academics, researchers, philosophers, and others who are strictly disciplined in what often looks to me like narrowness of vision — by which I mean adherence to what they would call "pure reason," "rules of evidence," the demands of "proof" alone. The intellectual stance that many professional thinkers adopt is unmistakably defensive. Those with a more relaxed posture seem always to season their lives and work with humor and an open, gracious mind.

I am reminded in particular of a scientist I knew at the University of Pittsburgh, a woman who could laugh at the pettiness of academe despite the carefully rationalized slights aimed at her by colleagues. I suspect her broader spirit was either the cause or effect of her ability to admit that she and her four sisters had more than once experienced things — dreams, foreknowledge, intuitive connections — that reason alone could not explain. She always seemed pretty balanced to me, able to function in a variety of settings, able to draw lines in the sand at work, able to protect her family and self and keep her priorities straight. In contrast, I can think of dozens of bright, critical minds that flounder, go numb, or inflict real harm in matters of practicality, human relationships, or common sense.

I guess I have my own defensiveness. I am reluctant to call down even the imagined scorn of people whose values I reject in turn. Still, I am awestruck by how many things have had to come so neatly together for this new life to take shape in this new place.

Though I have no idea where it really began, I can pinpoint a Sunday in January 1996 as the locomotive that has hauled a series of changes through my life like freight cars, the first carrying cargoes of pain and anxiety, the next ones bearing excitement, adventure, delight, and thanksgiving—but all of them, I have learned, rumbling on a solid track.

I have been a Quaker for twenty-some years, a declared one for fifteen or more, but I had been attending Meeting for Worship only rarely when I renewed my commitment that January. Adam was ten, and I wanted him to learn the history and values of the Religious Society of Friends within a Quaker community. I also needed that community in a big way myself, and I wanted the distance from my own woes that getting involved would bring. My husband and I had been trying for almost ten years to revive our near-dead marriage, and it wasn't working, despite two years of insightful counsel from a gifted therapist. We each had our own way of trying, but neither of us could adopt the other's. Our defenses were too high, our resentments too deep.

That turning-point Sunday, after attending my third consecutive Meeting for Worship, I went for a walk in the bright cold, taking advantage of the winter sunshine that is all too rare in Pittsburgh. I covered eight or ten blocks in our neighborhood and eventually found myself on a short, narrow, dead-end street lined with a half dozen neat brick houses and ending at a hillside above the city's busway. The last house on that street was for sale. It had a charming air of mild decrepitude, two big firs out front, deep eaves, and lots of windows. It was not the house I ended up buying, just two months later, but it was the one that ignited an urgent determination to be free of the mournful, oppressive air inside the house where I had lived for eighteen years. I stood on the sidewalk, peering into the windows of that other house, the one I had stumbled upon, and I thought: I want to live right here with Adam, just the two of us.

That was the real moment of decision, but it had been struggling to the surface for a long time. It was one of those gradual instants, able to break through only because of everything that had gone before, all the counseling, the trying, the sorrow, the rage — and the Internet. Some weeks before that Sunday walk, I had gone surfing for something other than the most widely publicized, invariably negative effects of divorce on children. Without believing it existed, I found what I was looking for, a saving grace. I found longitudinal studies indicating that children of divorced parents do as well academically, emotionally, and psychologically as children from intact families, if they are spared the common accompaniments to divorce — custody battles, domestic violence, nasty fights, substance abuse, emotional tugs of war. I was confident that Adam would neither witness nor suffer those hazards. I knew protecting him was the one thing his father and I still had enough love and will to accomplish together.

I had long avoided the full truth about my marriage because I believed that Adam could not grow strong and healthy unless he was safe in an intact family. The problem was, we were not intact, and not really a family, even when we all lived in the same house. Adam and I did many things together. Adam and his father did fewer things together. The three of us did almost nothing together — not meals, outings, vacations, games, errands, or chores. The pretense of intactness and the fear of an honest dismantling took an awful toll, as lies will always do. Happening upon that Web site killed the lies by exposing them to hope. Happening upon the house for sale gave shape to the hope.

Other happenings followed rapidly. I confronted my husband, who was not surprised. We agreed that Adam came first, and, although it took some mighty effort, we agreed on the terms for ending our marriage. I found the Arts and Crafts house on the second day out with a realtor, and I got a good price on it because I was a cat lover, willing to continue caring for a feral family (Emmylou's kin) that the owners were forced to leave behind. Adam and I moved in on the first of May, less than four months after my Sunday walk. We spent that spring, summer, and fall settling into new patterns and routines. The divorce was final by the holidays. Just before Christmas, Adam and I had a winter solstice party, and our sixty-some guests brought candles to celebrate the slow, seasonal return of the light that would begin after that longest night of the year. The house rang with voices and glimmered with a hopeful incandescence.

After the party, too jazzed to sleep, I called an old friend on the West Coast, someone I had known since college. He told me bluntly that the last time he had seen me I had seemed stale. I had lost my spark, my sexual confidence, my pizzazz. He was right, or had been, before the divorce. So that January, a year after my Sunday walk in the cold, I made a pact with a friend named Carol, another divorced working mother — she was a reporter, and I worked at the University of Pittsburgh, writing about educational research for teachers, school administrators, and congressional staffers — that we would reach out together for new connections.

To be honest, Pittsburgh had little to offer two middle-aged professional women with kids. Our few dispiriting forays — one of which landed us in a group of aging single professionals in which the men spoke mainly to our breasts and the women spoke mainly to each other — eventually urged me farther afield than I had ever anticipated going. By the end of that month, operating by celestial navigation, I had found Alan, a continent away, in Oregon. Or we had found each other. Everything that has happened between us since then has taken place with such ease and so many coincidences that we can only conclude we are meant to be together. I can hear some of the researchers and academics with whom I once worked sniffing derisively — *Yeah, right.* My old college friend laughed at that notion, too.

I have always, even at my angriest or most despairing moments, believed in a sustaining, creative mystery at the heart of the universe, but I had little faith, earlier on, that the mystery would sustain *me.* Now, serendipity, amazing grace, divine coincidence, good timing — call it what you will — has so infused my life, and the life that Alan and I live together, that to doubt some divine shuffling of our cards would be to spurn the winning hands we hold. To doubt, whether by taking good fortune for granted, focusing on the surface irritants that are inevitable in life and relationships, or rejecting what reason cannot grasp, would be to see our lives only through the windows of our house at night and to ignore the view of the stars from the rise outside.

Wood

The full story of amazing grace is long and a little hard to believe, even for the two of us who have lived it. It needs plenty of practical relief, strong periodic doses of life's mundane and earthy stuff, as a counterbalance. I have always thought that one way to keep proportion in our lives is to tune in to the miraculous in the commonplace and to recognize the mutable, clay-foot qualities in the people and things we most adore. To me, the famous words of E. M. Forster, "Only connect," advise us to see the prose in the passion, the passion in the prose. It keeps things in proportion.

Yesterday, I did some very prosaic work in this place I passionately love. I lugged and stacked firewood for three hours, almost finishing the three-cord load we ordered to supplement the two cords already here. The old part of the house, the former cottage, is heated by woodstove, the new by a high-tech kerosene unit with a thermostat and timer. Five cords of wood seems a huge amount until I remember that Sarah and Joe and their five kids used to burn twice that much each winter, relying exclusively on the stove in their kitchen to heat their whole two-story house and a tower bedroom. Now, with the children grown, Sarah and Joe live in town and have a switch on their wall that starts or stops the flow of heat as they please. They don't even have a fireplace. One day, we too will have a switch, but for now we need our seven-foot-tall piles of beech, maple, and birch cut in stove lengths and laid three deep.

Alan has been a woodworker and carpenter for at least twenty-five years, so wood has long been a presence in his life. Now wood figures centrally in our life together. While I stacked yesterday, Alan burned brush and saplings on the other side of the house. The woodsy scent of the fire reminded me that all my work will go up in smoke by the end of the winter. Our stove wood will dictate chores all season — keeping the outdoor piles covered and dry; retrieving wood from under the tarps to replenish the supply in the wood room; transferring a day's worth at a time from wood room to stove; building fires and keeping them going when it is bitterly cold outside; adjusting the damper for the temperature and rate of burn that works best at each time of day or night; shoveling ashes out of the stove and trudging with them out to the compost bin.

During the winter, the logger we will hire will take out many of the taller, spindlier trees, especially those precariously near the house. He will skid most of the felled trees out of the woods, load them, pay us for them, and haul them off to sell. We'll keep some hardwood trees and have them milled, so that Alan will have big boards of maple, birch, and ash to work with.

Someone with a portable mill will charge about fifteen cents a foot to cut the boards right here. At Home Depot, a clear maple board is about five dollars a foot, more than thirty times as much.

We'll need hundreds of spruce or pine boards to build the rest of the house, but that utilitarian lumber won't come from our trees.

Alan has already brought in truckloads of two-by-fours, one-by-sixes, supplies, and aluminum roofing from which he has built his sixteen-by-twenty-four-foot wood-working and carpentry shop and an attached storage shed. The shop houses a different sort of wood for a different sort of construction, a dozen or more pieces of burl that Alan scavenged in Oregon. Some of the burls are bird's-eye maple, some redwood. Some are more or less whole, with the bark removed but the spikes and whorls of the root systems left intact. Alan will make bowls from these, hollowing them out and polishing the insides to a satin sheen, bringing out their intricate grain patterns. The largest pieces of burl are cross-sections — smooth, flat, continent-shaped slabs with rough outer edges — that will probably become table tops.

The first gift Alan ever gave me was a redwood bowl made from a driftwood burl he had found on the beach in southwest Oregon. The

outside of the bowl — the wood revealed when the bark was removed —
is covered with smooth peaks and wavelets the color and sheen of burnt
meringue. The inside has a marblelike finish and patterns that look like
clouds and the shapes one sees in them — but these clouds range from
deepest reddish brown to a soft sand color, and in their midst is a tiny
resin window, a translucent pane that might have been there for a thousand years or more. As Alan told me in an e-mail message, the tree from
which the bowl is made might have stood when Jesus himself was on
earth. According to St. Thomas, Jesus once said, "Cleave a piece of
wood; I am there."

It is impossible to cleave, burn, stack, or fashion a piece of wood
without knowing it was once alive and still needs to breathe. Alan dislikes seeing wood encased in polyurethane or plastic. It suffocates. Even
the pieces — split, cloven — that we will burn to stay warm this winter
still feel alive as I carry them to the woodpile from the jumbled heap left
by the dumptruck. The ones with bark attached bear the same colors as
the mountains do in winter, when their life is slow and banked against
the cold, but still strong. The bark and the fungi and lichens that grow on
it are not just dull brown or gray but colored with a soft spectrum of
sage, amethyst, cinnamon, silver, mauve, and grayish pink, just like the
winter hills. Occasionally there is a tinge of acid yellow, or turquoise.
The naked inner wood has straight or curly grains that show the way the
tree once grew — its branches, roots, knots, and rings. The colors of the
wood are blond, red, brown, and even black, like human skin or hair.
The shapes in the grain invite sculpting, they suggest faces, bird wings,
animals — and trees.

I realize that I notice these details now, when heating with wood is
new to me and stacking it is a physical pleasure. I also know that a year
or two from now I will blindly lift-pitch-stack, lift-pitch-stack without a
thought to the colors or shapes of what will simply be fuel, unromantic
and necessary. So I want to appreciate the magic while it lasts.

Wood not only heats but also frames our living spaces. It is the first
thing we see in the morning — the planed and polished lumber that forms
our high pine ceiling, or the standing timber outside our cherry-framed

bedroom windows. Wood provides income and a resource for us, and others, and for the state. It surrounds us and marks the seasons. The trees on our ten acres keep at least some of the wind from us and muffle the noise from Route 12. The trees that cover Vermont rustle, sway, and speak; attract tourists in the summer and fall; shelter birds, animals, and people; are mirrored in still lakes. They fall, and if no one hears them, they still make a sound. It is only when we are arrogant that we can't imagine any reality without our witness.

October

Tool Guy Seeks Martha

Recently, Alan and I spent a disappointing morning looking for a truck, driving a good ninety miles to inspect rusted-out, hard-used heaps in scattered towns. He sold his 1994 Dodge Ram diesel last week, having cherished it and kept it pristine for almost five years. It was a brilliant, pulsing red, with a matching cap over the bed. It had a forties-like grille, reminiscent of fire engines Alan had loved as a child. The first time he saw it, he was as bedazzled as Toad, in *Wind in the Willows,* at his first breath of gasoline exhaust.

So why sell the truck? I was dumbfounded when Alan first said he was "thinking of it," which in Alanese means the deed is as good as done. He had his reasons. The Dodge was the wrong truck for his purposes now. He needs something he can leave out in the snow, beat up, bang against trees, add a winch to, yank stumps with, and haul house-sized loads of lumber in. He couldn't stand to abuse the Dodge so severely, and he couldn't justify devaluing an expensive vehicle when a cheap one will do. He figured he could get top dollar for his dream machine (a rare, rust-free beauty on the heavily salted roads of Vermont), fatten our financial cushion, and buy himself a workhorse in its place, something he won't mind using hard to its last coughing shudder.

I have known more than one man who, in Alan's place, would be calculating how to mortgage our house to keep that truck. The fact that this sacrifice was Alan's idea, that I tried to dissuade him, and that he followed through anyway, tells me he is more focused on our shared fate and circumstances than he is on himself. I got everything I dreamed up when I was mentally composing the man I would like to meet. And I got more, too, qualities I would never have thought of that are at least as important as the ones I did.

We met in cyberspace, the same territory that had led me to freedom by relieving my maternal anxieties about the effects of divorce on Adam. I had not thought another shining pathway could open there. But after Carol and I despaired of expanding our social lives in Pittsburgh, I told her I was going to extend my reach. Half daring myself, I posted an anonymous profile at a now-defunct Web site called Intermingle (I liked the pun). I made a determined effort to represent myself there as a person of multiple quirks and virtues, not just another beach walker and mooner over sunsets — if that's not a mixed metaphor. I talked about Adam, our house, my work, my politics, my feeling that the world and one's spirit open up after the age of fifty. Then I closed my eyes and described the person I would like to meet, someone smart, funny, kind, clean, fond of animals and children, emotionally responsible, grown up at last, carrying relatively light baggage. For some reason, I pictured a long, lean face.

I didn't ask for someone who would move to Vermont with me. I didn't ask for — though I daydreamed about — someone who worked with wood. I didn't ask for someone who lived in Oregon but had gone to a grade school five miles from mine in Ohio, had sat in the same Saturday matinees at the same movie theater, had lived in several other states at the same times I did, and had almost crossed my path a dozen times throughout the country in forty-some years. I didn't ask for someone who had never been to a Friends' Meeting but was deeply and instinctually a Quaker. I didn't ask for someone who had left the mainstream twenty-five years ago in obedience to the promptings of his soul. I didn't ask for someone who would read my mind and finish my sentences. I didn't ask for someone who would be hijacked by his own computer and held hostage until he opened the Web site on which I had posted what I did ask for.

Less than two weeks after I ventured onto the Web, Alan was sitting in his house in the Oregon woods, researching something online, some topic relating to Native American cultures that he hoped he would find at the Web site for the Intertribal Council. The system crashed, as it often did in his rural, newly wired area. When it came back up, the screen said *Intermingle*. Alan hit the "back" button, but nothing happened. He hit it several more times with no more effect. Finally, thinking he just might be getting a nudge from the universe, he opened that Web site and then found he couldn't get out of it without joining up. Before he finally escaped, he read my post. He posted a profile of his own, and he answered mine: "Hello. My name is Alan. I read your profile with great interest. Mine is under the user name N'Wester. If I interest you, please respond."

I searched for N'Wester and learned — no surprise — that Alan lived in the great Northwest, that he had long ago given up a promising (or compromising) career in PR and journalism, that he liked the clean air, simple living, low crime rate, and slow pace of his life. His wife had died the year before, just weeks before I ended my marriage, but his capacity to love was intact and sought an object. Stuff he liked included music, gardening, and reading. Stuff he didn't like included war, violence, and tofu. His only baggage was Lucy, a "neurotic bassett hound." He hoped to find someone who would be a friend first, perhaps a life partner later.

I responded. He wrote again. We e-mailed each other almost every day for four months, amassing a correspondence that eventually ran to 853 pages (442 by Alan, the other 411 by me — the only time he has ever outtalked me). Neither of us knew what the other looked like, beyond the hair-and-eye-color descriptions we had posted. We never exchanged photos or phone calls until we had revealed so much of our inner selves that we had already, tentatively, skittishly, begun to love each other. We learned each other from the inside out. We had none of the distractions or rapid judgments that physical proximity and appearances can breed.

Had we met in the usual ways, we might never have recognized each other. We might never even have spoken. I was mainstream, middle-aged, middle-class, middle-sized, mortgaged, employed, encumbered, and playing it safe, or so I thought, even as I sold little pieces of my soul every day. He was weather-beaten, watchful, patient, wary, shy, and largely silent. He was his own boss, on his own time, and he traveled light, without debt, guilt, shackles, or neediness. He told me once, in an e-mail, after I had complained about the spirit wounding that went on routinely where I worked: "Am currently brushing mine w/ Colgate — invisible protective shield. My spirit refuses to be wounded anymore, not even w/ kryptonite." Alan had been using his soul Colgate for a long time. I was just beginning to detect the need for a tube of my own.

In what I later learned was a piece of careful angling, he told me he was renovating his house in Oregon. "Although I am a great carpenter, plumber, electrician, am somewhat lost when it comes to choosing the 'software'— carpets, drapes, color schemes. Where is Martha Stewart when I need her?"

I replied that I in turn wasn't a very good tool guy but could muster Martha-ness as needed. Eventually, I discovered that I was just transcribing my part of a script we both were writing — or one that was being written for us — which would lay out the kind of life we now live, in which each of us designs everything from living spaces to daydreams in full partnership with another whose values and spiritual quest match our own.

"If I'm ever cruising in your neighborhood, flag me down," Alan wrote. "I'm the guy in the red truck w/ toolbox on the back and sign — 'Will Fix Things For Food.'" Likewise, he added, "If you're ever cruising up my lane, stop in. Free advice graciously accepted. It's the red house that clashes badly with the old yellow backhoe that's broke down on the half-dug new leach field in the front yard."

We were keeping it light, easing into our connection, neither of us presuming anything about the other, but each of us hoping. We had only each other's words to go on, but as the months went by, the words began to hum, and we tuned in to the music as much as the lyrics.

The Stone Bridge

In the beginning of our connection was the word. Alan and I had nothing but words at first. We had none of the interpretive benefits offered by voice, inflection, body language, or facial expression. I know how dangerous that can be, how easy it is to find in another person's writing your own best hopes or worst fears, whether they are there or not. The word is frail, at best, and subject to gross misreading. In cyberspace it seems especially ephemeral and risky, too easy to erase, work over, overstress, or understate. How can we ever really communicate in such an abstract plane?

The questions arise only in retrospect. At the time, all four months of it, I never doubted Alan's sincerity or truthfulness. I never misread a word he wrote. He never failed to apprehend my messages. There was something solid in what we said to each other. It turned out to be faith. Alan was far more willing than I to be led by intuition. My gradual certainty that he was a true kindred soul was unique in all my life. I had never *not* second-guessed myself and others.

The word is frail, but the Word, and the fact that Alan and I share rather an unconventional understanding of it, is strong. I was reassured by one of his first messages — "Tell me about your Quaker faith." He could have been calculating his effect on me, playing to this larger concern. He could have been a scam artist, a criminal, a serial killer, or just another manipulative, me-first kind of guy. I am not sure when I knew beyond question that he was none of these, but I sensed it immediately and immediately trusted my senses. That was not like me at the time. Having hung around so many heavy thinkers, especially in my job at the university, I tended to be more skeptical and restrained than that.

What spoke to me most compellingly was imagery — nothing airy or disconnected, but real-life images, born on the ground yet bearing wings. Again, the example that comes to mind is wood and the power of its presence in Alan's life. It was central to his best childhood memories, which took place during summers at his grandmother's rustic cottage in Wolfeboro, New Hampshire, on Lake Winnepesaukee:

> Grandpa had this sleek old mahogany Chris Craft that sliced through the water like a knife — Uncle Bud's Comet sailboat that he built himself in the garage, me underfoot and in the way, hiding under the piles of sweet-smelling shavings, long transparent ribbons that spewed out of his hand plane . . . Tool Guy? Uncle Bud was the original — stubby fingered big blocky hands. Uncle Bud could turn a screw with his thumb nail — this is *hero* stuff in TGdom.
>
> This is for sure where my reverence for wood came from. (*Reverence for Wood* is one of Eric Sloane's books; ever read this or any others of his? *Barns and Covered Bridges? Our Vanishing Landscape?*) Remembering the textures, the turpentiney smell of fresh planed pine . . . knew nothing, until a week or so ago, about the "cleave open a piece of wood" stuff, but obviously . . . soul was there.

We always wrote to each other about prosaic things, past and present — what he was building onto his house, who was buying his wooden bowls at the artists' market each weekend, what I was doing at work, who peopled our lives, what we had felt while growing up — but passion and spirit ran through it all, like Jesus in a piece of wood. Our writing, though it was goofy, pun-ridden, heavily illustrated with emoticons, and filled with e-isms — a personalized cyber-dialect given to down-home lingo, contractions, and telegraphic sentences — became poetry, at least to us. Images reverberated. They tended to be images we shared. "What's this *thing* you have for rivers?" Alan once asked me, admitting that he also found them compelling. The unsaid was loud between us. There was as much between our lines as in them, and I trusted the indirection.

Some of my friends found this alarming. When I said I had met someone online who intrigued and entertained me, they said, echoing each other almost verbatim, "How do you know he's for real? He could be dangerous, a predator, a maniac." A few told me stories of online romances that had ended in sick disappointment, shock, even murder.

Alan's friends were cheerleaders. "Go for it!" they said. "That's great!" they said, never considering (or else being too polite to mention) that I could be a black widow, a ball-breaker, a whiner, or a pain in the ass. Most of his friends were artists and crafters, many with advanced degrees in medicine, physics, or biology, former heavy thinkers themselves who did not like where their thoughts had led them. With varying degrees of deliberation or debilitation, they had finally fled to a simpler, if not an easier, life.

Maybe the double standard was still at work. Maybe my friends worried because I am a woman and presumed a likelier target of predatory humans than a man would be. Or perhaps Alan's friends had more direct experience with faith than my doubters and fretters. I imagine that many of the people he knew, having abandoned their training and lifelong expectations for lives they patchworked together without much security, understood that trusting your instincts, a close relative of faith, can bring miracles. The "leap of faith" we hear so much about seems like a true leap to me, a willing if terrified plunge into what our senses, intellect, and lifelong habits of knowing and defending cannot perceive.

I keep thinking about that scene in *Indiana Jones and the Last Crusade*, where Harrison Ford, led by an ancient Latin text, steps over the edge of a bottomless, echoing abyss, only to be held up by a rock-solid optical illusion, a stone bridge made invisible by its perfect blending with the walls of the chasm.

One friend, Emma, told me, even after Alan and I had been together for almost a year and were planning our move to Vermont, that my actions were "rash and risky," that I was not listening carefully enough to the warnings she and others were issuing. I could not explain adequately that I had considered such warnings on my own, long before they were uttered by others. I could not convey to her satisfaction my profound sense of rightness. I am sure my protestations only made me seem more obdurate. I could not show her my stone bridge except by stepping out onto it. I did. It holds me up.

Boxes

Emma and another friend, Ellen, are the only ones who remain uneasy about the radical changes in my life. I tried with each of them to explain that this new life reflects an obedience to my soul, which in the past few years has been making its requirements known to me in clear, unprecedented ways. They don't seem to understand, and I am not sure why, except that each friendship has always had both its joyful times and its tensions. It's possible that the three of us never knew each other as well as the long confluence of our lives led us to think we did. It is easy to feel close to people who outwardly resemble you — people who aspire to similar things, who hold similar political views, and who have shared struggles, fond times, and pastimes involving writing, mothering, gardening, running, jobs, families, and social events.

Sudden change can challenge all of that. In the space of just eighteen months, my life and pleasures went from resembling Emma's and Ellen's to looking altogether different. I divorced, I met a stranger online, that stranger moved into my house after less than six months, and then that stranger swept me away — or so it would have appeared to others — from my new house, my job, my friends, and the life I had meant to occupy for good. In the whirlwind course of these events, I realized how constrained and confined I had felt for years.

Work, especially, was always a looming question in my life. I had bills to pay, a child and a way of life to support. It all seemed necessary, yet the need to earn a living had always felt like a prison. I felt guilty when I complained about the bars. Who was I to want freedom from wage slavery? I used to walk to work in the early years of my job as a writer at the University of Pittsburgh, and each morning I would watch others making their own way to their offices, labs, or desks. An old Hoyt Axton song would run through my mind — "When the mornin' comes and you gotta get up, how you gonna find your shoes?" I would picture people in their houses or apartments, hunting their shoes, shaking the wrinkles from shirts or pants, brewing coffee, feeding kids or pets, being alone or being hassled and bustling. I would find everybody brave except me. I worried that I was never as productive as I thought I should be, even in an uncongenial setting. When I met Alan, I began to see that my prison had doors, and all along the key was within my reach.

Alan had grasped his own key about twenty-five years earlier, when he had listened to an inner voice that warned him away from the compromises his work kept insisting that he make. Somehow, he found enough confidence in himself and trust in his own soul to escape altogether the compulsive, competitive get-and-spend world of careers and commercial success. He couldn't stomach what it took to keep making more money, so he figured out how to need as little of that toxic stuff as possible. He taught himself carpentry, plumbing, wiring, and woodcraft. He worked at construction, demolition, bar tending, and art fairs. He built or renovated his own houses, bartering and scavenging what he could and producing beautiful, artful structures. By the time we met, he was doing exactly as he pleased, working on what he chose to work on, keeping his productivity high but only in obedience to his "Inner Boss Man."

Even so, Alan told me that he sensed he had long been living in a box, a confined space that kept him from a full surrender to faith and the promptings of his soul. That box began opening up when his wife, Judy, died. She had esophageal cancer, and she refused conventional treatments, choosing to stay at home, where Alan cared for her. He told me that at the moment she died, her soul did a dance with his:

> She passed over quietly in her sleep cradled in my arms. I had an experience that still, in memory, fills me with wonder and awe. I felt her soul leave her body, and as it ascended, my soul left my body. We were, for a period of time — could have been an instant, could have been hours — suspended in this warm time-warp-bubble. She let me know she was OK. I let her know I was gonna be OK. And we parted.

This event let a beam of light slide past the last of Alan's resistance. My divorce and the serendipitous events that led to it were my counterpart stimuli. I think each of us felt we had a large capacity to give love but no partner to receive it. I was lucky to have Adam at home, soaking up love, but Alan's immediate, step-, and surrogate family members were widely scattered.

Alan wrote his description of Judy's death early in our correspondence, in answer to my questions about how she had died and how he had dealt with his mourning. I acknowledged losses of my own, and somehow that established the beginnings of trust between us. Alan wrote, a week or two into our correspondence:

> Still a little bit puzzled about what it was in your short "profile" that gave me the sense that there is a comfort zone here — that it's perfectly OK to share your deepest thoughts and feelings with someone who is, in effect, a perfect stranger.

We were indeed the "perfect strangers" for each other. We soon shared space on a plane that neither of us had ever investigated with another person. Before long, I felt my hibernating soul begin to stir in that space:

> Morning again, after a night of the weirdest dreams, prompted by a constellation of things on my mind, from some new books, to you and this correspondence, to realizations that I've put the lid on a hell of a lot and now that heavy old thing is creaking open, letting daylight shine on stuff I had always thought not-right-about-me, which turns out to be the stuff I am *made* of, the stuff I love most. I rejoice and am nervous and full of excitement — that old sap rising.
>
> I have to wonder why I left it all alone for so long — for decades — in order to surround myself with analytical, agnostic, atheist, intellectual types, some of them dour, rigid, and contemptuous of the things that I resonated to. I have been realizing, with a sense of release, that my spirit is finally beginning to recognize itself again (and maybe know itself for the first time).

I think about Emma and Ellen, and I begin to understand that I stepped outside their expectations for me and their thoughts about who I am. I stepped beyond my own boundaries, too. The surprises in my

life, which must mystify them, showed me where the key to my confining space was hidden — in the faith, love, and risk that lay beneath my
defenses and fears. I didn't earn or ask for the key or the things that
uncovered it. I was simply blessed. I have no idea why.

Quakerism — Roots of Faith and Practice

I never expected Quakerism to lead me onto a path of miracles. When I
first started going to Quaker Meetings almost thirty years ago, I was
drawn by much more worldly concerns. I was attracted to what I viewed
as the Friends' social agenda, which reflected their underlying "testimonies"— statements of principle that include or lead inexorably to pacifism, racial and gender equity, fairness in all dealings, respect for all people, and an avoidance of excess, whether material or behavioral.

I knew little about the faith from which Friends' testimonies and
related practices grew, although I did feel a longing for some kind of
spiritual home in which I would not be seen as wrong-headed for my
social and political values. I liked very much the fact that Quakers had
always regarded women and men as equals, had renounced slavery early
on, and had often stood almost entirely alone against war — sometimes
while serving *in* war as medics, drivers, counselors, and other noncom-
batant personnel.

Eventually, I came to understand that values and actions are inseparable from faith for people who try to follow the deepest truths they
know. Friends have made this their goal from their first beginnings, in
mid-seventeenth-century England, a time and place in which both
church and state were shaken by dissent.

For more than a century, the Protestant Reformation had been blowing through Europe on a questioning spirit that gusted into every area
of established thought, from the pope's religious autocracy to the position of the sun to the powers and proper role of government. That spirit
came in handy for King Henry VIII, who pitched a fit when Rome
refused to grant him a divorce from Catherine of Aragon. In 1534 he

declared himself, rather than the pope, sole head of the Church in England. His daughter, Elizabeth I, later formalized this split with Rome, and anti-Catholic sentiment deepened after Mary Queen of Scots, a Catholic, was executed in 1587 for plotting against the English Queen Elizabeth, her cousin.

New religious thought emerged everywhere during the Reformation. By the seventeenth century, many Protestant sects were turning inward, in search of direct spiritual revelation and away from prescribed doctrines and the teachings of religious authorities. Among these were the Puritans, whose faith began in personal grace and the belief that a loving God would redeem all sins through Christ. Unfortunately, the Puritans came to feel that they alone had been chosen for the "grace" part of that equation. Before long, they could see only sin and depravity in everyone but themselves, and they made every holier-than-thou effort to eradicate evil and bring the wayward into their ranks. During Elizabeth's reign, their self-appointed mission was to cleanse the state religion of any icons or rituals that still stank of popishness. Their zeal translated into power both in the church and in Parliament. After Elizabeth's reign, they opposed her next two successors, James I and Charles I, the son and grandson of the treacherous Scottish Queen Mary.

Charles I was automatically suspect because he was married to a Catholic and believed in the divine right of kings. Yet he was also tightly allied with the Church of England's Archbishop of Canterbury, and he fought back against the Puritans and any other nonconforming religious groups. He conflicted so bitterly with Puritans and others in Parliament that he ruled virtually without that body's support or involvement for more than a decade. In 1642 these disputes launched twenty years of intermittent civil war in Britain. In 1649, Charles I was tried and executed. In 1653, Oliver Cromwell, one of the most outspoken Puritans in Parliament, was made Lord Protectorate of England.

Under Cromwell's rule, the Puritans persisted in abusing, imprisoning, and tormenting the members of any religious group whose beliefs departed from their own. They usually did this at the local level, since Cromwell himself, though he cracked down energetically on religious dissent, could also be persuaded to let some sects worship more or less in peace as long as they did not disturb the peace of others.

As a result, some religious sects both flourished and suffered in these years, persecuted less by Cromwell than by lower-level judges, bishops, and prison personnel. One such group called itself variously the Children of Light, the Friends of Truth, and, eventually, the Religious Society of Friends. The man most commonly regarded as the founder of the Society was George Fox, born in 1624, a weaver's son from Leicestershire with great personal charisma and physical power, whose guiding spiritual vision came to him only after a long struggle characteristic of his time.

The religious ferment that surrounded the young George Fox arose mainly from Puritans, Anabaptists, Mennonites, and other sects designated "spiritual," and also from a tiny — but loud — group called Ranters. The Ranters held to no doctrines or Scriptures but rather to the idea that God is present in all of life and that humans, by virtue of this holy diffusion, partake of the divine and can know it mystically. The Ranters did not feel themselves bound by civil or moral law any more than by spiritual dogma, and they acted accordingly, seizing rather than petitioning for liberties. Their justification lay in the idea that people who communicated directly with God Himself could not be ruled by human institutions.

In such times and amid such radical influences, it is no wonder that Fox found himself wary of established thought and all its representatives, including the Church of England, its bishops and priests, its many interpreters of the word of God. By 1647, when Fox was twenty-three and Charles I was two years away from execution, he had despaired of finding anyone who could help him in his search for God's truth, a matter of the deepest personal discipline and discernment.

Eventually, as Fox wrote in his journal, he heard a voice that said to him, "There is one, even Christ Jesus, that can speak to thy condition." Fox understood this voice to be the very same one from which prophets and sages had taken holy dictation and had then written down Scripture. He understood it to be the voice of God. He felt confirmed in mistrusting the ranks of intermediaries who pretended to sit between God and the mass of humankind. Though he himself had "read the Scriptures that spoke of Christ and of God," he nevertheless knew them for himself only "by revelation." Fox, in obedience to the voice that spoke to him, began to seek for himself "the pure knowledge of God and Christ alone, without the help of any man, book, or writing."

Fox's developing vision was a refinement of beliefs held by Puritans, Anabaptists, and even Ranters. He reduced these beliefs to their purest essence. He did not focus on human depravity, nor excuse himself or anyone else from God's law. Instead he sought direct contact with what he called — and Quakers still call —"that of God" in every person, starting with himself. The Puritans, especially, had set themselves up as holy intermediaries of a new kind, whereas Fox, through his personal experience of God, was fully convinced that illumination by an "inner light" was not only available to all who sought it but was the single reliable source of spiritual truth.

This was so radical a notion, and so readily conflated with some of the Ranters' and others' more disruptive views, that it soon, and often, landed Fox in prison — for interrupting a church service in 1649, for blasphemy in the 1650s, for other civil and religious offenses through the decade after that. His journal describes the conditions of one imprisonment in 1653:

> [The gaoler] grew very devilish and wicked, and carried us and put us into Doomsdale, a nasty stinking place where they said few people came out alive; where they used to put witches and murderers before their execution; where the prisoners' excrements had not been carried out for scores of years, as it was said. It was all like mire, and in some places at the top of the shoes in water and piss. . . . The gaoler would not let us cleanse the place, nor let us have beds nor straw to lie on; but at night some friendly people of the town brought us a candle and a little straw, and we went to burn a little of our straw to take away the stink.

When Fox was not incarcerated, he traveled on foot or horseback "preaching" to interested seekers. He spoke only to guide them to their own light, not to set down spiritual laws nor to propound upon Scripture as the only communication available from God. In 1652, during one of the periods when he was at large, Fox climbed a steep incline in Derbyshire, called Pendle Hill, where "the Lord let me see . . . in what places he had a great people to be gathered." Later, at a nearby inn, Fox's vision narrowed down to an adjacent riverside, where he saw "a great people in white raiment . . . coming to the Lord."

Soon after, Fox's role as the leader of such a people—that is, the founder of a religious society that has now lasted three and a half centuries and is represented on every continent—crystallized during his visits to Swarthmoor Hall, near the town of Ulverston, in what is now Cumbria. This Elizabethan house was the home of an influential judge, Judge Fell. Fox convinced Judge Fell's wife, Margaret, of his truth and its soundness, and he earned the judge's respect, if not his conversion. While the judge was alive, his stature gave at least limited protection to Fox and his followers, who met often at Swarthmoor and spread out from there to broadcast their word.

Despite localized persecution and arrests, Fox's followers grew in number and strength during Cromwell's rule and even after Cromwell's death in 1658 ended his uneven religious tolerance. The royalists soon regained power and restored the monarchy, in 1660, by enthroning Charles II, son of the executed King Charles I. Charles II promised religious tolerance, but it was long in coming. Religious abuses continued, but the Friends nonetheless survived. By the late 1660s, they were building meetinghouses and schools and providing a stable presence in many towns and villages.

Finally, in 1678, the first London Yearly Meeting was convened as the oversight organization for Friends. From that event grew the structure by which the Religious Society of Friends is still organized worldwide. Yearly Meetings—which might cover whole countries or large geographic regions like New England—consider the broad spiritual and practical concerns of Quarterly and Monthly Meetings. Monthly Meetings, based in individual meetinghouses or homes or community centers, meet weekly or more often for worship and hold Meeting for Business once a month. Groups of these Monthly Meetings belong to a Quarterly Meeting that convenes every three months both for worship and for conducting business.

That first Yearly Meeting in London established the "Quakers"—so-called, derisively at first, because they trembled in the presence of God and while delivering God's word during Meeting for Worship — as an organization with principles, processes, testimonies, and structure. In 1689, the Toleration Act finally overturned the harsher religious laws in England and made way for greater religious freedom. In 1691, George Fox died, leaving a flourishing Society of Friends.

Quaker Meetings

Knowing some details of George Fox's and the Quakers' early struggles, I appreciate more fully than ever the clear, unbroken link between the silent Meeting for Worship that I so value and the man from whose vision it derives. Silent Meeting is simply the logical result of Fox's belief that no one's voice can speak more truth than the voice within. Anyone attending Meeting for Worship can make this inner voice heard when it demands to speak aloud. Such testimonies are not sermons in any standard sense. In fact, they often represent a reluctant obedience to spirit on the part of speakers who must overcome shyness, modesty, or self-doubt in order to break the gathered silence of other Friends.

There are at least four Friends Meetings that I could attend here in Vermont, and I have only been to one so far, in Plainfield, about a half-hour drive from here. The other Meetings are farther away, in Glover, Burlington, or Middlebury. With Alan's and my weather-imposed deadlines nearly met and our household finally up and running, I can spend some time visiting Meetings to decide which one feels most like home. Somehow, the Meeting in Pittsburgh always felt tense. I loved it, and I miss it, but it tended to erupt into crisis fairly often.

The meetinghouse in Pittsburgh is an immense, soot-blackened stone structure that a hundred years ago was a single-family home. It has been carved up and ill used in the past, and what is now the meeting room is an addition to the original house. That room has a hardwood floor, big leaded-glass windows and doors, dark wainscoting and, of all things, reddish-black velvet on the walls. The ceilings must be fifteen feet high, with shaded lights suspended from them on three- or four-foot cables. The combination of dark walls, big windows, and soft interior lighting often creates a serene, shadowless glow. Trees are visible outside, and in summer birdsong comes floating in the open windows along with street sounds, neighborhood children's voices, and the drone of lawnmowers. In winter, the radiators hiss, the air is closer, the silence and the spoken ministry of gathered Friends are somehow more inward. From fall through spring, the Meeting's children can be heard in the First Day School upstairs, and there can be great disagreement among Friends as to whether that sound impedes or enhances worship.

When Alan asked me about Quakerism, his question launched a conversation about faith and God that threaded its way through our whole correspondence. "Do you feel that the light shines with more intensity in a group situation?" he wanted to know. I answered:

I do find group worship a completely different, and complementary, kind of practice than the solitary sort, and I try to get both in on a regular basis. In Meeting for Worship, all I know is, it can be deep or shallow, annoying or profound, and the real challenge is realizing and then acting on the fact that it's up to me, not the other Friends, which it *is* for me. There are always Friends who are trying to get the silence itself to be perfect — no comings and goings or stomachs growling or babies crying or chairs creaking, please, and no inappropriate ministry (really, one MUST quake first, or how do you know the message is from God?). Oy, to borrow a phrase. I have come to think, over the years, that all ministry is from God and if it's annoying, then the message is, get over yourself and love that Friend, and try to get past the annoyance to the heart of the need that is being manifested. And as for the silence, I now believe it is always there. The image I often have is of a river, with lots of surface noise and traffic — boats, birds, waterbugs, kids skipping stones — but with a silky, silty bottom to which one can sink like an old trout. The river is always there. Where we go in it depends on our discipline and our choice.

I am always struck by how extraordinary it is that five or ten or a hundred people, regardless of their differences or even their conflicts, should choose to sit together on Sunday morning for an hour of deep silence, united by the belief that the silence will speak volumes to any who open themselves to hear. The first time Alan went to Meeting, two days after he arrived to visit me in Pittsburgh, he said afterward, "I've never felt anything like that." He described his sense of the silence falling as electric, a current that ran through him from his scalp to his feet. Since then, he has gone to Meeting with me almost every time I have attended, but in general he is less in need of that group experience than I am. As he wrote to me:

> My own faith consists of a profound *personal* relationship with God that brings me inner peace and serenity. Not always so — for me it was an intense struggle. At a very early age, I sensed the hypocrisy of the church (Sunday School) environment that I was dragged into. Made the big mistake of equating God with "religion"— tried to throw them both out of my life at the same time. Jumped through every kind of hoop imaginable —"intellectual atheism" (intellectual at age 18, yeah, right), Eastern philosophy, mysticism, Aquarian woo-woo-ism, peyote in the sweat lodge — in essence, "anything BUT God." He waited me out.
>
> When I feel a specific need to talk to God, I tend toward one of the structures he created — my place at the ocean or a redwood grove between here and the coast — massive spires that rise straight up to heaven — don't think man has yet been able to create a cathedral quite that magnificent.

Hypocrisy certainly does exist in church, temple, mosque, or meetinghouse, no matter how ornate or plain the edifice might be. I am often aware of my own hypocrisy, especially when I read something like that e-mail passage above and realize how frequently I stray from my best intentions and find myself annoyed or unable to quiet the critic inside. All the other human failings manifest themselves in church as well. A looming question for me is whether, like Alan, I will stay detached from the inner workings of a Meeting and seek spiritual fulfillment in mainly solitary ways. It is tempting. On alternating days I am pulled toward fellowship with Friends and then repelled by the petulance and pettiness that all groups finally must deal with. In particular, it is hard to suffer fractiousness and sanctimony, both of which thrive in religious soil.

One of the founding members of Pittsburgh Meeting, a woman now in her eighties who in my view epitomizes honest, caring, tough-minded Quakerism, once said snappishly, in response to those who would perfect the silence almost to the point of banning coughs, "We're supposed to be able to worship in a subway car!" Another Friend gave ministry one week that celebrated the Quaker notion of a movable, personal, silent Meeting. He said he took advantage of every lull—waiting in the grocery line, stalled in traffic—to sink into the spiritual stream that refreshed his outlook and calmed his soul. These are only two of the countless gifts the people in a Meeting can offer. I have brought many gifts with me from Pittsburgh Meeting.

But that Meeting was also full of strife. Ironically, difficulties among Friends can actually deepen in the face of the Quaker commitment to unity—not because of the commitment itself, but because it is not always easy to tell the difference between a spiritual impediment and one that arises from any of hundreds of human frailties. Quakers do not vote; rather, they seek "the sense of the Meeting." The ideal is for worship and dialogue to put all doubts and questions to rest—in effect, to achieve full unanimity. What is more common, and more realistic, given the nature of any human enterprise, is to seek an accord in which anyone who feels uneasy about an act or decision becomes willing—often after long prayer and consideration—to step aside and allow the action to proceed. But if even one Friend, out of the few or many who may be present, feels he or she must conscientiously oppose an item on the agenda of the monthly Meeting for Business, then that item must be shelved until the path to unity finally opens—if it ever does. This can take months, if not years, and resentments can easily flourish in such long holding periods, all the more if the members of a Meeting begin judging one another.

The idea behind Quaker process — the effort to reach unity — is that a matter of deep discernment must be respected, even if it is perceived by only the tiniest minority of Friends. The Quaker belief that there is that of God in every person means we each possess a piece of the ultimate truth that all human beings, together, embody. Thus to override the concerns of any one person could be to override that person's truth. But Friends being human, it is not always easy for an individual or the Meeting as a whole to discern when or whether conscience represents the inner light or is more a matter of ego, arrogance, crankiness, or just plain confusion.

I respect the struggle, but I would like to find a Meeting in which there is less of it. This could be a vain desire, given the nature of human groups. On the other hand, much has been written by Friends about healthy and troubled Meetings. Pittsburgh, in all the intermittent years in which I knew it, had qualities of both. It had a good cross-section of elderly Quakers and younger ones, of lifelong Quakers and newcomers, of singles and families. It had devoted, energetic people willing to fill committee seats and organize events. It had a long series of conscientious, insightful clerks, the spirit-led CEOs of Meeting who — at least in Pittsburgh Meeting — served a two-year term after having been assistant clerk for an introductory year.

But Pittsburgh Meeting also had a history of division dating back at least to the Vietnam War. As a group, it was not overtly warm to newcomers, and many who sojourned with us said how hard it was to get to know anyone. It had moral disagreements about who could marry or form a household with Quaker blessings. It continues, as I write this, to struggle over the meetinghouse itself — whether to sell it and relocate to a smaller, simpler building or stay put and gather rental income from the other groups who use it during the week. The Meeting suffered terribly when one member turned hideously violent against another. Some people urged forgiveness above all, while others, devastated by the perpetrator's utter betrayal of Quaker testimony on nonviolence and respect, insisted on consequences, including revoking the person's membership if he showed neither remorse nor a desire to make amends. These things penetrated the soul of the Meeting so deeply that it was hard not to feel some tension in every gathering or piece of business.

Sarah, the person who first introduced me to Friends, belongs to Barton-Glover Meeting, an hour's drive northeast of here. She knows and loves the people there from long association; she lived in that area during her first four or five years in Vermont. She quit going to Meeting regularly when Joe was out of work a couple of years ago and she didn't want to spend the money on gas. Now perhaps she will go with me.

Still, I miss Pittsburgh Meeting. A newsletter came a week or so ago, with photos from a recent gathering, and I felt an unexpected pang at the sight of all those familiar faces. It is time Alan and I started getting to know more people here, Friends, friends, associates, acquaintances.

Yankee Virtues

I recently went with Sarah to help her choose new glasses frames. She wanted my Martha-ness, limited as it is when compared with the real, time-consuming, endlessly inventive (but for what?) thing. That reminded me of my move to the Arts and Crafts house in Pittsburgh, which Sarah flew down to help me accomplish. For nearly a week, she assembled bookshelves, dressers, and end tables from IKEA while I unpacked boxes and arranged the rooms.

Sarah and I first met in Toronto in 1968. I was living there with my first husband, Ned, who was working on his master's in English literature while I worked for an architecture magazine and later a textbook publisher. I was a dutiful and supportive young wife; Sarah was a free spirit, traveling light, getting by on almost nothing, working as a waitress. She was friends with people Ned met through the English department. I took one look at her grin and wanted to get to know her.

A few years later, in 1971, when Ned and I had moved to the coast of

Maine and were living miserably in the midst of all that natural beauty, Sarah helped me leave that failed marriage. She drove me away in her black VW bug, to stay for a while with friends even farther north, in New Brunswick, Canada. From there I went to Boston for a while, and finally ended up in California for several years. Sarah joined me in California but didn't stay long. She moved back East in 1973 and has been in Vermont ever since.

Decades later, as she watched me unpack in the Arts and Crafts house after my second divorce, she asked, "How do you know where everything goes?" She surveyed the clutter. "When Joe and I moved into town, things stayed wherever the movers put them down."

People call it the nesting instinct. Some have it and some don't. Martha has way too much of it (she would surely disagree, considering her profits). I have all that I need. Sarah has more than she thinks she does, but five kids and a never-quite-finished Vermont hippie house didn't let her explore it much.

There may be full-blooded Marthas in Vermont — women who devote themselves to devilishly detailed artistry in cuisine and decor — but I have never seen any, not since moving here and not on any visits over the years. Perhaps they live in the southern part of the state, where an elegant appearance is valued and people have more money to spend and more stylish places in which to spend it.

In southern Vermont, outlet stores now inhabit immaculately restored clapboard houses in perfect, tree-sheltered, New England town centers. But people in central and northern Vermont tend to be scornful of these southern towns and their commercialized charm, fearful that the tide of corrupt or merely yuppie values will rise into their own areas. Bad enough (and good enough, given the state's reliance on tourist dollars) that there are ski towns and summer resorts throughout the state and that the fall foliage brings tour buses in an endless stream, most with darkened windows so you can't see who is seeing you and your town and your hills.

Not surprisingly, Vermont politics tends to follow the money, with some upscale tourist areas being among the most conservative. What is surprising, at least to me, is how conservative some of the poorest areas are. I would have thought that struggling Vermonters would support progressive ideas like universal health care and higher educational standards, but in fact many people in out-of-the-way villages and on small farms cling to the kind of Yankee pride that resents any institutionalized change — that is, any change foisted on them against their traditional ways of doing things. They especially dislike policies that have been introduced by the flatlanders, including politically progressive people who began settling here in significant numbers during the sixties back-to-the-land movement. This deep-seated resistance to change is understandable in light of the higher taxes and the influx of unfamiliar ideas and faces that accompany it.

My impression is that many old-time Vermonters, whose families have been here for four or five generations, still yearn for the days when small farms were numerous and viable, when neighbors took care of each other and the state didn't have to, when everyone knew everyone else, and most private lands were not posted against hunting or trespassing. In fact, if you ask directions around here, your answer will often be couched in the past: "Oh, just go on beyond where the old union store used to be and turn left where Joe Smith's barn burned down a few years ago. . . ."

But it's complicated. Many of the sixties newcomers to Vermont have worked incredibly hard to protect small farms. For this, they are respected. They have also worked hard to improve education, and for this they are sometimes scorned: "Why should Vermont kids have to learn about Bosnia when they'll never *go* there? They'll stay right here and live the way Vermonters are supposed to live." The worst controversies tend to erupt over issues of bureaucratization — the state telling people what kinds of signs they can and cannot erect to point to their businesses; the state redistributing property tax burdens so that poor towns, which until 1997 had to levy taxes as high as 8 percent of property value in order to fund their schools, no longer had to pay more heavily than rich towns, which raised enough money with rates as low as .1 percent; or, the state even *considering* whether gays and lesbians are discriminated against. Yankees have long been willing to accept people as they are, but they don't want the law telling them they *must* do that. They also don't want private business made public.

Meanwhile, many people from old Vermont families depart from these attitudes altogether and are counted among the most progressive thinkers in the state. There are no clear boundary lines among conservatives, centrists, liberals, and progressives, much as it would be simpler to think so. There are just human beings with different degrees of tolerance and different values, all sharing a very small state.

But back to the matter of Marthas. If there are any in Vermont, they surely do their baking and decorating farther south. Up here, in central Vermont and into the Northeast Kingdom — the quadrant contained within the protuberance bounded by the Canadian and New Hampshire borders, a rugged area with only about seven people per square mile — it is almost a point of pride to have a funky house. As Adam has made friends, and as the parents of these friends have dropped them off at our house on a Saturday or Sunday, the adults have examined our home with some satisfaction, laughingly pronouncing it a typical Vermont house. I take them to mean it is not only unfinished, but cluttered with unsorted stuff, impossible to keep clean, and barely worth the effort. I try, but no sooner do I wash down the painted plywood floor in the mudroom and the cottage room, our temporary office, than two filthy puppies romp in, or Alan sloshes coffee on his way to his desk, or Adam scuffs in from school shedding shoes, leaves, twigs, and backpack. The newer parts of the house are a little easier to maintain, but I am less inclined than ever in my life to keep after them.

Vermonters, including many still seen by the native-born as flatlanders, seem to value process over finished results. Process is everywhere, in politics, in landscaping, in building, in the seasons. Much that is lovingly undertaken is never finished, but never fully abandoned, either. What matters is practical things like warmth, shelter, comfort for family, a welcome for friends. Wherever there is too much design or too careful a cleanliness, those essentials lose their place of honor, supplanted by a polished appearance.

I do aspire to more space, better organization, and clean, well-lighted rooms, but only to the point where those things serve practical and humane values. Too often in my life, I have filled an inner void or subdued frustration and loneliness by planting, cooking, bedecking, refurbishing, arranging, cleaning, or organizing material and botanical *things*. Hence my development of certain Martha-like skills. I have even practiced retail therapy, not with the best of shoppers (since I never liked the chase, just the purchases), but with a hunger that was never entirely appeased.

Lately, I experience none of the urge to buy. Alan's example has me watching money as intently as his inner Scotsman has ever done (well, almost). As he points out, frugality is not the same as cheapness. He volunteered three thousand dollars for new kitchen appliances almost as soon as he joined me in Pittsburgh. He was eager for our self-indulgent days on the coast of Maine just after we got married. He likes good food and is pleased to spring for treats. But why pay full price when there are sales? Why buy a new chain saw if he can get one used? Why not clip store coupons when there are so many waiting to be clipped?

This is new to me. I think I have perceived money as an emotionally charged matter, not simply a practical one — but I am an eager apprentice. Last month, I went to a clothing exchange with Sarah, who has always lived a simple, frugal life. The exchange, a semiannual event, was held in a community sports center set up with five tables, each at least twenty feet long and all of them piled higher than eye level with contributed clothing sorted, sort of, into men's, women's, children's, outerwear, and accessories. We volunteered to unpack, sort, and stack up the donated items, and in the meantime we were free to plunder the tables.

Everything was free, for us and everyone else. I got Alan a clean, serviceable down jacket for winter chores, as well as a new-looking wool-lined barn coat, a Banana Republic windbreaker, and some sweaters and flannel shirts. I got myself a never-worn J. Crew barn coat, a like-new Woolrich storm coat, a denim jacket, flannel pajamas, and a heavy, soft twill shirt in a dusty plaid that is now my favorite piece of clothing. Since then, I have been to rummage sales and yard sales with Sarah and to discount department stores with Adam, but nothing has pleased me down to my bones the way those freebies did.

Sarah said, as we scooped up articles of clothing for ourselves and our families at the exchange, "There's no reason for anyone around here to go naked." Vermonters pride themselves on their frugality. Without intrusive self-righteousness, they embody the Quaker admonition: "Use it up, wear it out, make it do, or do without." They do just as the bumper sticker says: "Live simply, so that others may simply live." That is extraordinarily difficult in a country whose economy depends on generating fears (Am I young enough, pretty enough, smart enough, clean enough, hip enough, healthy enough, fit enough, successful enough?) and then producing — *voila! honest!* — just the items that will put those fears to rest, for a minute or two. I was never exactly extravagant, except perhaps by Third World standards, but it wasn't until I moved to Vermont, where the predominant culture supports and applauds plainness, thrift, and an absence of self-decoration, that I stepped fully into a leaner and simpler life.

Imagine what would happen if more people in more states every year said, "Hey, I really don't *need* all this stuff. I never wear most of the clothes I own; I never use a quarter of the cosmetics I've bought; I take out that salad shooter about once every two years and the electric knife at Thanksgiving. I know at least half the gifts I give on birthdays and holidays end up in closets or at yard sales, and I know this because half the ones I *get* end up there. I know I don't really *need* a new car until the five-year-old model I'm driving now unfolds around me like a rusty flower in another ten years. And by the way, I know my baseball team doesn't *need* a new stadium, and my downtown doesn't *need* a bypass or a busway, and my city doesn't *need* a new airport."

Two thirds of the U.S. economy depends on consumer spending. Now that we are no longer a manufacturing nation, now that we no longer deal very much in real, durable goods, now that we are largely a service economy, what does that mean? How much of what consumers buy, even if you can actually heft it, wear it, or drive it, has any real value, any worth set by one's degree of need as opposed to desire or anxiety?

If consumers didn't spend so much, what would the economy depend on instead? What would it look like? Is there some immutable economic law that says the only security is in growth? What if we grow ourselves right off the planet, pushing all those "developing nations" off first?

Even if we live modestly — say, with basic appliances, the clothes and food we actually need, and comfortable furniture in enough warm rooms to keep the family from each other's throats — our lives are still blessed with wealth and comforts undreamed of by (I'm guessing wildly) at least 90 percent of the people who have ever inhabited the planet and another huge proportion of those who still do. Why isn't *that* enough?

Local Soil

Saturdays here are bracketed by two things I look forward to each week — the farmers' market in the morning and Adam's piano lesson in the afternoon.

I have missed the farmers' market only twice since we moved here. It is held each week, from May through the end of October, at its outdoor site in downtown Montpelier, a small lawn and parking lot at the corner of Elm and State streets, next to the courthouse. It is held one last time, just before Thanksgiving, at an indoor site, and the accent then is on holiday goods.

I went to my first farmers' market with Sarah when it opened for the season. Alan and I had driven up to close on our house and show the place to Adam. It was raining, chilly, and many weeks too early for local produce, but the market was thronged. There were crafts, maple syrup, bread, cheese, baked goods, and seedlings — herbs, perennials, vegetables — for sale. Everyone seemed in a festive mood, happy to be at the front end of the market's six-month season, the half year in which there *might* not be snow in Vermont.

This week the market was thinner than last week. The two or three killing frosts we have had recently meant almost no eggplants, summer squash, or tomatoes — but the brussel sprouts are sweetened by the cold, and the broccoli, winter squash, potatoes, onions, and even greenhouse peppers were there in abundance. Apples were everywhere, dozens of mouthwatering varieties, both heirloom and modern. Some I have never met anywhere else. Femieux, Honey Crisp, Macoun, Monroe, Paula Red, and others are all new to me, all juicy and flavorful whether red, green, streaky, or mottled. Others, like Northern Spy, are just plain hard to find in city supermarkets. The familiar Macintoshes, of course, were plentiful. Here, though, they are not mushy and bland, have not been kept since last winter, but are firm and tart and fresh from the trees.

I bought out the market's remaining eggplants and zucchinis (yes, those, the ubiquitous, can't-give-'em-away zucchinis that we'll soon grow ourselves!), along with onions, some late-season thick-skinned tomatoes, fresh parsley and dill, and a mess of peppers — Anchos, Hungarian wax peppers, and some sweet reds almost as big and shiny as Alan's sadly missed truck. As soon as I got home I started right in on six or seven quarts of ratatouille, stewing all the market stuff with two whole cups of olive oil, much garlic, a little red wine, and some cans of Italian plum tomatoes. I froze this colorful glop in batches, so we can taste summer in deepest February — if the batches last that long.

Later, Adam and I headed north to East Craftsbury for his lesson. This weekly outing represents more serendipity in our lives. Adam studied piano for five years in Pittsburgh, the first year with a pretentious woman who taught him nothing, the other four with Ray, whom I found by sheerest chance through an ad in a newspaper that I almost never read. The ad said a Juilliard graduate was available to teach piano. I called. Ray answered. He came to our door a few days later, wearing shiny new loafers, a sport coat, and too much after-shave. He gave Adam a brief sample lesson and eagerly took him on as one of the four students he would teach that year. Adam was eight then; Ray was somewhere in his mid-twenties.

Ray had just moved to Pittsburgh from New York. He was a first-year medical student at the University of Pittsburgh, and he was also finishing his Ph.D. in performance at Juilliard. All that year, he made trips to New York to present and defend his thesis. He was a gifted teacher, an accomplished and disciplined man, and a warm person. He came to the house every Saturday for an hour, and we always chatted after he had finished Adam's lesson. Ray's mother, I learned, was about my age, so Ray might have been like a son to me. Instead, he became a good friend. Adam and I went to parties at Ray's house, and Ray and his friend Will came to ours for dinner. Ray, who was tall, articulate, funny, and good-looking, managed to be both outspoken and courtly. He had been raised in West Virginia, mostly by his mother, because his father was often away. When Ray got frustrated with Adam, he would say, "Mercy!"

All along, I worried about who would take over Adam's music instruction after Ray's four years of medical school were over and he moved away for his residency. I just never thought that Adam and I would be leaving town, too, at exactly the same time. When I told Ray, who was headed for California, that we were moving to Vermont with Alan, he exclaimed, grinning, "But the best teacher for Adam on this *planet* lives in Vermont!"

That teacher is Mary Anthony Cox, who now meets with Adam for an hour every Saturday. Ray himself studied with her at Juilliard, where she still teaches three days a week, flying back and forth from the Burlington airport, a ninety-minute drive from her home. She lives in East Craftsbury, thirty-five miles from our house over secondary and dirt roads. The drive takes just under an hour each way, will probably take longer in the snow. The lesson takes an hour. I cherish all three hours, both for the easy, intimate time Adam and I can spend together in the car and for the opportunity he has — to be thirteen and studying with the director of Juilliard's ear training program.

Mary Anthony's house is a good Vermont structure, a long gray clapboard building with the rooms, from what I have seen, loosely strung together. The furniture is clean, comfortable, shabby, and not color-coordinated. Potted plants are everywhere, some lush, some leggy. I sit in an enclosed, heated sun porch, and the lesson takes place in the next room, which is dominated by a ninety-year-old Steinway grand visible to me through a large window. I can see the top of Adam's head as he sits at the keyboard, and I can overhear the music and tones of voice but not all the words that Adam and Mary Anthony exchange.

Ray, no doubt inadvertently, had prepared me for someone intimidating, saying Mary Anthony would not stand for the games and laziness Adam offered up to him from time to time. It is true that Mary Anthony is precise and demanding, but she also laughs a lot with Adam and is not above giggling, even as she stops him, corrects him, starts him over, questions him, praises him. When Adam asked her how she wanted him to address her, she told him that at Juilliard she is Miss Cox, no exceptions; but here in Vermont she is Mary Anthony, Miss Cox, or even Miz Rowell (her married name). "Just don't call me anything that chokes you," she said, laughing.

Last year, in Pittsburgh, music was a struggle for Adam for the first time. He was overwhelmed at the arts magnet school he had just entered. He had a second piano teacher there, as well as teachers for percussion, theory, music history, all the academic subjects, and the usual add-ons — health, gym, citizenship. He had too many subjects, too many teachers, no friends at that school (at least at first), and a new, major figure in his life at home, once Alan came to stay.

This year, so far, the pace of life and learning is slower. The pressures are more manageable. Adam has already made a half dozen friends, most of them in his core academic group and the school band, and he is following the interest in percussion that he first developed at the magnet school last year. He seems to be enjoying piano again. For the moment, at least, we argue less over practicing, and he has a new focus when he sits down to play. I love listening to him. He is learning a Mozart sonata, the first movement of which he will perform at a gathering at Mary Anthony's in a couple of weeks, an occasion for all her local students and their families to meet each other and share their music. The seventh-grade band concert is also coming up, on Wednesday night, and Adam is playing five or six percussion instruments in the three pieces they will perform. He talks about it often, with animation.

Adam's enthusiasm for music is divided between piano and percussion, and he seems to be having a great deal of fun with both. He practices the drums informally, playing at a friend's house and on the instruments at school. He plays percussion in the school band, which has no keyboard slot, and he enjoys jamming—not a thing that happens much with classical piano! I also think that on drums Adam can sound pretty good without lessons or a lot of hard work. With piano, he has reached a point where it's all hard work and discipline.

Regardless of the direction Adam follows, I hope he will cling to music. In a couple of years, he may want to join the senior jazz band at school, where he *could* play piano. This group, I gather, is hot—their performances are well attended, and the players are respected by classmates and adults alike.

Though the decision will be Adam's, I would like to see him follow both jazz and classical. He already says he wants to attend Carnegie Mellon University, in Pittsburgh, where his father teaches, to major in computer applications and minor in music. Ray was a good model for this kind of split—a passionate musician who did not want to earn his living by either playing or teaching. He wanted a more reliable livelihood than that, and he had a genuine interest in medicine, as Adam does in computers.

Stepfamily

We have had almost two weeks of respiratory nastiness here. I was down most of Sunday and Monday, after thinking I had already conquered this ailment. Now it's Wednesday, and Alan is suffering the worst of it. Adam has seasonal allergies, and ragweed pollen is rife here, but he has escaped whatever germ or virus has invaded Alan and me.

I am a better nurse than Alan, more solicitous, more forthcoming with the poached eggs on toast. He is generous in other ways. Before he got slam-banged with the worst symptoms, he was the one who got up in the dark and woke Adam and drove him to the bus stop. It is still hard for me to accept such an offer. I have spent most of my life and all of Adam's, until Alan, taking on too much. I think it makes me a little tiresome sometimes. I hesitated before admitting it would be wonderful if Alan got up and dealt with Adam and let me sleep. Once I gave in, I was rewarded with a grin that said: It's about time! Now we have agreed to take turns driving Adam the mile or so to the bus stop at the end of our road, when I don't drive him all the way to school.

Most mornings so far that is what I have done, mainly so we can have car time together. There is something about gazing straight ahead at the road that is conducive to unstrained parent-child conversation. Adam and I get that on the way to Mary Anthony's as well. We seldom talk about important things, though now and then I get a casual word in about values or beliefs or things I want to see Adam working on. When he was edging up on thirteen, I mentioned that I was sorry our culture — Western, Quaker, middle-class, white, WASP, whatever — does not have a proper rite of passage into a time in his life when he might want to get purposeful about the kind of man he hopes to be. He attended a friend's Bar Mitzvah in Pittsburgh but he seems uninterested in any similar ritual for himself.

Last year, after he and I had already been through a year and a half of heavy changes — which I had chosen and he had not — we were now and then at a loss with each other, an almost unprecedented thing. I yelled too much. Everything was a struggle — schoolwork, music, chores, bedtime, showers. Every kind of responsibility met huge resistance. The whole concept of having to earn anything, whether privileges or goods or allowances, seemed utterly foreign to him and was a very large sticking point for Alan, once he joined our household.

I felt defensive. I knew I had tried to instill in Adam a sense of cooperation and the need to consider others besides himself. But I also knew I had gone overboard with maternal sympathies and the effort to understand my son instead of holding him to account. Because of the odd dynamics between us, Adam's father and I fell into a one-sided pattern in which I did nearly all the parenting, and I think that, too, made me reluctant to be the perpetual bad guy. Seeing the results through Alan's eyes, and realizing that he was going to play a part in the parenting from then on, I felt insecure and sometimes resentful of what I perceived as his judgments of Adam and of me. I realize that Alan was observing, not judging, but for quite some time I could see only my failings, the ways in which I had overcompensated for being Adam's only full-time parent. I saw every error I had made and none of what I had done right.

Alan has no children of his own, but he raised or took care of four kids before Adam. Two of these were his wife, Judy's; they are now grown. One was his own nephew, who is also an adult now. Another was one of Judy's grandchildren, left in her care and Alan's almost from birth, until he was reclaimed by his mother at age twelve. Alan has very good instincts with kids and strong values to go with these. He is able to keep his hot buttons well hidden — if he even has any. Mine, on the other hand, are in plain view, and Adam has been pushing them all his life. He has often gotten his way just because he has greater energy and persistence than I do and so can wear me down.

Alan doesn't let that happen; he doesn't buy into the endless negotiations and manipulations in the first place. He cracks a sly one-liner or pokes fun at Adam in ways that take him by surprise and suddenly defuse everything with laughter. This happened when Alan went with us to Mary Anthony's recently. Adam had not eaten enough that day, and sitting in the backseat of the car he got queasy and started complaining. He was still carrying on as he got out of the car at Mary Anthony's. I kept quiet, not wanting to make it worse. Alan suddenly bent double and issued a variety of dramatic, disgusting barf noises. Adam started giggling, reluctantly at first, and then with a pure, gusty hilarity that I could never have drawn from him because I am so damned sympathetic.

Fortunately, Adam is good-hearted and good-humored. The annoying stuff is surface noise, mostly a product of early adolescence. Like any self-respecting kid, he will get away with what he can, but the things he wants to get away with are pretty innocent — extra TV, extra time on the computer, lots of leeway and bargaining and the acquisition of goods. When I worry most about the kind of man he will be, I remind myself that I have never seen him be mean to another person. Bossy, yes. Know-it-all, sometimes. Mean, never. He can be thin-skinned and sometimes edgy. My greatest hope for him is that the bossiness will evolve into leadership, the touchiness into a broader sensitivity that will apply to others' feelings as well as his own, the know-it-all quality into an ability to express and defend his ideas and feelings. Already, I see signs of what I hope for.

In our car talks, I have learned that Adam follows local politics with greater interest than he usually lets on. He asks about the Vermont governor's race, which pits the centrist Democrat incumbent, Howard Dean, against a far-right Republican, Ruth Dwyer, and wonders what a "side judge" is (I gather it is someone who tracks various judges' decisions and actions — a sort of quality control person). He likes the Burma-Shave–style signs that Henrietta Jordan, our district's Democratic candidate for the Vermont legislature, has put up along the back roads. His favorite of these is "I looked over Jordan / and what did I see? / The one I want / to represent me!"

We also talk about the foliage, other drivers on the road, percussion instruments, the friends Adam is making, and — endlessly, until my eyes glaze over — the computer games he likes, the infinite capacities of his beloved Hewlett-Packard. To give Adam credit, he will watch me during these high-tech talks and eventually say, "Your eyes are glazing over, aren't they." Then he will move on, perhaps to Thanksgiving, when he will be in Pittsburgh with his father and will see his friends.

We never talk about girls. Adam may be thirteen, but that is not a subject that interests him yet. He has not started studying himself in the mirror, or worrying about his wardrobe, or showing any interest in changing his straight-banged haircut. He does not spend any time at all before the mirror.

Last year, Alan, Adam, and I had a lot of work to do, getting used to the new dynamics that Alan's presence set in motion. This year, it is easier among us, though ups and downs are sure to keep rolling in like sine waves. It helps that Alan and I got married. Adam introduces Alan as his "stepdad," instead of having to flounder in search of some other identifying term. That simple word clarifies the role Alan plays in Adam's life. It also helps Alan and me establish the united front that Adam's father and I never managed. Adam now rides squarely in the backseat of the family car (the metaphoric one, not the nausea-making one), where any child belongs. He has some say in our timing and destinations, but not in the driving. Until Alan came along, Adam and I were a twosome by default. Each of us was the other's primary relationship. It wasn't the best arrangement for him or for me, but it was comfortable, loving, and secure — so not all bad, either.

Dogs

Annie and Hank are three months old now, pictures of bliss on these fall days. They chase each other, grinning and tumbling, their ears flying. They must run ten miles a day. I join them outside and work on getting commands to register. Hank is very quick, Annie is a dreamer. They know what "Sit" means, and "Down." I have been getting them used to gentle constraint, sitting down with one or the other between my knees and holding him or her around the chest and saying "Stay" until I let go. They don't seem to mind.

I use the Monks' techniques but not their single-minded focus. They work with their own dogs, German shepherds, for hours every day. We neither need nor want highly disciplined dogs, just polite and biddable ones. I try to work with them in the course of daily interactions, not in set-aside training sessions. When I go outside with them, they attend fairly well to the focused instruction I give, but their main concern is delight in human company and the opportunity to play. I think they have their priorities pretty straight.

God

The news these days is full of the murder of Matthew Shepard, the Laramie, Wyoming, college student who was beaten, burned, and left for dead in the desert because he was gay. Matthew's funeral was marred by vociferous, intrusive antigay demonstrators. A commentator in the

Sunday *New York Times* wrote that no homosexual anywhere can afford to feel safe. *Time* has a cover story on the controversy over gays.

I think about numerous gay or lesbian friends and acquaintances, about Ray, about Harriet and Sandra, about same-sex couples with and without children who have "married" within the Friends Meeting in Pittsburgh—though not before the Meeting went through long and searching struggle over the sanctity of traditional marriage and whether such unions could likewise be regarded as sacred. What prevailed, as I recall, was the strong sense that all love is a gift from God.

Another couple in Pittsburgh Meeting, Jan and Mary Lou, entered a conventional marriage twenty-some years ago, when Jan was John, before sex-change surgery. They have stayed married, offering the Commonwealth of Pennsylvania a precedent it would rather not honor, that of two biological females legally wedded to each other. Of course, if Jan and Mary Lou should ever divorce, the state will not allow them to change their minds and marry each other again.

Every one of these people is decent, caring, hardworking. They have the same fluctuating proportions of virtue, flaws, and blind spots that most people do, but the only way anyone could truly, viciously hate them would be through a determined effort not to know them.

I often think that willed ignorance—the obdurate refusal of insight and understanding—is the only pathway to hatred and that the only target of hatred, without exception, is difference, otherness, anything we find incomprehensible. Diversity, in other words. The ignorance that gives rise to hatred is rooted in fear, which casts out love.

They say God is love, which casts out fear. It follows, for me, that God is also knowledge and diversity. I can't help but see the three qualities, love, knowledge, and diversity, as inseparable. We fear and hate what we do not understand. We can truly love only what we know, and I can't think of any way we come to know things except through different-ness, through comparison and contrast. It is more comfortable to think we come to know what we most identify with, but from our first breath we depend on otherness—other people and unfamiliar phenomena and experiences—to teach us every lesson. Left to singularity or selfsameness we would never walk, speak, question, calculate, explore, discuss, investigate, or rejoice. All our lives, we compare ourselves to mentors and models, striving to be like them. We measure our performance against that of skilled people whose ranks we would join. We seek the approval of friends and family. We learn who we are and what we can do only through contact with people and things outside our own skin and our own experience.

When we want to control the nature of the otherness through which we learn — when we want to deal only with others who think like us, or with whom we are comfortable, or whose values or skin tones match our own — we not only limit what they can teach us but also reveal our fears, suspicions, and insecurity. From these emotions hatred, given a chance, will grow. Hatred would do away with the diversity we need in order to develop and learn. Hatred thus denies the nature of the universe and the God who created it. It denies that we are all one, that each of us needs others in order to learn who we ourselves are.

In a prolific and exotically diverse Creation, every example is bound to have counterexamples; every rule, myriad exceptions; every kaleidoscopic view, a hundred others just as colorful, just as jewel-like. If we have one gender, we will have not only two but several, so we will live on a continuum of heterosexual, homosexual, bisexual, transsexual, asexual experience. If we have one race we will have several, and they will mix, so we will have every shade of skin color that ivory, brown, red, copper, black, bronze, and alabaster can combine to produce. If we have one code of morality and ethics, we will have a hundred, and they will all give rise to as much wrong-headedness, crime, and dishonesty as goodwill or social conscience. Likewise, if we have one religion, we will have a thousand, and they will breed love and hatred, peace and war, in varying proportions, always reflecting their members' capacity for love and degree of fear.

When I trust my intuitions — which Quakers would call the inner light — about the nature of God as it is revealed through love, knowledge, and diversity, I can only conclude that religion is a human creation, not a heavenly one. There are so many religions claiming the exclusive truth about one God, and they have forever been willing to torture and kill blasphemers and heathens to prove their claim. *Love? Knowledge? Diversity?* Being a Quaker, I also believe every religion has a piece of the truth, as every human being does, even if it is difficult for outsiders, or even insiders, to discern. Troubles arise when we mistake our own small piece as the whole and regard the truth in others' possession as upstart lies.

Creation may be infinitely varied, but the only way it makes any sense to me is to believe that the Creator Herself is — or began as — one, a limitless singularity containing all potential. Our muddled, fractious, faction-ridden thinking about God comes from our limited, fragmented human vision. Only God is all-seeing; we are not.

I have heard that God created the universe out of loneliness and a desire to experience otherness — something, everything, that is not-God. So if God is love, and God learns the way we do, through otherness, then God must have created hatred, indifference, and evil. This raises the thorny question: How could a God who is perfect love have conceived of evil, let alone permitted it to enter Her creation?

The nearest explanation that I can intuit is also my strongest evidence that God exists at all, and that explanation runs more or less like this: Only that which is can engender that which is not. Only an eternal, singular, unattended, uncontrasted mind could, in its isolation and purity, create something from the nothing-yet, or the all-potential, that has been itself; could explode its own singularity and perfection into a universe of trouble and complexity. Only perfect love can devise its own antithesis, and in fact it *must* do so. It must willingly open itself up to loss, betrayal, and disappointment in order to reveal itself as pure, and purely loving.

God wished to observe, learn, and also reveal Herself through comparison and contrast, through a rubbing-up against a diversity as great in magnitude as God's undivided self. All of this — this explosive creation — would have required God's own cosmically terrifying leap, a plunge into fragmentation and away from the comforting but invariable oneness and allness that God had been. Perhaps our human experience, our dependence on diversity for all our knowledge, is simply a dim mirror of God's own creative urge and risk — God's own leap of faith.

If God is love, and love seeks an object, then God had to create that object through otherness, separateness. The greater the love, the greater the diversity and number of the objects of love. The greater the diversity, the greater the knowledge — of both other and self — that it can generate. How else could God-the-infinite know Herself but to create the whole universe as both a mirror of Her mind and antithesis to it?

I believe it is possible, then, that when God fragmented oneness into the multifarious universe, She gave both Herself and us, out of boundless, risky, heartbreaking love, the only possible route to knowledge and understanding: comparison, diversity, opposition, contrast. I do not for an instant believe She forbade knowledge. That story about the off-limits apple is nothing more than a fable, one that creates in us a fear of curiosity and knowing, which is a fear of our very nature. Fear casts out love, and so the forbidden apple becomes a dividing image. Yet our best salvation, to my mind, lies in a long journey, as individuals and as a race of God's children, out of division and back into a knowing harmony that encompasses everything we are, have been, could be.

Increasingly, then, it seems to me that the God of Creation is pure paradox — that creating required and embodied not only the possibility but the fact of destruction, especially the destruction of God's insular, integral oneness. God would have *had* to relinquish control. She would have *had* to open Herself to some vast version of what arises in any human endeavor, which is the possibility of unanticipated glitches, spin-offs, problems, complexities. With infinity as Her raw material, She would have had no choice but to create everything not-God, including violence, division, cruelty, suspicion, arrogance, ignorance, and intolerance. Creation *is* fragmentation, first. To make anything — a house, a quilt, an omelet — we first have to break, cut, tear, collect the pieces or ingredients. Perhaps our job on earth is to find as many scraps of original truth as we can and fit them together again. Perhaps that is how both we and God can come to know Her.

If we lived in a perfect paradise, as in the tale of the apple, how could we know it as one without some experience of pain and loss to serve as a defining opposite? We cannot know hot without cold, joy without sorrow, comfort without pain, intimacy without loneliness — or love without fear and hatred. Opposites are usually not separate things but aspects of each other. We hate this idea. We love polarizing.

But we are all part of the diversity that God created in order to know Herself. We are all made by God, of Godstuff, and we all have feet of clay, too. We are deeply, inextricably twined into this not-God universe. This helps explain to me our dichotomous tendencies, our insistence on having things purely black or white, our resistance to shades of gray, to paradox, to ambiguity.

But what could be more paradoxical or ambiguous than an all-powerful, all-loving God who had no choice, once the creating began, but to engender Her own antitheses?

We think we are either angels or devils. We are male or female. We are right or wrong, saved or lost. If we are right, those who differ from us are wrong or misguided, even evil, and therefore to be hated and feared, not tolerated, not treated with compassion, and certainly not loved.

Real love is neither sentimental nor easy. It manifests through action and challenge; it requires a muscular moral struggle every inch of the way, but it is the only way. It is hard enough to love the lovable. It takes incredible energy to love, because it means putting ourselves in the loved one's place, imagining another's reality even, or especially, when that person annoys or disappoints or frightens us. If it is so hard to love even a beloved other as ourselves, especially when we are exhausted or angry, it must be the hardest thing in the world to love the unlovable. It must take a Jesus, a Buddha, a saint to do it well. The rest of us have a smaller capacity because our spirits are constrained by fear and by the ignorance we hang onto as a defense. The more we learn, and the more we welcome the truths that others carry, the more we enlarge our spirits and make way for oneness instead of division.

I perceive Jesus, Buddha, and every other famous or unsung holy one as both divine and human. This seems perfectly plain. To the extent that

I believe Jesus was God in a human body, I can be counted a Christian. But in believing that the rest of us, and all our various faiths, carry a share of divinity, I probably don't qualify. It is a matter of degree — a very large matter, a mysterious and holy one, but still proportional — the difference between most of us and those we revere. The holy ones might have had much larger shares of inner light to begin with. They surely tuned in more deeply to that of God in themselves and in everyone else. They kept their focus on spirit, becoming more Godlike the more they discovered the truth in their own and others' being.

Focus

I am learning the power of both focus and choice. When I train my mind's eye on a spiritual question — when I am deliberate about exploring, thinking, envisioning — I discover my faith by watching it appear in words on the computer screen before me, words I believe originate beyond my mind. Much of what I write comes to me because I have chosen to train my attention on a particular issue, such as diversity. But in the process of seeking and articulating, I learn more than I ever thought I knew. If I have just enough faith to begin writing about something, anything, of compelling spiritual concern to me, I will be rewarded by insights that deepen the faith that got me started. Where the insights come from I can only intuit, but I intuit God.

Such acts of faith and discernment are to me the very heart of Quakerism; they reflect the central concept that the inner light exists in every person. Invoking the light, praying for it to illuminate my doubts and questions, I come gradually to an understanding beyond the power of words and intellect to convey. This understanding, which I have just described as best I can in terms of love, knowledge, and diversity, moves me to my soul and seems in fact to shine.

Holy Pronouns

When I speak of God sometimes as She and sometimes as He and sometimes as It I am being neither flippant nor doggedly feminist. There is no satisfactory pronoun in our language. No he-she-or-it that we use for the animate, inanimate, and bounded things of our earthly experience can remotely convey the eternal, unknowable entity that is God. Yet I believe God is *apprehensible* to us, because we all carry that divine spark that Quakers call the inner light, which is that of God within us. We have within us direct access to our eternal origin, a way to hear the voice of God, not literally but by indirection, inference, and logic. I infer God from the patterns of my life and their connection to much larger patterns. They all unfold until, for me, the existence of God becomes the only thing that makes sense — both the ultimate logical conclusion and the mystery our minds can't grasp.

The patterns I speak of are formed by the dichotomies I have mentioned, the polarizations that create the terms in which we ask almost every question, silly or profound: Does he love me or love me not? What is right, what is wrong? Are we innately good, or are we born in sin? What does it mean to be male? female? Is there a God, or not?

I believe most dichotomies represent a futile effort to reduce our complex world to simplistic pairs, splitting it down the middle the way Solomon suggested splitting that baby. I believe genuine simplicity embraces everything; it is *both/and*, not *either/or;* it admits that we can do good and do evil, can love one day and fail to love the next, can be outwardly male or female but far more alike than different.

In only one telling instance do I believe the dichotomy is absolute and our view of it utterly defining: Is there a God, or not?

I am reminded of some work done in the research program where I once worked, on the nature of learning in physics. It was apparently very difficult for newcomers to the subject to grasp concepts that contradict everyday perceptions; for example, the nature of heat and cold. It is not easy to understand that heat is a phenomenon in its own right; it has identity and reality, whereas cold is merely the absence of heat. Heat is something; cold, when you get right down to it, is nothing. For anyone who has eaten ice cream or experienced a New England winter, that is indeed a difficult concept. Cold certainly *feels* like a presence, not an absence.

But when I think of the God-versus-no-God question in this framework, I have to rephrase it: What is the ground of our being? Is it something, or nothing? For something to come out of nothing makes no sense to me. It violates our cherished laws of science and logic, laws that to me reflect the mind of God. There may have been "nothing" before Creation — no substance, space, or time. But there had to have been mind, desire, and intention. This is surely why all *human* creation begins with thought and imagination. It is why, in its purest efforts, the human mind can change reality simply by envisioning, without devising blueprints or schedules.

Another way I sometimes think about the existence of God is through one of the commonplace questions about God: "You mean you believe in a God who hears you, pays attention to you, is able to track your life personally among the billions of lives on this planet?" The question always reminds me of what children ask about Santa Claus when they begin figuring out that he is fiction: "But how can he get to all those houses in one night?" In fact, the fictional Santa Claus bears a strong resemblance to the fictional God who sees everything we do, punishes us for our sins, rewards us for our good deeds, has a long white beard, and lives in some distant unreachable place.

When, as children, we write a letter to Santa, our parents intercept it and selectively make our wishes come true. When, as adults, we pray to God, and our life changes — not according to a specific wish list but in deep thematic ways — there are no intermediaries, there is no deception, however benign. When we pray, when we seek God patiently and without an agenda, a personal relationship is indeed established, not because there is an anthropomorphic figure seated in a heavenly throne taking calls from below, but because we have made contact with the mind that moves the universe; we have drawn on that of God within us to establish union with God Itself.

It is impossible for me to have any picture of God. I believe I am made in God's image, but only in the sense that God is a maker, a source of love, and an entity who wishes to know both Itself and whatever exists outside Itself. Beyond this notion, I am aware that everything I believe or speculate about in connection with God is as much my imagination — my envisioning capacity — as any knowable reality. To me, though, my imagination *is* that of God, so it is my best way of intuiting what God is. When I seek relationship with God, it is through these qualities in myself, as they connect me to the eternal mystery beyond myself, the mystery from which I come and to which I will return.

This is why I cannot call God exclusively He, She, or It; these pronouns have too many earthbound associations. I do not see God as a man or woman, a mother or a father. God is both and everything, endless and endlessly loving. Nevertheless, when I seek most intently, I feel I am answered, and I feel the answer comes to me because I have willingly and faithfully entered the connection to my source, which is also my solace and my power.

"Bless and Release"

Yesterday, I asked Alan why he had never seen his biological father — who was divorced from his mother before Alan really knew him — between the ages of five and a troubled seventeen. I knew the outline of his biography as he had sent it to me in early e-mail, in a style both telegraphic and rollicking:

> Born in Lakewood, Ohio, on the west side of Cleveland. Lakewood was a burb before the term was coined. An old burb. Ethnic food in this neighborhood was Spam and Velveeta on Wonder Bread; I remember Granny apoplectic when a Jewish doctor bought a house on our block. Daddy was off to war (and never came back — not to our house anyway, but with new wife he met in D.C. — he was mostly a desk-bound sailor).

Actually, I was an unplanned product of a frenzied coupling before off-to-war, conceived pretty danged close to Pearl Harbor Day.

Moved to Bay Village, Ohio, at six w/ Mom and new Nazi stepfather. B.V. was famous as the home of Dr. Sam Sheppard. Dr. Sam vaccinated us kids. We think he didn't do it.

To East Lansing, Michigan for junior high. Hot soul food: lather both sides of your spam-vel sandwich w/ Imperial marg and grill it. Had one black kid in school — daughter of the maid of the president of Michigan State. Major life-changing experience: seeing James Dean in *Rebel Without a Cause* — and I changed into being a cool, pomaded, Marlboros-in-the-T-shirt-sleeve, horny adolescent with fantasies about Natalie Wood in that pink angora sweater.

Nazi stepfather runs off to California w/ bimbo, bimbo dumps him, he comes back tail between legs, drags us off to San Francisco. I enroll next semester at Balboa High School. HOLY ****!! — instant cultural adjustment required here. "Uh, excuse me, but what part of the school-yard belongs to you, uh, Pa-chu-co guys?" Daily motivation switched from getting straight A's (to avoid wrath of Nazi stepdad) to getting to and from school ALIVE.

Nazi step hooks up w/ bimbo again in L.A., dumps us in fringe-of-the-Mission funky place. Whitebread Mom freaks at the environment, moves us to San Mateo. My punky rebellion period — I'm into booze, scoring, and fast cars . . . Angel-on-shoulder period — should not have survived drunken drag races over Route 92 to Half Moon Bay, Skyline, Highway 1 in the fog.

Get in a bit o' a jam w/ police for prying screen off back of Chinese restaurant and swiping a few cases of beer to fuel a beach party. The juvie division guys offer me the choice of boys' ranch or go live in a better enviro w/ an uncle in Cleveland.

Bungee back to Cleveland, get reunited w/ natural father, who lives near uncle . . . find out I have two brothers . . . they find out about me . . .

Why didn't Alan's father, James, maintain contact with him? Until Harvey, the "Nazi stepdad," moved the family to Michigan when Alan was twelve, James lived only a few miles away. But for those seven years, he was wholly absent from his young son's life.

Turns out, James did visit Alan every week for a while after the war. I gather the relationship was awkward. Alan never knew James very well, having been born while he was away in the Navy, having never lived in the same house with him, having another man, Harvey, in the role of father. But it was Harvey's idea, not Alan's or James's, to break that first paternal connection. Harvey made Alan, five years old, tell James one week that he didn't want him to visit anymore. And James never visited any more.

Many years later, after the shaky father-son reunion in Cleveland had gradually mellowed into a warm connection, James said he always thought Alan had had a comfortable, stable life with his mother and Harvey. But here is how Alan told it to me, prompted by my asking him whether he had ever read either Geoffrey Wolff's *Duke of Deception* or Tobias Wolff's *This Boy's Life* — both books about the same father:

Whoa! Didn't read (hadn't realized Geoff had written a book also) but DID see the film version of *This Boy's Life* — w/a sense of creepy-crawly déjà vu that made my hair stand up on the back of my neck — DeNiro as Dwight, Ellyn Barkin as Mom, and Leonardo di Caprio as Toby/Jack — who had me right down to the pomade and duck's ass haircut. My "Dwight" [Harvey] got me a paper route at age 8. From 8 to 14 I got up every morning of my life at 4:30. When snow was too deep to bicycle through, I pulled the papers on a sled. He too took all my route money to save for "college." When he split so did "my" bank account. Didn't trade my Winchester for a bulldog — Harvey's version went thusly: I wanted a new bicycle — *needed* a new bike, 'cause the one I had had plain worn out pushing papers. The bearings had fallen out of the wheels. He made me a "deal": he'd split the cost of a bike w/me, his "half" being my Christmas present. He took $60 from my account as my "half." Later I found a receipt for the bicycle on his desk. It cost $39.95. I didn't suffer the same kind of physical abuse as Toby/Jack; Harvey used a belt instead of fists. I made it a point to stay as far away from him as I could.

I love Alan, so I resent anyone who has done harm to him. But Alan himself, though he carries a lot of hurt, has no self-pity. I think that is what rescued him from the common cycle of abuse, in which victims end up harming others. But I don't think he forgives, either — maybe because forgiveness so often has a self-righteous aura that doesn't do either party any good. His method is to "bless and release." I think, literally, he utters a prayer for those who have hurt him and then dismisses their sins from his mind. The sins return, I am sure, but are banished again. It must be a constant effort. To my eyes, it is a clear example of difficult, strenuous love at work. Such love is not tender, not soft, not easy, and certainly not joyous, but it is full of respect for both self and other.

Autumn's Colors Fade

We have had some ferocious winds this past week, and now the leaves at our elevation are gone. Here and there a lone yellow maple glows like a candle against hills that are otherwise clothed in the dark green of conifers and the gray of leafless hardwoods. Those few remaining flamelike trees do not deceive; the cold will take over, they cannot stop it.

I remember how hungry for color I was in Pittsburgh winters. Everywhere, I saw only infinite variations on gray, taupe, and brown under damp, oyster-colored skies. When friends and coworkers learned I was moving to Vermont, they almost all said the same thing: "But how will you stand the winters?" I would reply that I could stand the cold if I could have three feet of clean snow on the ground and a blue sky overhead. It was the urban chill, the soot of exhaust, and the parade of damp gray days with temperatures in the thirties and forties that got me down.

Now that my airy proclamation is about to be tested, I am eager for the first snow, leery about the ones that might still be coming in April. Alan once said in e-mail, "Much as I love New England, best way to live there is to spend three months in the Bahamas." I think he meant January, February, and March — those three months.

But the Bahamas are out for now. We have blown most of our cash on two houses, with just about enough left to pay for construction supplies next spring, and we do have to keep Adam in school all winter. We are more likely to spend the winter hustling some freelance clients, making things out of wood, reading stacks of books, building cardboard models of our house and adding onto them in varying configurations. Graph paper is not enough; we need to see this structure's odd angles and peculiar upstairs-downstairs correspondences in three dimensions.

Alan has often lived on very little and in primitive conditions, always by choice. He, his late wife Judy, and whatever children and animals shared their household full or part time lived for several years on some mining claims in the mountains of Northern California, a proper homestead built from scavenged and bartered goods and lumber that Alan cut and milled himself. There was no electricity on "the claims." Conveniences were limited to a propane-powered refrigerator and stove, coils of black hose on the roof to solar-heat water (diverted from a stream uphill), and a fairweather washing machine that sat under a tree, attached to a small generator. In the winter, Alan drove to the laundromat.

People who visited the homestead said, "But this is *camp;* no one really *lives* like this."

Alan said it was so quiet there that they could hear individual snowflakes hit the ground. A bear once settled down for his long winter's nap in their greenhouse. Every morning, to get his stepdaughter Edie to school, Alan drove her to the bottom of the mountain in his truck, walked with her across a log bridge spanning a high stream, transferred her to the car they kept waiting on the other side, and then drove her to the bus stop. On snowy mornings, he plowed first. Edie — who is thirty at this writing, a computer whiz, happily married, and the mother of two girls — credits Alan and that spare lifestyle for her emotional strength, her resourceful self-reliance, and her skills as carpenter, plumber, auto mechanic, and electrician. Sam, her husband, is the cook in the family and is almost as handy as Edie.

Where Alan and I are now is far less remote than "the claims," but it is quiet enough that I could hear the dry leaves falling during still moments this fall. It is far enough from even the nearest neighbors that only one other house is faintly visible through the bare trees. It is wild enough that we can expect to see moose, deer, rabbits, skunks, fishers, and porcupines, and I have already heard foxes — or something — yipping at night.

We are private without being isolated, but the New England winter will still be a challenge to one who has been away so long. Sarah and I plan to make quilts this winter, a new experience for me. I will draw, write, and knit as well. Alan will read, complete the indoor tasks that the outdoor ones have preempted, write, and stay tuned to Matt Drudge, Molly Ivins, and Sam Smith on the Internet. Except in the bitterest cold, I will continue my walks outdoors, on snowshoes when necessary. I would like to go sledding with Adam.

I hope I will not even think about the Bahamas.

Plans for the Land

This morning, I woke to a wet fog. The leafless woods through the windows looked like a soft charcoal drawing, the hemlocks darkest, the birches and maples just pale strokes against the surrounding mist — hundreds of branches and twigs, jumbled and overlapping like kindling in a box.

By the time I finished my walk, the Indian summer sun was coming out, and Alan and I stood together and peered into our woods, amazed at their density. Nearly all the hardwoods are so overcrowded, and have been for so long, that their trunks are ridiculously spindly. Trees fifty to seventy feet tall are only eight to eighteen inches in diameter. Their branches don't start until thirty or more feet from the ground. At eye level, as you gaze into the bared woods, the ranks of leaning and upright trees look like crosshatched calendar markings on a prison wall, all superimposed on one another into the distance. Clearing the crosshatch, and creating a view of the Worcester Range on which to rest our eyes this winter, will surely help cancel that image of confinement.

As you look generally west from the rise in our clearing, toward the North Branch of the Winooski River and Route 12, the trees begin in a line roughly perpendicular to the front of the house. Those nearest trees define the upper edge of the first in a series of sheer, rocky bluffs that alternate with level ground. The level areas are now carpeted in leaves and needles but are thick with undergrowth in high summer. Alan has revised his plan for thinning and clearing a wide sweep of this difficult terrain. Though he has spoken to a couple of loggers about coming in to do the task, he has all along feared the torn-up land and the mess of brush and branches that might be left behind. What's more, he can't stand to think of all that hardwood being ground to pulp or burned to ash in someone's else's stove. He plans now to do most of the clearing on his own, cutting the trees, bucking them into stove lengths, splitting the wood, and stacking it. He will mill the prettiest wood himself, too, now that the portable sawmill he ordered through the Internet has arrived. Attached to a monster chain saw that Alan still needs to purchase (used, if possible), it will cut timber into boards, posts, or beams, anything up to sixteen inches.

To fell the trees, Alan has equipped his new-old truck (a dark blue '82 Ford with reasonable mileage and a renovated body) with a winch; or, rather, he has paid a welder to attach the winch, which the man did without any apparent use of a brain. He was supposed to construct a new front bumper and bolt the winch to that, leaving the bumper exposed except for a couple of protective bars to keep it from dents and dings. Instead, he welded a big, ugly slice of black steel over the original bumper and then welded the winch — instead of bolting it, so it could have been moved — inside that piece of junk, stringing the cable through a hole in the front. Alan spent a whole afternoon snarling and sweating as he struggled with this sloppy setup. He had to rewire the winch and attach its control box somewhere other than the site designated by the manufacturer, the welder's ingenuity having blocked access to that preferred location.

Alan finally got the winch working, only to have the truck's front axle break. The repair shop can't take that job on for another week, so now he is left with the prospect of glorious weather this weekend and no chance to test his equipment against our woods. He may not be able to resist doing it anyway, driving the crippled truck just far enough to hook some cables and pulleys onto the nearest trees atop the nearest ridge, sever their skinny trunks with his chainsaw (not the one he will need for the portable sawmill, but a smaller one he already has), and aim their crashing fall into the clearing but away from truck, house, and other trees. This is an artful job, one that requires him to get all the angles — cables to pulleys to trees to truck — just right.

I know he is going to start this despite the obstacles. The sun has burnt away this day's fog as I have been writing this, and sun draws Alan like a magnet. He used to joke in his e-mails that a sunny day turns him into Energizer Bunny (as opposed to Crusader Rabbit, another of his alter egos). This irresistible pull, coupled with the knowledge that today and tomorrow might give us the last of our good weather for a long while, will surely lure him into a major project, and logging is the one with his name all over it on this drop-dead gorgeous Saturday.

And now here comes the man himself, dressed in overalls, sweatshirt, and purple baseball cap, heading for the mudroom and his work boots. Grabbed those truck keys en route, so it looks like I am right. I will head outside myself. Sandra stashed perennials all over the place, amid ferns and wild blackberry, alongside the drainage ditch, atop rock outcrop-pings. I plan to find them, dig them up, and put them all in one spot for the winter, a nice, high plateau above the plastic-covered slope, in full sun. Next spring, or the one after that, I will start moving the plants again, to halfway houses if not permanent homes. A real landscape design could take three or four years even to lay out sketchily on our property. Today, though, the flowers are my own excuse to stoke some light and warmth for the winter that's coming.

Reflections in Older Eyes

Yesterday I hung one more year on the line — as Paul Simon would have it. I am now fifty-four, an unparsable, abstract number that seems a very odd measure of my time on this planet. I know what people mean when they say they feel younger than their ever-accelerating chronology tells them they should, yet I also feel every minute of my age. I am stiff and arthritic, despite regular walking and stretching. I can no longer fall into bed at night and not move until morning; now my joints complain loudly enough to wake me at uneven intervals. My metabolism has slowed. My hair and skin have lost some of their light. I can never remember where I put my keys. But I *understand* much more than ever before, and I find it ironic that so many lessons of late middle age keep me feeling young, adventuresome, alert, and joyful.

The biggest lesson is the sudden, calm surprise that I am only one of billions of people, living and dead, and that my life is mainly insignificant in the vast scope of the human struggle. I find this awareness operates peculiarly, making the deliberate, good use of my time and life seem more important, not less. I think with awe of all our ancestors. The debts we owe them date to dimmest prehistory and gather interest every day. I also know that I will *be* an ancestor before so very long. We ride on a sea of those who have gone before, who have built us an ark from their commonplace and extraordinary insights and discoveries. Every time we brew tea, listen to a saxophone, drink from a glass, or plant our garden, let alone surf the Internet or undergo laser surgery, we are in debt to the thousand thousand generations that have preceded us. When we forget this, and look after the needs of only one generation in ways that can harm the offspring of offspring not yet conceived, we abuse not only our future kin but our own souls.

This, I believe, is one reason I have wanted for so long to live in a natural setting. I remember telling Alan in an e-mail about my reactions to *The Spell of the Sensuous*, by David Abram:

> It begins with author's description of stepping out of a hut, at night in Indonesia, into a surrounding rice paddy, with stars above reflected below, with the middle air filled with fireflies, all of which sent him into a weightless vertigo, an overwhelming sensation of floating in space. This echoes an experience I had in a rowboat on a lake in northern New Hampshire when I was in high school. I was sitting in the boat late at night, on glassy water, with the stars above and below, like a space voyager. That was a peak experience for me, one of three or four I will never forget.
>
> The book is a long consideration of the industrialized world's loss of connection with a living world of nature and mystery; this is the source, according to Abram, of our cultural ills, from violence to immune disor-

ders. At one point he says that we have made the earth and natural world a mechanical, spiritless place without sensation or soul and as a consequence we have removed spirit to either heaven or the inside of our own skull.

I want to be closer to spirit that is abroad in this world, and so I want to live here, in the woods ("Cleave a piece of wood. . . ").

When Alan and I first began discussing where we would live, we thought about both the mountains and the ocean, and we considered, at least briefly, territory ranging from western North Carolina to Virginia to the coast of Maine. Water was somewhat more important to Alan, the mountains and woods more important to me. He decided, when we found this place, that he could make do with the rivers, streams, and nearby reservoir — as long as we visit the coast at least once a year.

I am more certain than ever that this is where I belong. I am attracted to the ocean but also intimidated and churned up by it. When Alan and I visited Maine during our first summer together, we spent a day sitting on rocks by the ocean, watching the tide and the sky. The water changes second by second, and the sky moment by moment. The woods change season by season, and the mountains eon by eon. I like the slower changes. They put my own life in perspective.

All of which is fine, but birthdays bring on less-than-lofty thoughts, too — thoughts about aging, loss, and one's diminishing allure and diminishing time on earth. This year I am thinking about what I have achieved in my life and wondering whether I would have done more or less without the baggage I carried into adulthood from my youth. I used to think I knew the answer. I used to think it was a given that I would have been free to do wonders. Now it occurs to me that the weight of the baggage might have given me muscle I would not have developed otherwise.

Having been pretty — not gorgeous, by any means, but all-American whitebread pretty — was part of the baggage. When you don't really believe there is much going on inside, and you have the kind of outward appearance that the culture values to the point of using it to hawk everything from tobacco to baby food, you can come to value yourself in only those superficial terms, trying to please or placate others in relatively shallow ways.

Alan and I wrote to each other about the matter of appearance long before we met in the flesh. We recollected and shared our adolescent angst, returning time and again to the differences between boys' and girls' coming of age in the fifties and early sixties. He said:

Think I understand the male half of the equation, but never have figgered out the female side. In the Rebel w/o a Causitiveness — I understood James Dean, never Natalie Wood (other than desperately desiring to get eyes and hands under that pink angora sweater).

I answered:

Well, not even remembering the movie, I can tell you that Natalie wanted to be described to herself in terms she could recognize *so that* she could take off that sweater, *so that* she could love without fearing exploitation, abuse, scorn, judgment, loss. Natalie had just as much lust and longing as James Dean but had been taught that that part was dangerous and the rest of her was not of interest.

Alan further asked:

Why does the virginal English captain's daughter have those "hot eyes" for the pirate with the big price on his head?

And I said:

Probably because she'll settle for an illusion of power, or a simulation of passion, or a straightforward romp if she knows she's unlikely to find . . . recognition and acceptance.

I might also have said the captain's daughter was in denial. She could convince herself that she and the pirate were star-crossed soul mates. This was close to what I had done in relationships, myself. As I said to Alan:

I am curious about the phenomenon of bad boys and good girls. When I was young I was attracted to the bad boys because of the vicarious sense of daring — they did stuff I was too scared to do. What does send people over the line and into people's faces? My rebellions tend to simmer until

I'm ready to act, and then I try to make sure I'm clear about what I'm doing. That's the adult pattern, though. In younger days, I simply indulged in mindless pinballing, all emotionally driven but without clarity. I went through jobs, lovers (well, not legions of them), dwellings, passions—all as if emotions were like the weather, intense but beyond my control.

The pinballing was very much an effect of thinking there was nothing much inside. It had led me into premature marriage, and afterward, while I still carried the shrapnel of that burst union, it led me across the country, into a murky search for myself, one I wasn't really aware of conducting. I formed a few uneasy, serial, sexual alliances. I made friends with some people who were good for me and some who were not. I kept my inmost self entirely distant from everyone, and I could not accept genuine affection. The longest relationship I had in California was with a man named Rich, an honest, generous person whose love I returned with criticism and aloofness. I remember one night in particular with wincing shame. Rich and I were in a restaurant with another couple. I aimed barbed comments at Rich all evening, thinking—really—that I was just being witty. Dimly, I saw the looks on our friends' faces; dimly I knew I was being a bitch. Rich never did a thing but care for me, and he paid for that by suffering my edginess and defenses.

In all those loose, spendthrift years out West, I was articulate about everything I did. I gave a good impression of a thoughtful person, but I felt I was a fraud, or some kind of idiot savant. So I skated by on my looks. I was satisfied to be looked at but not known. That lasted for a long, dangerous time, nearly eight years.

All that has changed. I care just enough about my looks to want what comes of being healthy, clean, well nourished, and reasonably fit. I like soft, comfortable clothes, or blue jeans; I will probably never again think much about fashion. I quit wearing makeup the day we arrived in Vermont. I quit highlighting my hair. I squelched the habitual *How do I look?* that had always accompanied me into the world, even to the grocery store. I surprised the hell out of myself.

Maybe I now care less about how I look because I have learned to value and recognize the other aspects of my character. I hear my soul more clearly. I also know that Alan likes my face unadorned and doesn't mind the softness enfolding a body that was always pretty angular. It is also true that my looks have been on a long hike and are fast disappearing over that famous hill. Why fight the inevitable, especially if those you care about don't care about it? Besides, paying less attention to appearances leaves me freer to contemplate what lies beneath them — to inquire into my truest nature, to ask what my soul requires of me at this time of my life.

Finally, I may be less concerned about how I look outwardly because I am in a culture that just plain loves plainness. I look around at the other undecorated women in Vermont and find them beautiful. When I see someone wearing make-up, it looks odd, false, stuck on. I don't have any figures to back this up, but I would risk a hefty wager that women in Vermont spend less money on cosmetics, per capita, than women in just about any other state. I believe this is because people around here are judged more consistently by their inner qualities and outward acts than by their appearance.

This is a radical notion, especially if you tend to suspect that women's insecurities about their looks are part of a giant socioeconomic conspiracy (whether deliberate or not) to sap their powers and plunder their pocketbooks. Most women here spend no more time, money, or anxiety on their appearance than men do. How amazing! It doesn't mean people don't care to a reasonable extent about their looks; it just means neither gender invests much more than the other to quell the anxiety or play up good bones. It seems also to mean that the men here, at least in my limited observations, care more about the content of a woman's character than about the special effects she can create with the contents of her bathroom cupboard. Who would not choose to be loved by being known rather than for outward attributes?

My own long fear of being known, deep down, in spiritual as well as emotional and philosophical matters, persisted until Alan came along. With my second husband I tried to share my mind, at least, and some of my emotional realities; but even when he invited conversation about

Quakers, about my spiritual life, I never was able to trust his sincerity. I always anticipated logical argument, not free and deep exploration. Now, with occasional relapses, I want Alan to see me for who I am, beneath all constructed appearances. Artifice can be creative, it can be enormous fun, it can make a person feel strutty and confident and full of mischief. I remember that well. I've just lost my taste for it. I'm taking pleasure in plainness. I'm reminded of something Bette Midler said in a television interview, that she would give it all up — the makeup, the face-lifts, the fashion — if her world would let her. Mine is letting me, and that is a great relief.

Artifice

We have discovered another benefit of this country life: The houses here are so far apart that Halloween will likely pass us by. Few trick-or-treaters will visit our door tonight, and Adam seems unconcerned about tricking himself out to plunder any neighbors' stashes of candy. We bought a small supply of sweets, just in case; but we have eaten about half ourselves.

In town, it is altogether a different story. Last year a steady stream of 300 children visited Sarah and Joe's porch. They ran out of candy and had to retire to the upstairs rooms, leaving the ground floor in unwelcoming darkness. Even in Pittsburgh, in both neighborhoods, I never had more than a few dozen kids ring the bell.

Alan dislikes Halloween — the costumes, the customs, the material exploitation, the lack of any compelling meaning to the holiday. Unlike me, I think Alan has never been one for artifice or fantasy. He can match any fifth-generation Vermonter for plainness, thrift, and truth telling. The idea of Alan in costume is as incongruous as (to borrow from Joe) tits on a boar hog. Not only would a costume be as out of place as said tits, it would also be too obvious, too overt a statement no matter what the get-up. Alan goes deep, but he isn't given to announcing what's down there. The way you find out is to apprehend and infer, not to ask directly or expect him to volunteer. You glean your information from his actions, his sly, dry humor, the content of his passionate rants against the news, or, if you ever get close enough, the incredible tenderness behind his eyes.

It should come as no surprise that not many people know Alan well. It is revealing, sometimes painfully so, to observe their reactions to his watchful, taciturn shyness. Emma and Ellen, two of the women I had known the longest in Pittsburgh, who had been my friends under many good and trying circumstances — from childbirth to the celebration of professional milestones, from the loss of parents to troubles at work — rejected him, either outright or because of the changes he and I chose to make. Everyone else accepted Alan, first on the strength of my attachment and respect, and later in his own right. Sarah said, regarding Alan's reluctance to talk much, especially about himself, "That's not how he lets you get to know him." She understood that Alan *does* let you get to know him in time and that his silence in general is neither judging nor secretive but comes from the heart of who he is. For Alan to be otherwise would be a falsehood, a costume.

Ironically, I know this, and I know the silent Alan, because I am the only person who has ever received a torrent of words from him, a rush that I referred to in an e-mail as his whitewater stream of consciousness. I realize that if Alan and I had met face to face, instead of through a pair of geographically far-flung computer monitors, I might have reacted to him much as my two unaccepting friends did. I was entirely a word person, a lifelong editor and writer, a weaver of stories about my own life and about the actions and thoughts of others who affected it. I depended on words to make sense of things; I came to think they were all I had.

I made other assumptions, too. I thought I was, for better or worse, a part of the mainstream, or at least the shallows along its banks. I was a professional, I lived an urban life that was scheduled largely by a job I did not like. I spent my free time with Adam or in my own pursuits: gardening, running errands, walking, reading, serving on Friends committees, having friends to dinner. My spending habits were well documented by Williams-Sonoma, White Flower Farm, j.jill, and other catalogue companies. My credit was perfect, and I thought I lived within my means — I paid my bills on time every month and slowly chipped away at the six-thousand-dollar plastic debt I had racked up during my move and divorce.

I regarded myself in these terms — a middle-aged professional, a single mother, an urban, independent woman — and when I envisioned a life partner, I assumed that if he existed at all he would be living in a similar fashion, like most of the people I knew. My friends and acquaintances and I were variations on a single familiar theme, despite differences in the tones or rhythms of our lives. Most of us were writers, editors, or academics. We had families and mortgages. We shared similar tastes in books, music, movies, and restaurants, and we tended to vote alike. So I expected to recognize any potential mate: He would look like the rest of us. The special qualities that would make him mine would shine out from a well-known pattern.

I had nearly forgotten other dimensions of myself. I had put aside my longing for rural New England. I had little hope that I could escape the need to get and spend. I could not imagine unhooking myself from my hated job and its generous retirement benefits. It never occurred to me that I might ever have a spiritual companion, a true partner to my soul.

It took challenge and surprise both to remind me of my confinement inside the box I occupied in compliance with social rules and economic pressures and to show me that there was a wider world beyond the lid. When Alan stepped out of his red truck on May 30, 1997, and stood before me in the flesh, looking nothing at all like anyone I could have pictured, nothing at all like a person living a life the least bit like mine — that is when I began to remember who I am. When he stood there, and we looked each other in the face for the first time, we were complete strangers for all of a split second. Then we walked into each other's arms as if we had been doing it all our lives, and we couldn't tell which heart it was that beat so fast.

In that split second before I recognized Alan I remember being startled. I think I saw him — so fast, it is hard to be sure — out of old habits of looking. In a flash, I took in details that spun out before me with absolute clarity. He wore a full beard on a seamed and weathered face that gave little away. He had blue eyes, set within deep lines, and they were guarded at first. His hands were brown but patterned with white scars from his years of working with tools and wood. He was nervous and shy, but he did not pretend to be otherwise. He did not try to be smooth. He wore jeans, sneakers, and a heavy shirt with a sweatshirt beneath. The sweatshirt had a picture of a wolf on the front, and it occurred to me later that that was fitting, because Alan himself looks rather like a wild creature, clear-eyed but not out to please. He was someone from very far away, and I was unnerved until I felt his heart only inches from my own.

For this reason, I suspect we would have remained strangers if we had met in conventional ways. As Jenny Diver sings in *The Three-Penny Opera*, "Ya never know to who you're talkin'." Jenny's observation is more sinister than benign, but the truth is, you never do know who lives there, behind the faces that spur our first, too-easy judgments and impressions. The world is a bigger place and the people more surprising and deep than we know. We forget that. We shrink.

November

Vermont Politics

The Vermont political scene has been both riveting and amusing in 1998, and the political season has just ended with my first Vermont Election Day. For the first time in my life, every person I voted for won — Howard Dean, the lukewarm incumbent, for governor; Doug Racine for lieutenant governor; Patrick Leahy for U.S. senator; Deb Markowitz for secretary of state; Henrietta Jordan for state representative; and Bernie Sanders for U.S. congressman. All are Democrats except Bernie, for years the only independent representative in the House of Representatives. Barney Bloom, the justice of the peace who married Alan and me, has been elected to the office of side judge, and that's another first — actually being acquainted with a candidate. It's not so remarkable here, though, because of Vermont's citizen legislature. State representatives and senators are not professional politicians and are paid merely a stipend for their service. Consequently, they tend to be people who hold other jobs and fulfill other roles in their communities. Occasionally, they are wealthy enough not to need that other income, but usually they are teachers, social workers, businesspeople, farmers.

The U.S. Senate race was a foregone conclusion, an automatic win for Leahy against the Republican Fred Tuttle — but what a primary! Fred — as he is known to everyone in Vermont — ran for the Republican nomination against Jack McMullen, a multimillionaire who maintains a near-fictitious address in Vermont while living in Massachusetts. McMullen apparently wanted to buy himself a campaign and a Senate seat. Fred, seventy-nine, is a dairy farmer and a fourth- or fifth-generation Vermonter (I have seen a photo of him holding a photo of his father holding a photo of *his* father — and all three Tuttle men are standing in front of the same barn in this triple shot). Anyway, Fred got talked into running against McMullen by his neighbor, John O'Brien, a local filmmaker who, a couple of years ago, made an underground hit starring Fred. It was sort of a Farmer Tuttle Goes to Washington (real title, *Man with a Plan*).

Fred and O'Brien, the filmmaker, decided to make life imitate art. Fred never actually wanted to win the Senate race, because then he would have had to live in D.C. Besides, he likes Leahy, who was running for his fifth term. Fred even voted for Leahy. He just didn't want McMullen representing Vermont. After all, McMullen, in a shameless set-up disguised as a press conference, flunked a basic Vermont quiz. Among other things, he didn't know how many tits on a cow (there are four, and he said six) or how to pronounce the name of the town of Calais. McMullen said it the French way, "Cal-LAY," but around here it's "CAL-lus," just like the leathery pads that form on a farmer's hands. In the end, Fred spent two hundred dollars on his primary campaign, to McMullen's million or more, and he won hands down. Bumper stickers everywhere said, "Spread Fred." Sarah is hoping that the name Fred Tuttle will come to stand for "none of the above" in any election, national or local. If you don't like any of your choices, just write in "Fred."

The Republic of Vermont

The Fred-versus-Jack McMullen campaign provides more grist for Vermont's reputation as a land of hard-nosed, resourceful, independent Yankees. It is surely warranted, that reputation, but I have learned that there are a lot of golden myths attached to its popularly stated origins and its heroes. I have been reading here and there, on the Internet, in the newspaper, and elsewhere, about Ethan Allen — best known for rebellious daring and even thought of as a statesman. I've been gathering rather a patchwork sense of Allen, his brothers Ira, Levi, Heman, and Zimri, their militia called the Green Mountain Boys, and their scrapes and skirmishes during the French and Indian War and especially the Revolution. What a tangle of a time!

The Green Mountains and the areas to the east and west of them might as well have been the Balkans. In the 1750s and '60s, the governors of New York and New Hampshire, both of whom had been appointed by King George III of England, feuded bitterly over the millions of acres that lay between them. The territory now known as the state of Vermont corresponds with much of this area, but in those early days most of it went unnamed, though not unclaimed. New York insisted it owned the territory entirely, even as Benning Wentworth, the New Hampshire governor, persisted in granting parcels of the disputed lands to settlers and land speculators, all the while pocketing enormous sums for the grants. King George put a stop to Wentworth's practices in 1767, whereupon New York insisted that everyone holding a Wentworth claim either pay up or turn over their lands.

Ethan Allen was one of these landholders. He and Ira, the two chief Allen brothers, owned the Onion River Land Company (named for the Winooski River, which means "onion" in Abenaki). Though Wentworth had granted the Allens more than 100,000 acres of the fertile Winooski River valley, the brothers could not pay outright for those lands. Like most speculators, they operated on a slim margin, having to turn around and sell land for profit in order to pay off the cost of the grants. Determined to protect their interests, they formed the Green Mountain Boys in 1769 or '70 and waged a long war of annoyance and bedevilment against New York — the "Yorkers"— over their claims. Thus, the Green Mountain Boys first came into existence not as champions of liberty but as a gang of troublemakers.

The Allens' claims and those of countless others remained unsettled nearly a decade later, when the Revolutionary War began between the original thirteen colonies and the British. Other rough militias like the Green Mountain Boys sprang up everywhere, as settlers, farmers, and woodsmen prepared to fight for contested lands that most of them felt they had bought or laid claim to in good faith. The Allens and the Green Mountain Boys gained heroic stature when, as part of a plan that was meant to push on into Canada, they took Fort Ticonderoga, at the head of Lake Champlain, from the British in 1775. The cockiness this bred in them was in no way diminished when Ethan Allen was jailed by the British a year later in the course of his ill-considered attempt to take Montreal nearly on his own.

That same year, 1776, as Ethan Allen was just beginning to serve his two-year sentence, the colonies' Declaration of Independence from England cast into doubt all titles to all the lands that had been granted in the name of the King—including the Allen brothers' holdings, granted by Benning Wentworth. The Onion River Land Company now found itself without even shaky title to the land that was the reason for its existence. And with the coalition of the thirteen colonies into a single nation, the large territory that the Allens and many others believed they had purchased fair and square found itself a rugged green island amid three suddenly more powerful neighbors who were now members of the new union: New York, New Hampshire, and Massachusetts.

The trouble was, this defiantly independent area could not remain an island entirely; it had to come to terms with its adjoining neighbors in order to protect itself against the British and their remaining claims to the land. But it did not want to join the neighbors' new union, either. Those with interests in the area moved cautiously. In January 1777, they named the territory New Connecticut and declared its independence both from Britain and from the former colonies' declared new nation. They chose their words carefully, wanting to remain on reasonably good terms with anyone who could prove a powerful adversary. Throughout the next several months, growing numbers of towns both west and east of the Green Mountains—including several on the east bank of the Connecticut River, in New Hampshire—joined New Connecticut. On June 30, 1777, they changed its name to the Republic of Vermont. All the while, they attempted not to offend the Continental Congress of the much larger new nation that was coming into existence around them. Clearly, they wanted to keep options for statehood open, even if they had no immediate desire to exercise those options.

Ethan Allen surely saw that any hope to regain legal title to his lands lay with this new republic, whose borders encompassed his holdings. He began serving Vermont's interests as soon as he was released from prison in May 1778. He was made commander of the Vermont Militia, and although he was never officially a statesman, he often negotiated with Vermont's former enemies and sometime allies. His dealings with New York, New Hampshire, the Continental Congress, and even the British were frequently tugs-of-war between his private goals and the concerns of Vermont. The most obvious example of this was his journey to the Continental Congress in 1779.

When Allen made this trip, he was alarmed by the imbalance of power between Vermont towns east of the Green Mountains and those to the west, which had different and often conflicting regional interests and political agendas. He himself was allied with the western faction, based near the town of Bennington, which represented twenty-six towns. This "Allen junto," as the other factions called it, was seriously outnumbered in October 1778, at the second meeting of the Vermont General Assembly, which had formed earlier that year. The eastern faction had thirty-five Vermont towns plus eleven towns on the New Hampshire side of the Connecticut River.

Though political power shifted with both the weather and the progress of the war in those days, Allen was unwilling to trust that it would change in his favor. He therefore made an independent deal with the state of New Hampshire, in which he promised to return New Hampshire's Connecticut River towns if New Hampshire would support a Vermont bid for inclusion in the new American Union. He sealed the deal upon his return from the Continental Congress by carrying word that that body would not consider statehood for Vermont unless Vermont gave back those New Hampshire towns — in fact, the Continental Congress might even order troops to invade the mountain republic.

This was all empty threats and exaggerations, but apparently Allen's distortions, along with later negotiations for a separate peace between Vermont and the British, gained for him both the power he sought and the lands he was trying to protect for himself.

Vermont never did ask for admission to join the Union at that time. The small nation struggled, nearly failed, and finally grew, until, by the end of the Revolution, it had tripled its population. Vermont remained a sovereign entity for fourteen years — from 1777 to 1791, when it finally became the fourteenth American state. Despite continued internal struggles, ongoing hassles with New York and New Hampshire, and further bluffs and interference by the Continental Congress, it conferred citizenship, wrote and enforced its own laws, had its own currency, and traded with other countries. Its constitution not only granted universal suffrage to all men, regardless of whether they owned property, but also outlawed slavery — the first of any constitution in North America to do so.

No wonder, then, that Vermonters still feel apart from the rest of the United States, still pride themselves on their independent spirit, and still consider Vermont a separate world and blessed in being so. More than a few Vermonters still regard statehood as a big mistake.

Radical Simplicity

The Republic of Vermont based its constitution on that of Pennsylvania, which was the most radical of any of the thirteen new states' governing documents. But Pennsylvania's constitution did not at first abolish slavery, and Vermont's did. Why?

I like to speculate that Vermonters knew about the teachings of an itinerant Colonial Quaker named John Woolman, who traveled throughout Pennsylvania and other mid-Atlantic states from 1743 until 1770. If so, and if the Vermont constitution reflected the ideas he put forth in all his travels, then that would be a perfect example of how Woolman worked — by speaking his truth and then leaving it to work however it would in the hearts of others.

Slavery was a source of keen anguish for Woolman, who traveled alone or with like-minded Friends through a vast territory to speak with others on this topic and present it to them in the light of God. He worked through the Quaker oversight structure in his spiritually led travels, always asking for the counsel and approval of Philadelphia Yearly Meeting or those Quarterly and Monthly Meetings he visited in his journeys. Woolman's spiritual mission tried his courage profoundly, as his journal repeatedly mentions. For instance, in 1757, in anticipation of a journey among slaveholders from Pennsylvania down through North Carolina, he wrote:

> The prospect of so weighty a work, and of being so distinguished from many whom I esteemed before myself, brought me very low, and such were the conflicts of my soul that I had a near sympathy with the Prophet, in the time of his weakness, when he said: "If thou deal thus with me, kill me, I pray thee, if I have found favor in thy sight" (Num. xi. 15). But I soon saw that this proceeded from the want of a full resignation to the Divine will.

After much prayer and reflection, Woolman finally "felt a deliverance from that tempest in which I had been sorely exercised, and in calmness of mind went forward."

Going forward took Woolman through Maryland and into Virginia, where he rode in the company of Friends to a Monthly Meeting in Camp Creek. Some of those Friends were slaveholders, even though London Yearly Meeting had warned against slavery as early as 1727, and American Friends had widely divergent feelings about it. One of those in Woolman's group of travelers gave him arguments that must have been tired even then—that the blackness of Africans was the mark of Cain and that their bondage was God's will, the reward for the murderous nature of their race.

Woolman wrote:

> I was troubled to perceive the darkness of their imaginations, and in some pressure of spirit said, "The love of ease and gain are the motives in general of keeping slaves, and men are wont to take hold of weak

arguments to support a cause which is unreasonable. I have no interest on either side, save only . . . in the truth. I believe liberty is their right, and as I see they are not only deprived of it, but treated in other respects with inhumanity, . . . I believe He who is a refuge for the oppressed will, in his own time, plead their cause."

Despite his sharp words, Woolman had compassion even for people of wealth, even for slaveholders. He remarked more than once in his journal on the "difference in general betwixt a people used to labor moderately for their living, training up their children in frugality and business, and those who live on the labor of slaves; the former, in my view, being the most happy life."

As Woolman continued this long journey in the southern colonies, he recorded the treatment and condition of slaves — the white people's disregard of black marriages and families; the ease with which they separated husbands from wives, children from parents; the brutal whippings; the inadequacy of food and clothing. Indignantly and in sorrow he wrote:

> These are the people by whose labor the other inhabitants are in a great measure supported, and many of them in the luxuries of life. These are the people who have made no agreement to serve us, and who have not forfeited their liberty that we know of. These are the souls for whom Christ died, and for our conduct towards them we must answer.

All of John Woolman's writings, but especially his journal, reveal a loving and humble soul, passionate in his search for truth and obedience to divine leadings, but never coercive or judgmental in delivering his messages. He would open his heart to those who aroused his concern, often doing so in trepidation and sadness. But once he had spoken, he "felt easy to leave it all to Him who alone is able to turn the hearts of the mighty."

Given Woolman's compassion even for slaveholders, whom he saw as heavily burdened and restless in their pursuit of wealth and power, he would surely be appalled at the heavy burdens of modern life as well — the seventy-hour work weeks, the two-earner homes, the pressure on children from an early age to succeed in school, sports, music, dance, and all manner of extracurricular pastimes. He would recognize bondage in our condition, because his antipathy to slavery came in part from his conviction that God never meant anyone to labor beyond the needs of body, mind, and spirit. He had a notion about "the right use of things" whereby an individual's or organization's pursuit of great wealth depended inevitably on the oppression of people and denial of spirit. He refused to wear cotton, because it was picked by slaves, or clothing dyed with substances "hurtful" to the dyers. Today, he would surely refuse to wear clothing manufactured in sweatshops.

It is easy to admire a man who lived two and a half centuries ago by the strength and challenge of his convictions. It is harder to admire such people today because they are so readily caricatured as weird, fanatical, naïve, or overly religious and therefore out of touch with reality. Even, or especially, among liberal and politically progressive people, I know of some who casually refer to women who act out of their faith as "church ladies," meaning no serious disrespect but simply being ignorant of the difficulty and passion involved in aligning one's faith and practice in this world.

An Imaginary Encounter

The stories of John Woolman, Ethan Allen, and the Vermont constitution connect on more issues than slavery, for Allen and many other revolutionaries possessed what Woolman would have called "a warrior spirit." He wrote about this in connection with the Indians — that is how he refers to them, without naming their tribes — whose hostile camps he occasionally visited on his own initiative, alone, carrying messages of brotherhood and peace. But he had no illusions about their willingness to wage war, even though he himself would neither fight against them nor pay any tax that supported such fights.

One day, in 1762, as Woolman visited among Indians in Pennsylvania who were warring with English settlers, he followed a trail through rocky ledges inscribed with tribal histories and stories painted in red and black. Viewing these, he reflected

> . . . on the innumerable afflictions which the proud, fierce spirit produceth in the world, also on the toils and fatigues of warriors in travelling over mountains and deserts; on their miseries and distresses when far from home and wounded by their enemies; of their bruises and great weariness in chasing one another over the rocks and mountains; of the restless, unquiet state of mind of those who live in this spirit, and of the hatred which mutually grows up in the minds of their children.

What if Ethan Allen had met John Woolman in person? It's not entirely out of the question if one assumes that Allen might have visited eastern Massachusetts, Pennsylvania, or Maryland near the beginning of the Revolutionary War, just at the end of Woolman's travels there. How would Allen have replied to questions that the quiet Quaker might have put to him about his desire for property and wealth, his willingness to fight with the "Yorkers" to recoup his losses?

"Friend Ethan," Woolman might have said, "I feel a tenderness in my spirit toward men like thee, who are compelled to struggle or even die for land and wealth. What need has thee of so much property?"

"It's my land, John. It was granted to me by the King's law, and I can sell it to whom I please. It will make me rich."

"Forgive my simple questions, Friend. Please tell me how the King came to own the lands that were granted to thee. Did he purchase them from those who inhabited them first?"

"I know not, nor do I care. Whether he bought them or took them, they were his to grant. And now they are mine to defend."

"Ah, so money and blood are equal currency to thee. And a man can own what God hath made? Does thee own, then, the creatures that inhabit thy land? And the water passing through it? And the rocks that house the mountain lions and the trees that are home to birds?"

I can guess that at this point Ethan Allen would have rolled his eyes, clapped John Woolman on the shoulder, and ridden away on horseback, amused but not moved by this plain man's naïve view of the world. Thus Woolman, in this case, would have spoken his truth to a deaf man, one who would go on to fight more deadly battles than the mild skirmishes he engaged in with his New York neighbors.

But many people did hear Woolman when he spoke, whether against war and slavery or on behalf of the poor and oppressed. Though he died a century before slavery was abolished, he convinced many Friends and others that it was wrong. He had no regrets about his work, though he did get discouraged. Near the end of his life, he wrote:

> [T]hat spirit which is of the world hath so much prevailed in many, and the pure life of truth hath been so pressed down, that I have gone forward . . . as a man walking through a miry place in which are stones here and there safe to step on, but so situated that, one step being taken, time is necessary to see where to step next.

But Woolman discovered in his trials that in "pure obedience the mind learns contentment in appearing weak and foolish to that wisdom which is of the world."

I imagine that Woolman practiced a version of Alan's "bless and release." He said what he had to say, then he released it to the hearing or deafness of others, knowing it was out of his hands whether his words would have any effect at all. These things take time. But it seems to me that nothing said out of love — for the truth and other people — can go entirely or forever unheard.

Yankee Independence

Ethan Allen embodied a split that still exists in Vermont, between the need or greed of commercial and tourist interests and a fierce Yankee loyalty to individual integrity, independence, and choice. Two hundred twenty years ago, the two tendencies often inhabited one and the same human body. Today, they often lead to the formation of separate factions and even, in at least a superficial sense, define separate parts of the state — southern versus northern Vermont, "gold" towns versus poor towns.

If it isn't sacrilege to wonder, where would Ethan Allen reside and what would he believe if he were alive today? With the liberty battle supposedly won for good, and his lands first secured and then sold for great profit, would he keep focusing on making money? Is that what any war boils down to? Would he oppose Act 60, the education funding act that now taxes rich towns at the same rate as poor ones, raising the burden on the former and reducing it for the latter? Or would he adhere most strongly of all to his Lockean fervor and support whatever equity requires?

I realize these questions are not simple. We all have to balance our ideals against our necessities — unless we lose our ideals altogether or have our necessities met by inheritance or the lottery. I find myself thinking a lot about that balance lately. Alan and I, especially Alan, work harder at the so-called simple life than one in which we would go to a job every day, bring home a steady paycheck, and pay to have the house completed, a furnace installed, the woods thinned. Alan rarely hires anyone for design, carpentry, wiring, plumbing, logging, painting, roofing, wood splitting, or anything else that two hands and a compromised back can do. The one recent exception was the welder who put the winch on the truck, and look what that ended up costing — both money and a lot of effort on Alan's part to reroute the wiring in the winch. Not only that, the botched welding job has cost him two cables. Alan discovered a few days ago that the guy didn't leave a big enough opening for the cables to thread through the steel box he installed. As a result, the rough edges of the opening saw through the cables after a short time — so now Alan has to fix that problem.

I don't know why he won't at least call the welder and yell at him, but I guess he sees that as further useless effort. Alan is not a man to waste his breath, or anything else.

So why do we do this, live as cheaply as possible, do as much ourselves as possible, and avoid calling anybody "boss" even though our
simple lives might actually be easier if we did?

We used to talk about it some in our e-mails. In fact, in Alan's very
first, here's-who-I-am-and-where-I've-been message, he wrote:

> I spent five years as a public information officer for a Fish and Game
> Commission. Based in the capital, I traveled extensively through every
> county in the state as an outdoor writer-photographer-cinematographer.
> Loved it, until they promoted me to chief of the division and put me into
> a cubicle at headquarters, where I learned, much to my chagrin, that my
> job was to head up the shovel brigade — chief prevaricator, equivocator,
> master of spin control. Not a happy camper! When I was assigned to do
> media spin on a case where a deputy fish warden had shot and killed a
> teenager for littering, I said, "Sorry, I can't do this anymore."
>
> Went to work as director of public relations for an aid organization.
> I was assigned to put spin on the fact that they knowingly released
> tainted blood that ended up infecting countless hemophiliac children. I
> burned my necktie and three-piece suit and ran screaming off into the
> wilderness.
>
> Armed with a stack of old issues of *Mother Earth News*, and a lot of
> naïvete coupled with tenacity and dogged determination, I succeeded in
> carving a beautiful self-sufficient homestead out of the raw woods. No
> electricity except for the spare amounts we generated ourselves using
> wind and water, home-made solar water heaters, wood heat, no TV —
> lotsa books. An adventure that would fill several chapters on its own. Am
> in a more "civilized" location now; the juice flows into the house via
> wires, but still rural, bucolic, simple.

Simple! We aim for simplicity, but we won't get there for a couple of
years yet. Dues first. The amount of work this place requires is overwhelming, and the money is getting tight. We have a thinner cushion
than we really need for all the construction that has to happen in the
spring. Our property taxes are high, especially on the house in town.
Phone and Internet charges are higher outside town than in. The car
needs snow tires. We are racking up dental bills, and Alan's recent phys-

ical revealed the need for meds that cost sixty dollars a month. Adam probably needs braces, though he is strenuously opposed to the idea. ("I've pictured myself in braces. I'll look terrible." He thinks every other kid who wears braces looks fine in them, but of course he won't. I can't convince him that every other kid feels the same way he does, thinks he/she is the only one who looks dorky in those full metal jackets.)

Our expenses are surprisingly high for people who have no mortgage and no other debts. Even without the braces, out-of-pocket prescriptions, automotive emergencies, or high-priced, high-deductible health insurance, our monthly budget is at least two thousand dollars, if you include property taxes, which total about four thousand dollars a year for our two houses. Two thousand dollars just about equals our monthly income from rent and a few other sources, so we'll need to bring in more income sooner than we thought, especially for building supplies.

Our costs will go down some next year or the year after, when we can begin growing a good deal of our own food. In the meantime, we cut out store coupons, buy second hand, and constantly toss around ideas for making more money. Both Alan and I can edit and write, so in January and February we'll start rustling up some freelance clients, either locally or out of state. I would like Alan to teach me some woodworking, so both of us can turn out items for sale through art fairs and galleries.

Alan has earned much of his living this way since burning his three-piece suit. In addition to his burl bowls, he has made and marketed nineteenth-century wooden toys, including unicycle-riding clowns on tightropes, tumbling clowns, and buxom acrobats, along with toys of more recent design, like hopping toads, lumbering gorillas, and interlocking kangaroos. The tightrope clown is my favorite. He has a painted wooden face, a fabric clown-suit (which Alan sews himself), a weighted balance bar, and a little wooden wheel that he rides along a taut string. When you gently push up on one end of the string, with an attached dowel, the clown trundles happily downhill, perfectly balanced and pedaling at comic, Chaplin-like speed. When he nears the end of his rope, you just pull the string down, and he pedals backwards just as fast and just as happily, as if he could see.

When Alan and I reach the end of our own rope, I guess we feel a little like those clowns, not always in control. And our balancing act is more than a matter of physics. We cycle through physical, emotional, and financial ups and downs, and we don't always see where we are going or exactly how we will get there. But we believe in ourselves, in each other, and in the choices we've made. We understand that a down cycle eventually leads to an up. We keep perspective, realizing that the tectonic changes of the last two years and the mountain of work in the next two will give way to still more choices and more freedom. We are grateful for the skills and options that will help us carve our Yankee independence out of this rocky terrain.

Vermont is full of people like us, people who decide how they want to live and then find any and every means of supporting their choice. This life will get simpler, because we will make it that way. The money will come, because we will work for it and because that is the way faith works. As Quakers say, "Way will open." You can't force it, but you do have to be alert to the moment and ready to hop to.

Way Will Open

Not forcing things is a difficult lesson, and it can't be forced either. By our fifties or so, we may finally understand, from all our efforts to the contrary, that we have control only over ourselves and only to the extent that we recognize that. Other things and other people will be just what they are — not what they seem, nor what they conjure in our hearts, nor what we insist they must be. Life will deliver gifts and sorrows without notice and without our consent. Lately, it has delivered Alan, Vermont, this house and clearing, and in these gifts I sense a convergence of life-long themes and some unlooked-for opportunities for discovery.

Wisdom comes piecemeal, its lessons are cumulative, and probably everyone's life is shaped by a cluster of central issues that take decades to understand and get right. Work, money, art, love, family, fame, power, knowledge, altruism, faith — for most of us, a few of these seem to drive the others. When we are young, these central themes may be the ones that feel the most urgent and are also the most hazardous, though we never see them that way, and that is why they put us in peril.

For me, the central themes have always been love, home, and a spiritual search. The first two were not fashionable when I was a young woman in the loose, lively sixties and early seventies — especially not in California — and so I could not admit them outright, even to myself. The third was all right if you were high while searching (c.f., Alan's Aquarian woo-woo-ism). I didn't fully understand how hazardously mismatched I was with my times for many years, because I so powerfully identified with the stated values of those years, the movements for peace, civil rights, feminism. It was hard to separate casual sex from women's liberation from antiwar marches from drugs from the desire for racial equity and fairness for all. So I tried everything, at least once, and everything became a big emotional tangle.

It has taken all *this* time — say, the past twenty years — to unravel the mistakes of *that* time, and in doing so to understand that not everything was for naught. Some things, if only the lessons learned, are worth keeping, even after disasters. The main disasters in my life, at least the ones over which I had some power of choice, were my first two marriages, born of my unexamined and subverted search for love and home. The lessons have been difficult to learn, because they have forced me to value myself so that I can value others properly, a thing I never could manage before two marriages failed. The lessons about love — self-love, love for others, love of life, God, beauty — keep unfolding, and they have produced the life I live now.

The decades of resentment and sadness that accompanied my marriages took the particular shapes they did because of my fear — rooted in an insecure and overly responsible childhood — of declaring my personal truth in a time not quite my own, a time in which the personal was supposed to be political and I could not connect the two. What I did declare, I could not accomplish. I said I wanted work, independence, social justice, all the things I was supposed to want in those times. But these represented aims and desires that could only come second. They were ideals I could never fully embrace until the prime movers of my life — love, home, and faith — were solidly in place. And they never could be, not until I was in a position both to acknowledge their importance and to act on it.

This comes as a surprise to me. I have never before thought about the central themes of my life or tried to identify them. But the three I have just named ring true, like a familiar tune, and I recognize in them some chords added by other concerns. Somehow this all relates to things I mentioned early in this book — to the outlook of the Monks of New Skete, to the parents who raised me, to the generation in which they lived, and to the ways in which we live out certain motifs of our forebears' lives, for good and ill, whether we know it or not.

I can see now that, despite my efforts at marriage, I could not allow love, home, and faith their places of honor in my life until I had lived out the influence of my own mother, and her mother, and probably generations of women before them, women whose values in turn shaped their daughters, nieces, sisters. The blood I have inherited from my female kin carries a heritage of constraint, both religious and secular.

In my early years, in a household where nothing of psychological or emotional importance was ever expressed overtly, I picked up on the vibes and became a fearful child and therefore one too fixed on being good. I knew God lurked and watched. I knew my mother and grandmother spoke privately about God. I knew my mother preferred God's company to that of any human on the planet. And because of overheard conversations in which my mother confided to my grandmother both her unhappiness and her commitment to staying in her unhappy marriage for the sake of her children — meaning my two brothers and me — I made my mother's well-being my job. She never knew about my self-assigned task, and I was ineffectual because I was a child; but my intense feeling of responsibility for her established a pattern in which, for decades, I found it nearly impossible to go after what I wanted if I thought someone else might pay a price.

Perversely, I longed for love and home because they had seemed to mean so little to my mother. I remembered her telling me once, when I was about Adam's age, that if she had it to do all over again, she would never have married at all. This from a woman born in 1915 of straitlaced parents, a woman who was never permitted to go to college, only to secretarial school as a precaution against the fate-worse-than-death of spinsterhood. She attempted to soften her hard truth by saying she was glad she had the three of us children, now that we were in her life, but I knew otherwise, or thought I did.

My mother's unhappiness made me unhappy, and so I needed to believe, still without fully articulating the belief to myself, that I could end the cycle by doing better than she the very thing that had brought us both so low. I didn't see how superstitious a fix I was after, or how impossible. My desire for the love and family that neither of us had had led me blindly into my first marriage before I had any emotional sense whatever. The failure of that marriage, after six years of belittlement, bewilderment, and battles, put off any sense-making years into the future. Instead of looking hard at where I had been and where I might like to take myself, I drifted mindlessly into those half dozen serial love affairs in California, followed by marriage number two when I was old enough to know better but did not.

That was how I spent my twenties, thirties, and forties. My second marriage was not unhappy at first, when both of us held on to cherished, hungry illusions. But eventually illness, family traumas, the late-pregnancy loss of our first child, and even the birth of Adam took their toll, pushing us into utterly separate lives, bedrooms, outlooks, and dreams.

Becoming a mother, after harrowing loss and struggle, was one way I finally learned something about love and finally broke the constricting bonds to my own mother, eventually replacing them with gentler ties of respect and affection. After sorrows ranging from a hormonal failure in my teens to an ectopic pregnancy in my twenties and that late-pregnancy loss in my thirties, bearing my healthy son and caring for him allowed me to start over, to create a mother-child relationship I had never experienced before. It was my first experience of unconditional love, a love of action instead of ideas.

Eventually, the insights I gained from motherhood ended my second marriage by blowing apart its ideas about love and its love of ideas. Adam's father loved him, and he loved me, as he often said. But I could never fully grasp why he was not able to participate in family life or make room for intimacy. Days would go by when his work schedule — late, late nights, mornings spent desperately grasping for sleep — prevented him from even seeing Adam or me for more than moments at a time. I grew resentful and impatient, which probably made him want to see me even less than he did. I lost compassion for him, which felt the same as losing love. Although these past two years have reminded me what a good friend he is, I could not see anything good about him then. We both — like my mother — put our love in a box marked "Do Not Open."

But there is more to this story, and it shows me again how preferable indirection is to deliberate maps and plans. Way will indeed open. Whether we see the opening depends on whether we surrender to love. I believe I could not love anyone well until I could love my mother, and by then it was probably too late for my husband, though not for Adam, who was still a baby when I began learning how to love.

It was through my mother's dying that I finally came to love her, unconditionally, in the way I once wanted her to love me. It was in caring for her in her last years that I stopped resenting that she had not been other than what she was, either with me or in her own soul and passions. I think I began *seeing* her soul, and understanding that it had its own business to take care of.

My true responsibility for my mother — the job I had taken on in childhood but was only at this point prepared to fulfill — came about when my father died. I was seven months pregnant with my late baby, Adam. Usually, people do not have to care for their parents until their own children are in their teens or grown. At forty, though, I was about to become both Adam's and my own mother's mother.

My parents were living in Washington State, and I was living in Pittsburgh, when my father died of an aortal aneurism. His death was sudden, and the shock further loosened my mother's failing grip on reality. She had long had symptoms of Alzheimer's disease — she left stove burners on, had started repeating herself, was unable to learn new things and retain them — but she did not make big forays over the edge until my father died. Theirs had been a disappointing marriage, but they had been together almost fifty years. My mother called me with the news, and she sounded lucid. A few days later, though, she asked a friend, "Did Jess really die? Or did I dream that?"

She could not stay out West, not with all three of her children — me; my older brother, Mike; and my younger brother, Steve — in the East. By default, I think, since I was the daughter, we moved her to Pittsburgh, where I found her an apartment in a seven-story brick building full of women her age. The deliberations that went into this were painful. Could she manage on her own? Should we put her straight into a nursing home?

My brothers and my husband and I decided to try the apartment, to give her every chance for as much independence as she could hang onto. I took her grocery shopping, managed her finances, found a young woman to keep her company in the afternoons, arranged for Meals on Wheels. I couldn't care for her in our house, with too little space and a baby on the way. I still regret that, though in an abstract way. Had I found the means and energy to care for my mother, the intimacy of that care would have invaded her soul somehow; it would have violated the character she had when she was fully herself — an intensely private character, especially about physical and emotional matters. Was I really going to change my mother's diapers along with my infant son's? No. Some children are not meant — are never invited — to get that close to some parents.

Instead of managing my mother's care directly, I read everything I could find about Alzheimer's. Among many other things, I learned that Alzheimer's patients lose, in exact reverse order, the skills that young children develop from birth through age ten or so. By degrees, if Alzheimer's patients last that long, they are left with nothing but the sucking and swallowing reflexes. I pictured my mother and my baby waving wistfully to each other in passing, Adam on the rise and thriving, my mother descending, failing. This was exactly what happened, though my mother's downward progress was hastened, when Adam was not quite two, by a stroke that left her in a semivegetative state for four years. Interestingly, she remembered how to play the piano right up until her stroke, even though she had forgotten most of the skills of daily life by then.

My mother was able to stay in her apartment less than a year, even with all the help we could give. She hallucinated. She began wandering. Twice I found her in her travels — once by happenstance, when I was out walking with Adam and simply encountered her in a street near my house, and the next time by driving the streets near her apartment after I had gone to see her and not found her at home. Then, just days before she was scheduled to move into a senior-care home, she disappeared for thirty-six hours. I searched and searched for her. Emma searched with me, to no avail. My mother was finally found in the woods, just below the Carnegie Mellon campus, near the railroad tracks. She had fallen down a steep incline and had spent the night in a semiconscious state beneath the trees. It was July, and thunderstorms moved through all night, drenching the woods and filling them with noise and stabbing brightness. I imagine she was terrified, but I can also imagine that she was not, that she was simply stoic and patient.

Eventually a railroad crew spotted my mother in the woods and called the police. When I saw her in the hospital, her hair was matted and muddy, her arm and shoulder bruised, her glasses broken, and her face pitifully naked and blind without them. The nurses asked her how old she was, and she told them, "A hundred and one." She looked it, and surely felt it, though she was only seventy-two.

From the hospital, she entered a senior-care facility in Oakmont, outside Pittsburgh. For a while she lived in what was called the personal-care wing, the place for residents who needed some level of help or supervision but did not require close monitoring or nursing. There she spent her time in the company of two or three women who still had their wits and took gentle charge of her. My cool, aloof mother had become sweet and childlike, grateful for their attention and their help. After her stroke, she went into the skilled nursing unit and never left. She was not expected to survive the stroke, and so I gave permission for her to be put on a feeding tube, to keep her comfortable.

Once the feeding tube was in, it stayed in until my mother died. Having it removed would have put us all — family, doctors, and caregivers — through a risky process that no one wanted to embark upon. I was told, accurately or not, that we could all agree to stop the artificial means that kept my mother in less than a half-life, unable to speak, care for herself, recognize her children, or even taste food, but that somewhere down the road a disgruntled caregiver or a dissenting relative could raise a ruckus and put us all in legal jeopardy.

I have been told since that this overstates the case, but the fact is, I would not have been able to stop the flow of nourishment to my mother even had the choice been entirely without legal risk or controversy. I say this not because I think it is wrong to withdraw life support from patients who will never recover, but because my mother had never told me what she wanted me to do. She knew she was losing her reasoning skills; she knew she was in for the same accelerating ride that had carried her own mother away. I never asked her what limits she wanted to set on her care, an inexcusable omission that I trace to the family habit of avoiding any discussion of important issues, especially personal ones. The fact that she never volunteered any instructions left me powerless to act as her agent.

So I would go to see her every weekend, and sit beside her bed and hold her hand and sometimes read to her, always wondering whether she still was there — conscious inside her locked body. I wondered whether she floated in a dream or struggled helplessly in a nightmare. I bought her a CD player and headset and classical-music CDs, hoping music would still have the power to reach her and give her pleasure.

It was during those visits, as I stroked my mother's hair and studied her face and watched her body contract steadily inward, more and more toward fetal position, that I began at last to see her as just another woman — not my mother but my sister, my child, a stranger, another soul. I knew so much about her but did not know her. I did not know what she might have wanted to be, had she not been bound for most of her life to the demands and expectations of others — her parents, peers, husband, and children, her place on the timeline of the century.

My mother had many gifts. She played the piano, she made puns and witty jokes, she was articulate, she loved to read. She had a light touch with pie crust and needle, and so — who knows? — she might have been a surgeon or an artist in a later time or a different setting.

I placed her in history and that is what made me love her without reservation. I could not have done better than she, perhaps not as well as she did. I *do* better, as a mother and a woman with choices, but only because she could not.

I believe I was able to understand something about my mother because becoming a mother myself had tapped a deeper capacity to love than I ever knew I had. I find it wonderful and sad that my son taught me the lessons my mother could not, and that she, in the end, became the beneficiary of her own grandchild. Who says that the cycles of life run only in one direction?

Hazards of Romance

A while ago, Alan, Sarah, and I went to see a recent film by a Vermonter named Nora Jacobson. It was called *My Mother's Early Lovers,* and it was the story of a daughter's discovery that her mother, a freethinking young American woman of the 1930s, had been raped by the handsome leader of a rural commune, had conceived a child, had married the rapist (the woman's own father), and had spent her life with him. The tale unwinds after the mother's death. The father, when confronted, never believes he did wrong. He wanted that woman, and he went out and got her. She married him, didn't she?

Literature on rape is full of such male thickheadedness. Men assault women and then, days or weeks or months later, call them up and ask them out.

The sorry theme of rape as romance is older than Scarlett and Rhett, older than our current epidemic of domestic abuse, old as the first upright humans — whether they really dragged their mates by the hair or not.

Because I had been writing and thinking about my mother, the movie reminded me of her. Her own marriage was not a rape but a theft. It robbed her of her outgoingness, it kidnapped a self-described "friendly girl" and left a changeling, a shy, remote, unhappy wife and mother. It stole her barely hatched desire to write, shoving it right out of the nest to make room for real-life human babies. It required her to go without a piano for most of a decade, when there wasn't the money for one. It made off with her spark and, like a packrat, it left an item of no value at all, the conviction that there was something wrong with her because she did not melt at the sight of her children's faces, did not live for and through her husband, did not wish to acquire ever-shinier appliances. This was the 1950s.

So many millions of marriages — begun in the flush of romantic love — have over time been based in lies, shoulds, wishes, or fantasy. My heart breaks when I think of the waste of just my own mother's powers, the draining of her brightness and energy. I feel fortunate, and I bless her and mourn for her. I bless and mourn for every woman who has ever suffered bound feet, bound hands, bound breasts, or bound spirit, because every one of them has made possible my — our — chance to grow unfettered, at least in most of the West. But women in India, in Islamic countries, in African nations, and elsewhere are still subject not only to male control but to culturally sanctioned murder and mutilation.

Here, we are free to make our mistakes without, in most but not all cases, the fear of death or torture. My own first marriages were bad ones, to be sure. They were begun in wistfulness, denial, and unexplored sadness, not in the genuine love that trusts in itself, and sees another person whole, and remembers itself even when beset. But those marriages taught me the limits of romantic love, and that has been an incredibly valuable lesson. I know now that love must choose freely, must act, must imagine, and must ground itself in faith — or in something larger than the personal. That is the only way it proves itself to be tough, unsentimental, and able to weather reality. "Love is not love which alters when it alteration finds."

Long before I ever met Alan, I wondered whether any man of my generation could love a woman his own age, could feel passion (and compassion) for her aging, vulnerable flesh, could open himself to a soul-deep love even as he himself loses muscle tone, stamina, and hair — could well and truly stand naked in front of another and not be ashamed.

Now I know there is at least one such man on the planet.

The Way of Words

Still, Alan and I began about as far from naked reality as possible. After all, we came to our first love for each other entirely through words, and what are words but representations of experience, not experience itself? I had no idea, when Alan and I were exchanging our 853 pages of words, that my association with him would lead me to scrutinize much of my relationship to language and perception, to question many previously unexamined assumptions and motivations. Alan's and my transition from words and ideas to shared experience — call it reality — has not always been easy, just inevitable. I have had no choice but to love Alan. This love rises from my soul and also takes me back into it, showing me larger vistas than I thought possible. It is analogous only to my love for Adam, whom I also loved without question before ever meeting him.

My first two husbands were talkers, men overflowing with their own ideas. I talked a lot, too. Being in love with language, I easily mistook my own and that of others for something real; I easily fell in love with the words of another and confused that with love of the person. Now, I love a silent man. I ask myself, How can this be? How can I know this is real if he doesn't describe me to myself, if he doesn't proclaim and pro-nounce his emotions, if he doesn't express every insight and invite me to share his innermost observations? Do I need to be told what I already know? Can I accept that I know it?

Usually, I can. Sometimes, when I feel needy or blue, I want more.

The questions go nowhere, though, because the fact is, I love Alan not for his words (few) nor his actions (many) but for himself, a seem-ingly unlikely man for me, someone I might not have been drawn to had I seen him before I loved him (before I read his words!), someone who does not match my earlier ideas about a mate but who speaks to my deeper, wordless self—whatever part of me lives free of language and perceives directly, without a diminishing interface. Perhaps this is the part of me that is capable of faith.

Well. I am using language to try to describe this, because it is all I have.

It has all happened, is happening, slowly—not my loving Alan but my learning how to live with loving him. At first, for several months, I would look at him in surprise, wondering at the apparent huge differences between us—differences of lifestyle and manner, habits and preferences—and at the fact that they did not diminish the sense that we were soul mates, brought together by some kind of divine intervention after a lifetime of not quite meeting on our own. He once said he had been nervous about our meeting only because he wasn't sure that someone like me could be interested in someone like him. I said, "You mean, a city girl?" He shrugged, and I knew he meant more than that. He meant our lives had shaped at least our outward appearance and behavior—he did not look or act like anyone else I knew, whereas I tended to fit right in with the styles and expectations of those around me—and he wondered whether we (rather, I) could get past the differences. On another occasion, feeling that I was fairly rapidly losing the good looks of my youth, I asked him how much it had mattered to him what I looked like, and he answered, "I didn't care what you looked like. I knew your soul."

That does seem to be the truth of it. Beneath our surfaces our souls understand each other profoundly. From the moment we met, we felt we had known each other a very long time. We are the same. You would think such an astounding thing could never be difficult, could never get lost in daily tedium and necessities. But I remember Catherine and Heathcliff, in *Wuthering Heights*. It was only in an agony of loss and parting that Catherine finally cried out to her childhood nurse, "Nelly, I *am* Heathcliff!" It was her ideas about how the course of love should run, and who she herself should be, that scuttled the passion of her soul.

Like Catherine, and with the added, endless help and interference of literature, television, movies, and especially advertising, I developed deep assumptions about intimacy and love and the way they are supposed to proceed. Given my sources, I naturally thought they proceeded through words — words of recognition, praise, affection, passion. What was I to do with this taciturn man, whose long Scots face and habits of silence can make him seem as remote as the farthest ridge I can see from the highest point of my morning walks?

It is only seeming, this remoteness, and that has been the hardest thing for me to learn about Alan. My love for him has forced me to new insights, among them the realization that words can deplete experience, shrink it, rob it of its directness and impact.

In the beginning, I wanted Alan to sing my praises, but I had ears only for a certain tune and lyrics. As I have educated my perceptions, I hear a formerly inaudible pitch, a hum of action, commitment, and feeling for which no words can be written or said. Alan has even admitted, "There are some things I just don't have the words for"— and this after 442 pages of words that won my heart and soul. So it isn't that he can't be eloquent.

Once, however, I would have thought that was the case. I would have thought his command of language wasn't up to the task of expression. Now, with Alan's help, I realize that experience is beyond expression.

I have known but somehow refused to accept this all my life. I was once driven to tears of frustration trying at the age of eighteen to explain to a boyfriend why I was so done in by the need to know why a tree stood near us instead of something incomprehensibly not-tree. Why was there yellow, blue, purple instead of some color our eyes have never seen? Why was *this* our teeming world instead of some other? The narrow specificity of actual things, and the infinity of never-to-be other things, was a burning matter for me. It isn't now, but I was young then, and both lonely and intense. I didn't *think* these questions so much as I felt them and lived them.

Such questions can't be articulated well enough to be asked, in any case. Wonder, awe, and the things that inspire them truly are beyond speech.

If we really tried to articulate our whole experience we would go deaf from all the internal chatter before we ever uttered a word or heard one from another being. We would have to make deliberate every involuntary and autonomic function of our organs, muscles, tendons, and appendages. We would need electronic computers to track the complex interactions of the internal systems that our brains now monitor without any conscious input from us. Odd notions, perhaps, but the more you think about what we undergo wordlessly, the more incidental language seems.

I couldn't admit this to myself, because it seemed a life sentence to loneliness. If we can't *say*, how can we love or know one another? Now, a little late, I know there are other ways. There are glances, laughter, touch, intuition, simultaneous utterances, banter, body language, actions. These say more than direct explanation or description. Only by indirection can we find each other out and only through faith can we truly love. We need faith in order to believe our own inferences, the things we intuit and apprehend, instead of needing to be told what's what.

We do not generally want to apprehend our lives or those who share them. It makes us, well, apprehensive. We would rather comprehend. We would rather be certain and be able to articulate our certainties until we have rendered them self-evident to others and need not fear misunderstanding. But everything that runs deepest in our existence, and brings us closest to the sustaining mystery at the heart of our being, requires apprehension — in both senses. Love and faith arise out of fear and conquer it, but not until we have taken that step off the edge of the abyss. We don't do this blindly. We have our intuitions and experience to guide us, hard though they may be to decipher. We have all five of our senses, our capacity for logic, our rational minds — and our souls. When we rely on everything *but* our souls, we cut ourselves off from mystery.

Nevertheless, I still do want the words. I still do say them and believe they are important, in tone and content, to the conduct of our daily lives and the expression of our feelings. I can't change my stripes altogether. This is cyclical. Usually, I trust. I apprehend. I look around at the life Alan and I share, and I never stop celebrating it. I am easy and content and I rejoice in the stretching I have had to do. Now and then something wells up in me and I pull away, lonely and sad, wanting from Alan the same kind of expression he offered so freely in his e-mails, when we had nothing else.

The other day Alan had to go digging down to the septic tank, seeking the cause of a stinking backup in the system. He was irritable, working in filth. I was irritable in response to his mood. But I realized I could check myself. I could stop and ask: Who is in emotional need, who can provide? I decided that I could easily let go of my surly mood and offer support. This kind of emotional marxism can work only with a totally trustworthy partner, one who will be equally conscientious about giving in and making room. It has never before worked, for me, in any other relationship. Perhaps this is why marxisms of money and power don't end up working — because they are enforced, not built on faith and trust. What a notion, to think that true marxism of any kind requires *faith*.

It is because I trust Alan that I can trust his silence. Again and again, I find that occasional loneliness is a thing that resides in me. It is not an artifact of what Alan does or does not say. When he does speak to me about his emotions, I know it is directly from his heart. He doesn't have to say much, because I can read the content of his heart in his eyes and acts. The universal loneliness is just a thing we all must live with, which no words can permanently allay.

Quaker Meetings

A couple of weeks ago, Sarah and I went to Barton-Glover Meeting, an hour north of here in the Northeast Kingdom. The Meeting is held in the basement of the library in Barton village. It is rather a dreary space, but the Meeting itself, about a dozen people, generated a deep spiritual warmth. At the rise of Meeting, when worship is over and Friends greet each other, everyone held hands in a circle and shared thoughts and introductions. There was a strong light about the group, a palpable sense of love, lacking in sanctimony or self-consciousness.

This is the Meeting Sarah belongs to. She has known people there for twenty-five years or more. I felt a sharp twinge of longing for that kind of history and connectedness, and I could understand Sarah's love for this group. But the hour's drive each way puts it largely out of reach for me, especially without that strong history. So Alan and I have been going to Plainfield Meeting, a different place altogether, but appealing. These Friends have a proper meetinghouse, only a few years old. It stands in a clearing near the fast, loud Winooski, the same river that runs through Montpelier. The structure is a gray-shingled cape with a small porch on the front and a deck in back. It is surrounded by trees and the sound of rushing water. Inside are a small entryway, kitchen, bathroom, library, and meeting room on the first floor, with space downstairs for First Day School and projects. The entryway is lined with Shaker-style wooden pegs for hanging coats. There is a small table with a guest book. Everything is spare and well lit.

The meeting room is wonderfully conducive to the silence of Quaker worship. It is about twenty feet square, with high, white walls, pine trim, a hardwood floor, and big windows on three sides. Green-cushioned pine benches face each other in a rectangle one or two rows deep on each side. Yesterday there were about twenty adults in attendance, and a half dozen children. Most were girls about six to nine years old; the two boys looked about five and ten. The children stayed with the adults for the first fifteen minutes of Meeting for Worship, a common practice in Friends Meetings, and then left for First Day School. They came in again after Meeting to report on their activities and present the Thanksgiving collage they had made.

This Meeting ended with a recitation of names and towns — who was from where. Only two or three people were actually from Plainfield; most were from Montpelier, a few were from Barre. There was no handholding, just the usual handshakes and smiles that mark the end of the silence. Announcements of potluck suppers and other activities preceded coffee and a spell of small talk.

Some of the older Friends we talked to have settled in Vermont from other places, having waited until middle age or retirement to move to the North Country. I like the mental image of older people taking different paths, some heading sensibly for Florida or Arizona, others making for this rocky, forested, cold, spectacular place.

Winter Prologue

Snow! We got only an inch or so the other night, and another couple of inches the next morning, but it was enough for a transformation. Snow turns the world into a photographic negative. What was dark before — the forest floor, the tree branches, the roofs of the house and shop and cabin — turned purest white, and what was pale became now dark against this brightness.

I got up and walked first thing that day. The stream that runs along the road at the top of our property was noisy, all its rocks, roots, boulders, and downed branches covered in white, the rushing water black beside them except for the foam at its breaking points. The air was still but filled with mote-sized flakes like a particled fog, a graceful, falling screen that blurred my vision.

I know that by March, with April still to go, I will have had enough snow, but that first brief snowfall was glorious. The hemlock outside the window seat in our bedroom looked more languorous than usual, its normally soft, drapy branches weighted with white, like something seen through Ansel Adams's lens. The silhouettes of everything were softened. It seemed quieter than usual. I don't think my pleasure was just that of a naïve, interloping flatlander. I think lifelong Vermonters feel it, too, no matter how winter-weary we all might become. The one does not cancel the other. Something about the first snow restores purity, renews the spirit, quickens the blood. Long before the last snow, we will be ready for another kind of renewal. With our blood thickened and slowed by the cold by then, we will long to feel it moving faster. It is all one thing, though, the first and last snows, the joy with which we greet one and our fed-up-ness at the other. I am in my chosen place, with the people I love most, and so it is easy for me to embrace these cycles. All of life is seasons, cycles, change, and restoration, and I don't see how we can live fully if we resist any of it, even the final changes of aging and death. These are our life, too.

What would happen if we stopped worrying about aging and embraced the changes it brings, seeing them as challenges, opportunities to grow and to keep learning even as our bodies give out? Wouldn't that strengthen and prepare our souls? It is almost as hard to imagine this as to give up our mainstream angst, our drive for goods and worldly success. Our culture is so obsessively youth-oriented that it must, by definition, be an immature culture. Why are we so willing to carve our bodies up—a nip here, a tummy tuck there, face lifts, liposuction—if not to maintain an outward appearance that must prevail against inward depths and a search for meaning? I wonder how our values would change if, as a nation and as individuals, we both grew up and let ourselves grow old. It seems unlikely, but perhaps not impossible.

Hunting Season

I took another walk in the snow recently—a fresh snow, boon to the hunter and bane to the deer, who must now leave a map behind them wherever they move. I saw many deer tracks, and the tracks of large and small birds, dogs, people, vehicles. As I came back home, down a hill, I faced the late-afternoon sun and saw a silhouetted figure walking up the road in my direction, carrying a rifle on a sling. I noted my instantaneous acceptance of this and thought how different my reaction would be if I were walking down a city street. Then, as the figure drew nearer and I could see it was a young woman, I did feel surprised. In spite of myself, I wondered why she was pursuing a blood sport, a chase I always associated with rites of virility.

I know that reflects my prejudice, which is no doubt uninformed and certainly runs far askew of the prevailing culture here. But I dislike the slaughter of wild creatures, finding it barely tolerable only if the deer population might otherwise starve, and in that contingency I would really rather some wildlife preservation group did the deed and made it clear that sport had no part in the killing. I would have no quarrel with this, as — when I climb down from my high horse — I also have no quarrel with people who hunt to put food on the table or to observe a generations-old connection to the natural world. Respect is the key. When Alan shot that buck, years ago, to feed a houseful of step- and surrogate children, he and the buck shared a compact, one that honored the need, the process, the hunt, and the blood. I have no doubt that that deer delivered himself into Alan's sights and that Alan made the kill with a prayer and not a whoop of triumph.

Sarah and Joe shush me when I mention my aversion to hunting, and they assure me that most people who hunt in these woods do use the meat and the hides. These local hunters, for the most part, are respectful and responsible. They are not like the worst kind of weekenders, city dwellers who tromp into the woods to drink and blaze away and take home a pair of antlers while leaving the carcass to rot or who shoot a deer in the gut and can't be bothered to track it down and end its pain. Sarah also points out that for many sons and daughters of local hunters, taking down a buck is a real rite of passage, a demonstration of mastery, an occasion for the kind of respect that some never get through any other avenue, not school, not other sports, not high expectations for success.

In a general store near here there is a "buck pool" with a chart that graphs the hunting season. Probably a hundred local hunters have paid into the pool; next to their names are spaces to enter their hauls. The last time I looked, only a day or so into the season, two men had each bagged a buck; one buck was a five-pointer that weighed 140 pounds; the other had six points but weighed 20 pounds less. I would guess the pool goes to the biggest pound-and-point totals, but I am not sure how their relative values are tallied.

I do know that buck fever is real. People can't seem to talk about anything else, in stores, gas stations, on the street, even at the dentist. Hunters' vans and pickups are parked everywhere beside the roads, wherever the woods are not posted. You see neon orange hats, pants, gloves, and jackets on half the men around and several of the women. Somehow, bear season did not heat up like this, nor did archery season for deer. Only buck season with firearms fuels this competitive heat.

There is always another side to the stories that trigger our visceral reactions. I recognize the prejudice in my gut revulsion against killing wildlife and in my stereotypes about bozo gunslingers going after prey that has more dignity than they do. And perhaps, in years to come, when deer are eating our gardens, I will feel differently. Some years ago, I did my level best to discourage, frighten, entrap, and even poison raccoons that leveled my city garden time and again. The difference, if it counts, if it mitigates the hypocrisy, is that I did not consider it a sport. Or maybe that deepens the hypocrisy. Maybe killing a raccoon because it damn well interferes with my landscaping plans is like eating meat from shrink-wrapped packages because I haven't the stomach to shoot it, gut it, skin it, and carve it up myself.

First Home

I hardly slept at all the night we watched Jimmy Smits's last episode of *NYPD Blue*. His character, Bobby Simone, died after weeks of struggling with a sudden, catastrophic heart infection, a random sweep of the scythe. The dying Bobby's dream images — symbols of flight, the unknown air, and the solid world he was soon to leave — all centered on the racing pigeons he once raised on a city rooftop and on the old man who was his mentor in that sport. His death was a letting-go and a sorrow, intensely and authentically expressed.

Still — it was only TV.

Still — there are days or weeks when life seems fragile and art just reminds us how thin is the crust around our earth. Just last week, a friend and coworker of Sarah's learned she had ovarian cancer. On Sunday night the friend died in an ICU in Hanover, New Hampshire. In less than seven days she had gone from not feeling well to falling into a steep, whirling, eternal plunge, like one of Bobby's pigeons shot in flight.

I feel all this the more because Adam is away this week, visiting his father in Pittsburgh. I know he is fine, but he is not experiencing this fineness within my range of vision. I know he will *be* fine and come home safely, but I know this in defiance of late-fall weather and the destructible nature of airplanes.

We all need memento mori from time to time. Part of being fully alive is knowing we will die and feeling that that, too, is part of life and its cycles. These recent events remind me of my own mortality and that of everyone I love, and the reminders are shaken like a crazy quilt by the wind at night. We have had some wild winds lately, and I lie in bed and hear the gusts approach from far off. They come with a dull and distant roar that gets louder and louder until the nearby trees catch it, and our temple chimes bong, and the chinks in the windows begin to whistle.

On the night Bobby Simone died, the wind in our woods battered our house so fiercely that the whole wood-and-glass structure felt flimsy as straw, truly capable of being blown away. This reminded me of a recurring frightening dream I had as a child. In truth, this dream probably played out inside my eyelids only two or three times, but I remember it as a common thing. In the dream, I walked down a wide street. I was six or seven years old, or younger — my age at the time. I was alone on this wide street, and suddenly the Big Bad Wolf appeared at my side to tell me, with a solicitous hairy paw on my shoulder, that the roof had blown off my house, and I had no home anymore. It was not the wolf that frightened me, but the prospect of homelessness.

An earlier dream of impending homelessness came to me repeatedly at about age four — a dream I actually remember as a vision, a thing I saw while awake. I shared a bedroom with my older brother, Mike, and our twin beds were on opposite walls. I would crawl into my bed and face my wall and then the image would come: I would see through my wall, and behind it there would be a tall, transparent man carrying a drum, which he beat slowly. Following this figure were a dozen or so little girls in nightgowns, all of them crying, all of them marching to the tempo of the slow drumbeat. I understood that these little girls would never go home again. I would pull my covers up tight around my neck, and when my mother came in to say good night, I would ask her if she could see my long hair or the lace on my nightgown. I never told her why I asked, but it was because I hoped the man might not know I was a girl, and might not take me from my bed. I also entertained the notion that he would take my brother instead, but I felt sure he would toss Mike back like a wiggling fish for not being female.

These dreams are the nearest I can get to the source of my lifelong search for home. I know very well that the longing for place arises largely from the emotional distances that characterized my family of origin and from the frequency with which the five of us moved from town to town and state to state, severing friendships and jettisoning keepsakes, mementos, and belongings (good word, "belongings"). But the deepest, threadiest roots of my rootlessness are a mystery to me. I don't know what childhood anxieties prompted those early dreams, with their omens of coerced and drifting loneliness, but they were the first announcements of this central theme in my life.

Later, the theme deepened with constant moving. According to my best calculations, I have lived in nine states, one Canadian province, twenty towns or cities, and more than thirty-five dwellings. The moving started before I turned two, near the end of World War II. My father was in the Navy in 1944, when I was born, and my mother was living with her half sister on a dairy farm just outside Princeton, New Jersey. My uncle taught me to walk. My aunt spoke to me in a voice more soothing than any I have heard since. My older brother, Mike, not yet four, trundled his red wagon full of hay almost to the East Farm, owned by a grown cousin.

I have no direct memory of this early time, but my mind has formed mote-filled sunny pictures of broad, towering shade trees; dim barns sliced through with shafts of light; horses, cows, dogs, and cats; wells with pump handles; dirt roads, a big frame farmhouse, and a smaller, tidier brick house. When Adam was little, I elaborately embellished the story of Mike and his red wagon, a favorite bedtime tale for my choosy son, who would not stand for stories from books but had to have his made up by the teller, nearly always me. The Mike story was one of the few Adam deemed worth hearing more than once, and I resorted to it when I was tired.

From that farm I moved with my mother and brother to another aunt's house in Indianapolis, to await, along with many boy cousins, our two fathers' return from the war. Next we stayed for a time in a small, clapboard hotel in Pomeroy, Ohio, beside a river, which is where I first knew my demobbed father and apparently resented his claims on my affection. I must have had no concept of what a father was or why one should intrude on my entirely satisfactory life with my mother and brother, aunt and cousins. Somewhere I have an account that my mother wrote about this quiet sojourn in Pomeroy. She characterized herself as outgoing and friendly, which, when I read the story in my thirties, I found remarkable. From the moment at age six or seven when I first became aware of my mother as an actual person, she was withdrawn, cool, and sad. It was then that I overheard her tell my grandmother how lonely she was. It was then that I made her my responsibility.

I believe we — my mother, brother, and I — went from Pomeroy back to Indianapolis, while my father went on to Pennsylvania to oversee progress on the tiny brick house being built for us in a postwar development. That house contains my first real memories — of Mike, the transparent man, and my mother, who at bedtime would "tell magic." She, like her own mother before her, like me with Adam, would make up stories, including one about a sprite from the moon who would slide down a beam of light and into our room to watch over us as we slept. She would also pretend not to see Mike and me, and she would wonder aloud if we were hiding in the bellies of the snapdragon blooms. I loved when she did that.

That house is where the roots of my love affair with language first dug into my life's soil. I remember sitting on the cement stoop one day, surrounded by the scrubby grass and dirt of the yard, with a question in my mind that was formed more as an image or a feeling than as words. It had to do with everyone encased in clear bubbles of perception that did not intersect. It had to do with the notion that when I said the word "green" and pointed to something green, my mother would applaud and affirm my communication. It had to do with whether my mother's eyes and mine worked the same way; whether what I saw as green would — seen through her eyes — appear to me suddenly as the color I understood to be red. I was not even three, and I would not have had the vocabulary for any of this. Still, the question was real, vivid, and utterly absorbing, so much so that I almost wonder whether that experience alone made writing my inevitable, resisted, difficult vocation.

I also remember an early awareness of differences between women and men from those days, and I am startled by its emotional content, which was already a bit dark. I remember that my father had little to do with the rest of us. He had outside pursuits. He played softball with neighborhood dads on weekends; he went to work on the other days; he stopped at the Green Lantern for a couple of beers on his way home from work each night. I knew my father's life and my mother's were as different as could be. I knew nothing at all about the quality of my father's life, but I already sensed that my mother's was not fulfilling.

I knew, too, at about this time, that my mother was going to have another baby. I remember arguing with Mike, then five, about whether the baby would be a girl or a boy, and I even remember my anger at his smug certainty that it was a brother and not a sister on the way. Worse, he was right.

When Steve was born, my mother's half sister, Fern, visiting from the dairy farm, drove Mike and me to the hospital, where we stood in the parking lot and waved to my mother, who held the new baby up in a third- or fourth-story window for our inspection. When she brought Steve home, he was not at all what I had anticipated. He lay in his crib and squalled, red-faced and bad-smelling. He was not adorable, but that didn't stop neighborhood children from coming to our door and demanding to see "the yittle Mayoy baby."

I had just started nursery school in a church basement, and Mike must have been in kindergarten somewhere else. We left the house each day, just like my father, but the message I got was not one of freedom or independence but of constraint. The nursery school was not far from our house. I think my mother walked me there. We children were not allowed to run from the sidewalk to the front steps of the church, and our teacher — not trusting us — would put her ear to our chests as we entered the building, listening for our telltale heartbeats and scolding us if a too-fast rat-a-tat betrayed exertion.

What a set of messages to take away from my first remembered home — that ghostly men will lurk behind one's walls, that language and perception are limited at best, that men have broader options and more fun than women, that running in sheer exuberance is bad.

We moved away then. I went to kindergarten in Elyria, Ohio, first grade through fourth in North Olmsted, and fifth in Cleveland, where I was given an IQ test and was moved from a classroom I liked to an "advanced" classroom that, because I was a shy newcomer and an easy target, I hated. That was my reward for being bright. I went to sixth grade in Stoneham, Massachusetts, and grades seven through twelve in neighboring Reading, where at last we stayed put until only Steve was still in school and living at home.

That was when my mother left my father for six months, confirming an air of instability and tension that had always pervaded our house. She left Steve, too, who was sixteen and could not forgive her for years. Her defection from the family coincided almost exactly with my first marriage, at nineteen — now there's an irony. She went to California, lived in a rooming house, got a job. Guilt cut short her middle-aged dash for freedom — a dash that preceded my own escape from my first marriage by six or seven years — and she returned. But all that is another story, one I will never know in full, and one that my father later said never happened that way at all.

In all those childhood moves, I looked out from behind the terror I felt at every new relocation and watched my mother perform her ruthless calm triage, the sorting, tossing, packing, and cleaning that always fell to her alone. Each time, she pitched everything that had not been used, read, worn, looked at, opened up, played with, or fought over in recent memory. She threw it all off like ballast, as if she could distance herself from Earth that way. She threw away too much, kept too little. Or so I always thought, accusingly.

But all of life is a moving from one place to another, and in the moving we must sort. We are forever deciding what to keep and what to let go of. I keep my fondest memories of my mother, in which she is either playing the piano (chubby rump rolling as she reaches up and down the scales) or giggling helplessly at some awful pun or piece of silliness that she herself or one of us has perpetrated. I also keep my commoner recollections of her, in which she sits with her chin in her hand and her eyes on midspace.

New life blooms on old wood. My life blooms on my mother's in the way I now see myself as her likeness turned inside out, from a barely decipherable negative to a readable image in a positive tone. When I moved out of the house that had contained my unhappy marriage to Adam's father, I pitched or abandoned more than my mother ever did. I kept no dishes, utensils, furniture, or linens, none of the housekeeping or homemaking things, just some cherished memorabilia of my own life and my son's, as if no marriage had ever happened. In that move I finally understood why my mother had kept nothing more than necessary, why she had tried not to weigh herself down. But I still think the hazards of too many moves include a growing ease of departure, an ability to sever connections.

Thanksgivings

I sent Adam an e-mail at his father's house on Thanksgiving morning, then baked pies before we drove into town at one o'clock for Thanksgiving dinner at Sarah and Joe's. Sarah's parents were there, along with Justin, the oldest of Joe and Sarah's blended five, and Justin's wife, Luisa, and their six-year-old daughter, Lina. Sarah and I have been friends for thirty years, but I don't think we have ever shared this holiday before. It was refreshing and peaceful, having someone else, namely Joe, cook the dinner, and hearing their family stories instead of my own — learning, for instance, that there is no such thing as whipped cream at their table. Ever since the year their Mexican friend Matilde first visited, the pies after dinner have borne only "w'eeped cream" (Matilde) or "w'upped cream" (middle son Thomas, correcting her).

For many of my last fifteen or twenty Thanksgivings, one or both of my brothers have traveled to Pittsburgh. My older brother, Mike, owns a sign-painting business outside Atlanta, where he has lived ever since his former employer, Eastern Airlines, folded. He was always sketching and drawing when we were little, and in high school and beyond, he made money pinstriping hotrods — not in straight, skinny banker's stripes but in delicately curving flourishes that followed a chassis's contours. Now his artistic skills have alleviated the worst effects of having twenty-five years of steady employment yanked out from under him. He works out of a small, one-man shop, producing artful hand-carved or hand-lettered signage for local businesses, either building and delivering the works or painting them directly on trucks, vans, windows, or storefronts. When he isn't working, he acts in local theater productions, and for five or six years he has been deeply involved in his church.

Mike's daughter, my beautiful niece, Heather, is twenty-seven as I write this, a ballerina-choreographer with North Carolina Dance Theater and also an adventuresome woman with great sweetness and humor. Mike has been divorced for about twenty years from Heather's mother, Judi, who remains my close friend. He has never remarried, not really. I tend not to count a subsequent disastrous brief union that lasted only until a house got bought and the bride could cleverly claim it. I wonder whether he will ever try again, after all this time.

Steve — my younger brother who squalled so as an infant but at fifty is subtle, witty, sharp, and loyal — was a bachelor until his late thirties, when he finally found and married Rita, a native North Carolinian with determination, strong spirituality, plentiful intelligence, a family riddled with "spooks and haints," and not a trace of southern belle about her. They have a son, Stephen, almost two years younger than Adam, an outgoing, enthusiastic kid who is the nearest thing to a brother that Adam has had in his life. The two cousins used to bicker constantly when they were together, but when asked to pipe down they would say, "We're family — it's our job." Then they would laugh and keep bickering. Now they have dropped most of that in favor of an easier companionship.

Last Thanksgiving, the first that Alan and I shared, both brothers came, and so did Rita and Stephen. Alan fit in fine and was admirably patient with the inevitable family recollections and sibling dynamics.

The Thanksgiving before that one — Adam's and my first in the Arts and Crafts house — my brothers and nephew, Stephen, came without Rita, who was finishing a paper for her master's degree. That year, in an atmosphere heavy with testosterone, I heard coming-of-age stories from both brothers that pickled me with envy.

Mike and Steve, it seemed to me, had gotten away with being bad — at least by the standards of the late fifties and pre-hippie sixties — while I had been painfully good, such a teacher's pet and source of parental pride. The things my brothers did wouldn't even count as appetizers on today's menu of teen misadventures, but compared to my adolescent activities they were wildly mischievous. Mike and his friends found a stolen '53 Mercury up at the sand pits, hot-wired it, drove it until it wouldn't go any more and then ran it into the quarry where all the boys of Reading, Massachusetts, went skinny-dipping. Steve drank and bragged and stole things from time to time and prowled Boston's Tenderloin District or hitchhiked farther afield for mischief.

I lamented my dull good-girl-hood, but my brothers assured me there had been prices to pay for their rebellions. Steve, in particular, shelled out four years of his life when, just after high school, he got picked up in Boston, high on LSD, and was more or less sentenced to the military in order to avoid prosecution. He and the Air Force never did get along. It was a long four years, made longer by a stint at Sonderstrom Air Force Base in Greenland. The nights alone — even summer nights, not just the months-long winter darkness — seemed a year apiece. The inhabitants of the base used to stretch every mundane task and function, even taking a crap, to its utmost length of time. They all suffered what they called "the Sondy suck-me-downs." Sarah was in the middle of an on/off love affair with Steve at that time, and she and I used to bake cookies and address them to Flyboy Maloy.

That pre-Alan Thanksgiving visit was pretty good except for the day Mike left. I returned from a walk that morning to a pair of silent brothers sitting at the dining table, eating leftover pie for breakfast and reading the morning paper. That seemed normal. But after I had taken Mike to the airport, Steve told me they had had one of their now-and-then contretemps over a story in the paper, a report on sexual harassment in the military. Mike thought women did not belong there in the first place, and Steve accused him of disregarding the simple, repeatedly proven fact that women are capable of most anything men can do.

In the way of families, perhaps of brothers in particular, such moments have seasoned the relationship between Mike and Steve for as long as I can remember. But in recent years, since Mike has become a Christian and has tried to influence Steve's thinking and my own, the frustrations have heated up on occasion.

At such times, Mike's religious views seem to heighten his big-brother inclination to redirect people he considers off the mark or dangerously in error. Such stray souls now include, by Mike's reading of Scripture, anyone who is not a strict and literal Christian and anyone whose passions or pastimes are outlawed or reviled in the Bible. I once thought that this was simple prejudice on Mike's part, justified by religion. But it is more complicated than that. Mike is sincere in his search for truth, and he does not mean to give offense. He is worried for those close to him, whose souls he believes may be lost. He and I have in common the desire to open ourselves to mysteries and light, but he is more willing than I am to follow established thinking—a thing that surprises me, given the independence of mind and habits, that marked his youth.

It is also possible that there *is* some bias in his beliefs. We three were not raised by liberals. Our mother, Elizabeth, grew up with a grandmother who feared the family would all be murdered in their beds by some "big black nigger," and I think she learned to be apprehensive, too. She never knew any people of color herself, and she did not seek them out. She was so apolitical she never even voted. She was always more focused on the next world than this flawed and puny one she shared with the rest of us. She spent a great deal of time in her room with God, leaving us all to manage on our own during those prayerful absences, which indeed cut big holes into our childhood. But perhaps the biggest gift she ever gave me came straight from her times away from us. That gift was her declaration that she did not believe in hell—that if even one soul was saved, then every soul would have to be saved, and that meant the souls of heathens, Jews, Buddhists, atheists, "primitive" peoples, and every persuasion and color of person in the human rainbow. Her prejudices were the fearful or condescending kind, not the hating kind.

Our father, Jess, was a Republican with every reason — three kids, low wages, no college degree — to be a Democrat. He too had plenty of prejudices, but at least he knew better. He preferred to hide them rather than teach them to us. He was not an imaginative man, and he was deeply insecure. His affectionate gestures came across as ineffectual and sometimes even pleading. But he was a sad man, not a bad one.

So it could be that some combination of inclination, upbringing, and religion has licensed Mike's belief that whole groups of people are forever left out of the light, people like gays, lesbians, drug users, feminists, Jews, Muslims, Buddhists, and New Agers — anyone whose beliefs and behaviors don't fit the notions of righteousness he has adopted. At best he might say that such people can be saved by repentance.

I on the other hand would say that if God is the light, and if Jesus, among other holy ones, is God in human form, and if we all have a portion of the light within us, then it is through *both* our portion and the original light that we are saved — and not from hell but from anguish and fear, which are hellish enough.

Obviously, Mike and I disagree about God. He would have me believe, as he does, that God is the kind of parent who can abandon His own children to darkness for being the way God Himself made those children — for being human and therefore, in wildly varying proportions, frightened, ignorant, passionate, greedy, fallible, selfish, violent, easy to tempt, and prone to hatred and suspicion out of fear and doubt. Mike insists God feels only anguish when a soul is lost, when a remorseless child of God's has fallen beyond reach.

I think this is what *human* parents feel when they give up on their wild or wayward children, assuming they haven't already forced their feelings down below the level of detection. But I expect God to be better than the rest of us. I expect God, under every circumstance and in the face of every imaginable human weakness or evil, to look at even the so-called worst of Her children and say, whether they beg Her to or not,

Come home, come in, get warm. God fails utterly if God withholds love, because God *is* love.

Mike would say that God does not withhold love but that we turn down the gift. I would say that when we do — when we deny God, soul, connection, diversity — it is only evidence of our human limits and our great need. It is not cause for punishment but for ever greater and more perfect love.

My brother Mike, whom I love in a cranky and highly imperfect *human* way, is afraid I will burn forever because I can't believe in a God who could burn me or any other creature. But that only makes me fear that Mike might suffer terribly because he believes in the justice of terrible suffering. Sometimes I fear he is suffering now but determined to deny it. Frankly, I wish Mike had someone else to love, along with God. That might bring him back down to earth with the rest of us.

I miss my earlier brother Mike, the one who was funnier, easier, less ready to sort people into sheep and goats. The one who, ten years ago, flew up on an Eastern pass every weekend to build a deck on the house I was living in then. The one who cracked jokes and now and then let his hair down. That brother seems more real to me, more generous and relaxed. I am pretty sure he is still in there.

Emma and Ellen

Sarah and I went to a new coffee house in town a few days ago and sat down with a friend of Sarah's named Cynthia. Women have it so much easier than men! I took one look at Cynthia's face, found it open and kind, and felt immediately at ease. The three of us talked much as Sarah and I do, about our personal lives and histories, the people we love, the anecdotes that we have saved and polished for their defining qualities, their ability to telegraph who we are. We fell into tones and topics that offer comfort and affirm something about our lives as women.

I have lost that ease with Emma and Ellen, my two old Pittsburgh friends, the ones who regarded Alan with such hesitancy and who found my intimacy with him incomprehensible even after we had been together a year. I have not been able to understand the rift that remains between us except to suppose that tiny fissures might have been there for a long time before cracking open amid the strong tremors of change.

I can see now that I am different from Emma and Ellen in deep-seated ways — in a restless craving for change, in being more introverted, in simply having moved so often, and often so compulsively. Certain aspects and circumstances of our lives converged tightly for many years, and so I never saw the differences until I surprised us all in these recent events. Then I began to think I had always tested the limits of these friendships, perhaps because my life was often murky, unstable, and crisis-ridden in the Pittsburgh years, whereas Emma and Ellen seemed grounded — their marriages were strong, their lives largely as they wanted them to be, their work rewarding. When I moved away, it probably looked to them as if I were rejecting everything they valued, everything they found gratifying themselves. It probably looked as if I were perversely pursuing more uncertainty and upheaval, just when they thought I had finally settled down, into my Arts and Crafts house, my necessary job, and the satisfactions of a full life as a single woman with a son. They had every reason to think I embraced that settling down, because I myself thought I had found my future.

Now it seems Emma and Ellen cannot forgive what seemed precipitous, selfish, and too surprising in my actions, and I am unwilling to keep trying to explain myself. So we are stymied, for now. Even so, the door is just slightly ajar. We exchange infrequent, abbreviated notes through e-mail — birthday greetings, announcements of news. We do not declare the death of caring, and so it survives, though frail.

December

Stepfamily

Adam missed about four days of school before going to Pittsburgh for Thanksgiving, two days for flu and two for the trip. He and I met with his teachers to collect all the assignments for which he would be responsible, and when he returned home from Pittsburgh Saturday night he assured me everything was done. Then, Monday morning, he rose more reluctantly than usual and stood as if stunned beside the living-room heater, looking like a boy who wanted to die. Miserably, he told me he had done nothing. "I don't know why I can't make myself work," he told me. "I meant to do it. I kept thinking I would do it. You and Dad are hard workers, I don't understand why I'm not."

Oh, the angst in that confession! I didn't hear it at first. All I heard was that he had not done what he said he had done. It has taken me a while to realize that, from his perspective, this was less an outright lie than wishful thinking: If I *say* it is so, perhaps it will *be* so. I think lies carry less moral weight in children's minds than in ours, because children haven't yet seen what lies can do. Our job is to teach them, to make them feel the consequences of their actions while trying not to cast them into doubt about their worth as human beings. It isn't easy. We judge so readily and pass that on before we even think.

The first thing I did when Adam confessed was yell at him. "What do you *mean* you haven't done anything? *Nothing?* Not one thing?" I was outraged. I rapidly forced myself to calm down, but my first reaction was out there, and we both knew it. I explained that I was angry about being misled, not about the uncompleted work. "If you're having trouble, we want to help. But you have to tell us. You have to ask. If you tell us everything's okay when it's not, that only makes everything worse."

I shifted into problem-solving mode and wrote to Adam's teachers asking for a meeting. Adam took the letter with him and delivered it contritely. Alan, Adam, and I sat down with his teaching team at a long table a few days later. Alan and I agreed to be more vigilant, to make sure the homework is done every day and that it gets done before Adam has any access to entertainments.

We have been expecting too much. If Adam is not a disciplined worker yet, it is because he hasn't learned how to be one. He needs to understand that at thirteen he will not work the way adults do. That is part of what he will learn in school and from us.

How we handle this is made touchier by circumstances of birth. Adam is the only, overdue child of an adoring older mother. Alan was undervalued, neglected, and abused as a child. Alan the man is compassionate and fair-minded, but he is also the bearer of lessons learned so long ago that they are virtually ineradicable. As lessons go, their content is good — they have to do with responsibility, truth telling, hard work, and self-reliance. But they were learned in fear and by coercive means, which taints them with impatience, a vastly diluted version of the harshness dealt to Alan by his own stepfather, Harvey. It must be very hard, when the lessons are good but the teaching cruel, to fully separate the two.

Sensing this, I realize that the trust I have in Alan depends on my trusting myself. I am able to trust Alan — his love for me, his observations of Adam, the affection that now and then emerges between this stepfather and stepson — only because I have come to understand, in myself above all, that all trust is a matter of faith as well as behavior and communication, and all faith entails risk. My faith in myself is relatively recent, and it does not deny my failings or fallibility — it is simply my best refuge and surest shelter amid the loss of friends, the ends of marriages, and the search for God. What I know about Alan is what I know about myself, that the search is genuine and that the heart and soul that guide it long for tenderness and truth.

When Alan and I talked to Adam about our expectations, we did not yell or berate him. We tried to be informative, and we spoke in low voices. We talked about the need for trust. We emphasized that home-work problems do not make us angry but being deceived does — even if he didn't wholly mean to do that. We said we are available to help him when he is stuck, worried, confused, or unmotivated. Adam was fleet-ingly defensive, but he let go of that almost immediately. He acknowl-edged the legitimacy of our concerns. He sulked briefly about some con-sequences we imposed, but within ten minutes or less had returned to his habitual good humor. He has an incredibly good nature. He is resilient; he never holds a grudge. My love for him feels limitless, a perpetual and humbling joy.

Still, it is probably a good thing our children don't know how unsure we are sometimes, how we occasionally have to build our confidence in ourselves as parents from the ground up every day. We can't let them know, and so we need each other. I have never had a full partner in par-enting before. It moves me that Alan has become that. He was calm and gentle during our talk with Adam. He reflects carefully about Adam, and he identifies, too, seeing in Adam's tendency to keep his own counsel a ghost of his own young self.

Outwardly, Adam and Alan are still shy with each other much of the time. But I see in their slow approach the beginnings of a bond. They have granted each other respect. Alan has not pushed himself on Adam. Adam has never once said to Alan, "You're not my father — I don't have to listen to you." He has never said to me, "Why did you have to bring *him* into our lives?" He may test the limits, which seems a necessary way of getting to know oneself and others. But he is also able to recognize when a limit has been breached and to accept the consequences.

Long Walks and Metaphors

Last week, our nearest neighbor called around noon to see whether I had had my walk yet. I had not, so she invited me to join her on some trails through the woods. So far, I have been walking on the dirt roads, ours and adjoining ones, feeling unsure about going in search of trails, not wanting either to trespass or get lost. The prospect of an alternative was good.

Kathy and I started by heading up the hill where I always begin my walks; but at the top, where our road turns left, we went straight, following a semiprivate road well posted with warning signs. Kathy assured me that the owners are generous with their land and trails; it is only hunters and total strangers they want to discourage. We went up that road about a tenth of a mile, then cut across an open meadow and followed a vague path into the woods. Once there, Kathy let Zeke, her golden retriever, off his leash, and he bounded loose like a kid let out of school, grinning and streaking far ahead of us. Now and then he would double back, as if checking on us, or he would stand beneath a spreading pine and gaze stockstill into its branches, eyeing a bird or squirrel.

The woods this time of year are pretty open — the undergrowth has all died back, and fair distances are visible through the leafless trees. Like our own woods, these were full of tall, slender, close-together trees — mainly maple, birch, and beech, with pines, firs, and clusters of gnarly old apple trees here and there. What I thought were white birch, which we lack on our property, Kathy said might be poplar, or quaking aspen. Somewhere, Alan and I have a field guide to trees, but we haven't yet found the box in which it is packed. Now, with the leaves gone, identification is trickier.

Kathy and I walked almost two hours, up and down, alongside a stream, and past a meadow and barn with a tiny herd of Scottish Highlander cattle — mild, shaggy beasts with long curving horns, heavy forelocks over their eyes, and big broad noses. Here and there, deep in the woods, we saw crumbling, disused stone walls, covered with moss, snaking through the trees that have grown up around them and obscured whatever fields or meadows they once marked off. We saw parts of a stone foundation lining a depression in the earth. We saw a household dump — a clutter of rusted milk cans, an old kettle eaten away, pieces of cloudy glass — all signs of a homestead now dissolved into earth and embraced by vegetation. We walked and clambered, sharing each other's histories even as we became curious about the histories of those whose hands had placed the rocks in the walls that we passed. Now and then, through the trees, we could see the Worcester Range blue in the distance and sharp as a Matisse cutout.

The pleasure of walking with Kathy reminded me poignantly of how I came to know Emma twenty years ago, in Pittsburgh, when her teaching schedule and my freelance work permitted long runs in the afternoons. We talked about our lives and everyone in them as we tore along the trails in Pittsburgh's Frick or Schenley parks or ran through the streets and around the reservoir. Eventually our circumstances and schedules changed, my knees refused to run anymore, and our friendship waned, for these and other reasons. I have blamed myself and blamed her and tried with hindsight to discern the first signs of the unraveling between us. But blame is not the issue. Second-guessing teaches us very little. Amid the changes life brings, Emma and I simply grew apart, though not without sadness, hurt feelings, and mystification. I suspect, as I have already said, that we never knew each other as well as we thought we did.

I walked again the other morning, traveling almost six miles around the base of our mountain, on dirt roads and paved ones, beside streams, rivers, and marshes, past flocks of sheep and a few horses, and finally over the bridge at the entrance of our road and back to our house. Because deer season is now open for hunters using muzzle-loaders, I now and then heard those weapons' muffled double thumps, sounding like somebody falling against a barn door. It was a less intrusive sound, or perhaps just farther away, than the crack of high-powered deer rifles.

Just a mile into my walk, with nothing around me but woods and a few houses off the road, I smelled cigar smoke — so unexpected and puzzling. In the city, on a deserted block, it might have spelled a threat. For an instant, I thought it was a hunter, but I rapidly realized that deer would smell the smoke before I did and have sense enough to bolt. The smoker was one of a pair of surveyors, both bearded, one blowing his breath out into the cold air, the other expelling the stink. I walked on, hoping they were not measuring for any radical change on the road I was enjoying. There is no zoning to speak of around here, but neither can any lot be subdivided into pieces smaller than the 10.1-acre parcel we own ourselves. That is at least decent protection against too many incursions, too much development.

There was no snow on the ground, just frost, so the colors and forms of rocks and vegetation were visible through the sugary white coating. I noticed, near streams and in marshes, the low-growing red canes of wild blackberry, which lent a richness to the general grays and browns. So did clusters of sumac fruits, lit by the sun and glowing oxblood red against a blue sky. Lowest to the ground were honey-colored grasses, some of them spiky, some soft, bent low, and twisted by rain and wind. Covered with last night's frost, they looked like tangles of spaghetti. Cattails looked like hot dogs on a stick, some with buns — their seed-bearing down coats — and some naked, the buns eaten away by wind. Milkweed pods everywhere had exploded to release their fluff-borne seeds — they reminded me of old-fashioned nuns' wimples, opened up to reveal flyaway white hair, a liberating notion.

Why this image-making compulsion, this reflexive search for similes and metaphors? I catch myself at it all the time, I just never questioned it before. Ever since I read Charles Frazier's *Cold Mountain*, which I did soon after I joined with Alan and entered his silences with him, I have recalled certain lines from that book. They are from a letter written by Ada Monroe, a minister's daughter raised in Charleston, South Carolina, but forced, during the Civil War, to survive on a rugged mountain farm in North Carolina in a place called Black Cove. From the farm she writes to a friend in town:

> Working in the fields, there are brief times when I go totally without thought. Not one idea crosses my mind, though my senses are alert to all around me. Should a crow fly over, I mark it in all its details, but I do not

seek analogy for its blackness. I know it is a type of nothing, not metaphoric. A thing unto itself, without comparison. I believe those moments to be the root of my new mien. You would not know it on me, for I suspect it is somehow akin to contentment.

I have always used metaphor to give form to passion, but recently I realize that images can dilute powerful feeling as well — which perhaps makes contentment more elusive. All words, even the most vivid and precise, are ideas. They are symbols representing reality, but they are not reality itself, so they put distance between us and our experience. There is so much more *there,* in every scene and experience, than language can ever capture — and cage. When we forget that, we stop looking for the unsayable.

In my earliest years as a Quaker, the silence sometimes overwhelmed me. It brought me straight to my unknown and ineffable self, all the parts that felt strange, chaotic, unfocused, intense. Only very slowly did I begin to suspect these were my spiritual components, the uncontained within me, the wild center where that of God waits. This is why Quakers sit in silence, after all, to find that center and hear the voice of God. They know that language distracts us and can rein in spirit.

Even so, words are one way to seek. They allow us to describe our search to others. Isaac Penington, an early Quaker of Puritan descent, said, "The end of words (even of Christ's own directions in the days of His flesh) is to turn men to the holy life and power from whence the words came."

Words alone are not sufficient, though. There are other ways to turn to what is holy. I find it in people I love, in mystery — and in nature. For me, the simplest natural phenomena have always been avenues to the sacred. I am moved by every branching structure and every grassy leaf that bends like calligraphy, the writing of God, inviting notice. With the early sun on my face, I can close my eyes while I walk and feel the sliding muscles in my body, feel a kind of giddy physical tiredness, a heightened sensation of movement, air, light, heat.

Or — I can sense infinity too close at hand and feel pole-axed with terror. Words are handy, then, for their distancing qualities.

I love living here, because spiritual stimuli are so close. They feed my soul. I tune my senses to every change in the contours of the land, every smell, the new things revealed when the leaves fall. The hills never look the same from one day to the next. The light comes in countless forms and colors — sometimes it is blown everywhere by the wind, in visible currents. We all have our light. Some of us are moved by cityscapes, some by bayous, some by interiors. I like being close to what God has made directly. I like the handiwork of humans when it strikes me that the hands are doing God's work. But so much human manufacture stinks of greed or exploitation that I am happy to be surrounded by relatively little of it.

Like Ada Monroe, I experience contentment. It is not a tame or self-satisfied feeling; it is more like prayer.

Winds Out of Season

Prayers, of course, get interrupted. Last night, hard winds battered the house, and the strange, wild weather continued during my walk this morning. It was sixty-eight degrees when Alan got up around six, the same when I went out at nine. Winds were gusting at thirty to forty miles an hour, and the sky could not keep still. Clouds gathered, broke, and blew around in shades of charcoal, dove, and white. The sun shone through, and then it rained so hard I had to put on a nylon anorak for a brief tenth of a mile. Otherwise, I walked on this December day in Vermont wearing just a short-sleeved T-shirt and light leggings.

I would rather be out in the wind than indoors listening to it. It is a spooky wind for this season, too warm, too heavy, coming at us from the wrong direction. I guess it compares to the Santa Ana winds in California, or the siroccos, which blow up from North Africa over the northern Mediterranean coast. It knots Alan's body into painful gnarls. He is a walking barometer, and this wind in particular has him edgy and lame.

Me, too — I think I felt it coming. I was down all afternoon yesterday, subliminally aware of the upper atmosphere. I was blue for no reason, near tears whenever I had a moment alone. It was a global sadness that I felt, a spiritual sorrow consciously bound up with thoughts of mortality, my own and others'. Sometimes the weight of the unknown comes over me like an ocean, and I can barely breathe. I wonder how we all can keep on from one day to the next, so small inside this opaque immensity, so vulnerable to losses that can come in a heartbeat. Yesterday, I felt prone to terror, wondering whether the God I intuit and love is real, or whether others, who believe in a more punitive God or none at all, know something that I don't, can't, won't.

Such moods pass quickly, sped along by the knowledge that everyone who has ever lived has shared them. On mornings like this one, when all the elements are in wild motion and I can be out in them, I regain perspective. The wind, once it touches my face, stops getting under my skin, and I admire the tenacity of us all, the way we bounce back. When I came home, I stood at the top of our rise and gazed at the light everywhere. Through our naked trees I could see three ridges of the Worcester Range. The nearest was the dark green of firs and the farthest was the deepest cobalt blue. The middle ridge, catching a wide band of sun through the racing and darkening clouds, was a brilliant tawny gold, every naked branch of its deciduous pelt lit up like a wand on fire. So much light! It changes minute to minute but it always reaches me, always makes it easier to turn my mortal form around and settle more comfortably into the human condition.

Dogs

Annie and Hank are now five months old. We can almost watch them grow. Hank consistently outweighs Annie by 20 percent, and he leaves her in peace only when he wants to sleep. She is more timid than he, but she is sly as well. When Hank grabs a toy or chewie from her mouth, she looks woebegone for a moment, watching him enviously with her head on her paws. Then she goes and finds a lesser toy and makes an exaggerated show of enjoyment, tossing it into the air, gnawing it, parading it ostentatiously in front of Hank. He, of course, cannot resist. He drops the desirable object and goes for Annie's ruse. She then grabs the coveted prize. Her victory is always short-lived, but it seems immensely satisfying to her.

These are endlessly sweet-natured dogs. They understand several commands, and they obey when they know we are serious in issuing them. This may be particularly important at Christmas, when Alan's stepdaughter Edie will be here with her husband, Sam, and their two daughters, Ellie, eight, and Mimi, four. When Alan spoke to the girls on the phone recently and told them about Annie and Hank, Mimi said, "Oh! Puppies! They will lick me!"

Indeed they will. I just hope they don't also get Mimi on her back, upside down, with her head or another body part in their increasingly large mouths. This is what they do to Emmylou, our full-grown but tiny calico cat. Emmylou — unlike Topper, who looks down his nose like a tuxedoed Peter Ustinov — invites such treatment and relishes it despite her melodramatic yowls and hisses. I have seen her seductively draw her tail right under the nose of sleeping Hank until he wakes and pursues her. She spends so much time in the dogs' mouths that her coat is usually a spiky do held stiffly in place by canine saliva. Hairdressers should know how effectively that serves as styling gel.

Quakers

Alan, Sarah, and I went to Plainfield Friends Meeting again this week. Alan and I have worshipped with them perhaps four or five times so far, and each time, someone has made a point of speaking with us afterward. So far, I don't sense tension or judgment among the Friends there — which doesn't mean there is none. It takes time to learn a Meeting's inner workings well enough to perceive such things. I would guess this Meeting is one fourth or one third the size of the Meeting in Pittsburgh, so if there are disagreements there might be more means and motivation to resolve them.

Quakers are no strangers to disagreement. I know several people who are Quakers to their bones yet disaffected from any Meeting and unhappy with the state of the Religious Society of Friends. Some of them feel that Quakers have lost their spiritual convictions, that they are ruled too often by ego or opinion, too rarely by devotion to the light. They feel that true Quaker process, a powerful gift to the world in its search for unity and universal respect in the conduct of business and practical affairs, has grown weak. Others suspect that any process or institutionalization by its nature dilutes spirit. These Friends avoid the business of Quakers but rely on Meeting for Worship for spiritual growth and insight.

Like any other religious group, Quakers have both modern disagreements and a history of quarrels over process and belief. In the United States today, Friends Meetings take a variety of forms, depending on the faction in which they have their roots — though all factions can be traced to George Fox and the earliest Friends.

Fox's direct communication with God, and his belief that everyone can accomplish this same thing through "that of God" inside, is the basis for silent Quaker worship and for a common Quaker distinction between the historic Jesus and the "eternal Christ," the light, the truth. Jesus the man, the holy one, has been seen by many Friends as a sort of lens through which the eternal Christ burns with greatest intensity and can be apprehended in its most concentrated energy.

Some Friends, over time, have objected to this distinction when they have felt the emphasis was too heavily on the Christ within and too lightly on the historic Jesus and the Gospels. The very first signs of division among early Friends appeared in discussion as to whether human reason was compatible with the inner light or corrupted it. The Rationalists valued reason in spirituality; the Quietists mistrusted it. Over time, factions arose, quarreled, and split off from one another, especially in the United States, until finally, by the mid–1800s, there had emerged Keithians, Lloydians, Hicksites, Orthodox Friends, Gurney-ites, Wilburites — a cacophonous array all calling themselves Friends but variously interpreting George Fox's original vision and journey into direct communication with God. At bottom, most of the splits and arguments were over the sanctity of Scripture, the call to evangelism, and the significance of the historical Jesus. It is rather sad that the splits occurred at all among people whose testimonies urge peace, discernment, and respect for one another—but I suppose the splits keep us human and grounded, aware of our flaws.

Today, some Friends are evangelical and actively seek converts. They have retained George Fox's belief that there is that of God, and thus the potential for salvation, in every person. They interpret Scripture as a more literal description of the Way than Fox did; he saw it as a guidepost. Other Friends do not evangelize, but they do emphasize Scripture, and they are led by pastors in what are referred to as "programmed" Meetings.

Friends who worship in "unprogrammed" Meetings, like the ones in Plainfield and Pittsburgh, adhere to Fox's belief that "that of God" (the inner light, the eternal Christ) is each person's access to all truth; the part of us that is God can be found by means of the silent "waiting on the Lord" that constitutes a Meeting for Worship. In such a meeting, the silence is broken only as spirit moves Friends to speak. The light is there for us all, and so no Friend is seen as more qualified than any other to draw upon it; no Friend is elevated above others as a pastor or minister, interpreter or expert. Neither is any Friend a spiritual law unto himself or herself. Each person carries a share of the light, a molecule of God, a fragment of truth; but no one has it all, which is why we come together as a group, in a sacred silence, to hear what might arise within and from without.

Conversing with God is difficult. Everything else must drop away. The voice within is faint and small and sometimes speaks in a language we don't recognize. Our disbelief, our personal will, and our habits of literal mind are powerful. Distraction insists, intrudes, grabs us by the face the way Adam did at two if I tried to talk to someone else while holding him on my hip. Sometimes that distraction can lead us to exactly what we seek; sometimes it impedes. How to know?

These puzzles are why a reliance on the light in ourselves and others is not an invitation to invent our own religion but a strenuous discipline forged in the midst of human uncertainty, pettiness, and judgments. It is tempting to resist the truth when it is delivered by someone whose personality rankles or opinions offend. It is difficult to know when a prompting is from God and not an expression of ego, denial, selfishness, or sanctimony, in the self or other people. The ministry of Friends ranges widely in content and quality. It can be self-serving, shallow, and annoying, or it can be wise and moving. The same ministry that changes one listener's whole world view can seem tedious or self-evident to another.

I did not understand any of this when I first began attending Friends Meetings, which I did sporadically in the years after I learned about Friends from Sarah. I went to Meetings in Toronto, in Cambridge, Massachusetts, and in Berkeley and San Francisco before landing in Pittsburgh for two decades. Now and then I would see the oddest behavior. One woman danced her ministry. Sometimes people ranted or wept. A blind woman spoke more like a deaf one, shouting her message into the silence and making some people jerk in their chairs or wake snorting from their half sleep. A con artist, who later bilked Pittsburgh Meeting and stole from individual Friends, delivered the funniest, most poignant ministry about his childhood. Some peoples' ministry was nearly unintelligible — mumbled, sung, ranted, or garbled; some arose from raw emotions bumping together like unmoored boats in a choppy harbor. Now and then someone delivered a long jeremiad against whatever real or imagined injustice he or she had suffered — police brutality, psychological abuse, institutionalized prejudice.

In various Meetings I attended, I knew there were half-mad people, homeless people, angry people, lonely people, childish people. I came to see that because Quakers were known for tolerance, simplicity, social action, and caring, they attracted waifs and refugees from the fringes of American culture and a few others. This was the obvious difficulty — dealing compassionately with disruptive or deeply needy people without also disturbing the foundation of a Meeting, its silences, its testimonies, its processes.

Less obvious to me, before I joined Pittsburgh Meeting and came to know it over many years, was how hard it could be to deal with stable, responsible, well-established Friends. Often, in Pittsburgh and elsewhere, I have heard Friends use Meeting for Worship as their soapboxes and sounding boards. I have heard longtime Quakers defiantly ramble on with self-indulgent complaints just because they wanted to create a disturbance. I have seen one or two people hold up a decision in Meeting for Business just because they felt resentment or needed to exert their influence, knowing no action could be taken without the necessary unity.

In other words, I have seen Friends be just as selfish and cantankerous as any other group of human beings.

I have also seen tenderness and compassionate action carried out quietly and competently, without calling attention to itself. I have seen wounds healed, have heard inspired ministry delivered by some of the half-mad and injured, have been moved to tears by simple naked truths spoken by a woman in her eighties, afraid to die. I have learned that a danced, ranted, sung, or babbled message can be true and profound even if I can't understand it. I know I have heard messages from God, some straightforward and others in code. I know I have felt the presence of God when the silence has descended and have found in my own spirit a calm intensity that is not of this world.

Hearing what other Friends are led to say, and seeing the examples set by them — both good and bad — is a kind of spiritual apprenticeship through which the powers of discernment can grow. Above all, group worship draws upon the light of everyone present, illuminating more truth, love, and wisdom than one person's share of the light can ever do. Time and again I experience directly and with poignant power the fact that we are all part of the same larger, timeless whole. *Together* we embody the truth.

Winter Solstice

Kathy and I walked through the woods again, ten days before Christmas, this time on trails that start down below her house. I was glad to get out; it was such a busy time, with packages to send and guests arriving soon. I told Kathy I was hoping for snowshoes for Christmas. She said Alan — my Santa — should come look at hers to see what features are important. I bought Alan books, CDs, yarn for a new sweater, a nightshirt with moose printed all over it — and two shocking-pink plastic flamingos. This began as a joke, but soon I knew he actually wanted them, perhaps to keep us (me) from getting too serious about this place we will probably spend the rest of our lives working on. Once we have plenty of deep snow around, I suspect we will look out our living room windows and see these tacky tropical birds glowing hot against all the white. Is this instead of the Bahamas?

On the Sunday before the holiday, Edie, Sam, and the girls arrived in the middle of housecleaning a few days after my walk with Kathy and hours earlier than we thought they could get here from Chicago. That was just fine, an excuse to put down the broom and dustpan. Things were clean enough.

We were a little cramped during the five days of their stay. Alan and I turned our bedroom over to the whole family of guests. The girls slept on the window seat, my favorite spot in our house, a deep, cushioned, bed-sized platform three and a half feet off the floor, next to an eight-foot window that looks down onto the wooded plateaus and rocky bluffs leading to the river. Alan and I slept in the loft on two mattresses; he hung a sheet across the entrance for privacy. We all made do with one bathroom. We didn't complain. Most people in this world have no bathroom at all or else share one with dozens of others.

It was so good to have Edie and her family with us. They joined us for the holidays in Pittsburgh last year, and they issued satisfying *oohs* and *aahs* over the many contrasts between there and here.

Alan is "Papa" to all four in that family. When he and I were getting to know each other, he wrote:

I'm Edie's Dad, because we both chose it to be that way. Edie is twenty-eight, currently (mired) in Wheaton, Illinois. Husband Sam, daughters Ellie and Mimi. These four are the brightest stars in the universe, still glowing in the heavens even through the darkest, stormiest night.

Alan's role as Papa and Edie's unmistakable love for him were a big part of my certainty that he was who my soul told me he was — not a psychopath or scam man. I loved watching this young family surge and eddy around Alan's calm presence like water near a rock. He is not given to roughhousing, bustle, or lots of talk, but they all came to him. They told stories about Alan, about "the claims," about Sam and Edie's teenage courtship and Sam's earnest attempt to ask Alan for Edie's hand. They admire him, which pleases me.

Adam clicked with Edie and Sam from the first minute he met them last year, and he restlessly awaited their arrival this year. Both Edie and Sam are self-described nerds — computer professionals and computer addicts. Sam likes many of the same computer games Adam does. Above all, they both like Adam, and they invited him to spend time with them in Wheaton, perhaps over the summer. Adam just recently figured out that Edie became his stepsister when Alan and I married. He takes enormous pleasure in this; he has never had anything like a sister before, and the fact that Edie should bear this relationship to him was like an extra Christmas gift.

The solstice came and went during the holiday week. The longest night of the year is a gloomy prospect except for the fact that the light begins its resurgence on the morning after. I am not sure what it is about the annual cycles of light, the equinoxes and solstices, that causes me to note them without fail. Perhaps it is their perfect representation of less and more, balance and excess, opposites defining one another. Just as the light is weakest, it starts regaining strength. In death there is life, in life the knowledge, always, of death. The seasons, which give and take, flourish and die back, have many rhythmic lessons to teach. Over the whole cycle, there is perfect proportion, but within the rounds are passion and excess, balance and calm, each promising the other.

These rhythms mean more to me than simple alternations of light and dark, warmth and cold. They imply a wholeness in everything, a unity made up of its parts but much bigger than them. The solstices and equinoxes, as they wax and wane like the smaller cycles of the moon, suggest to me the interlocking curves of the symbol for yin and yang.

Where one narrows down, the other opens up, and it must happen this way, in harmony; it can't happen otherwise. Where light fades, darkness must pour in. Darkness can swell only so far before it must fade and light must enter. The timing and the rhythms are the heartbeat of all existence, and I find them comforting. All is as it needs to be, and it has been so since the original act of Creation also destroyed what had been before, the infinite silence and oneness.

It may be a stretch, but somehow I intuit from the irreducible necessity of paradox and pain in the cycles and counterpoint rhythms of life that there are no tragedies in this world. If existence can be no other way and yet is also the gift of a loving God, then even nature's red teeth and claws may not represent violence the way we humans think of it and inflict it on each other. Perhaps, like the deer that offered itself to Alan that northwest winter, animals in the end consent to their sacrifices. I think we consent to ours, too, but have no memory of having done so. I believe there is awareness — or some form of "life" — not only after death, but before birth, too. I believe we are eternal creatures; we have never not existed since the moment of Creation. Perhaps we can bear our immortality only through endless rounds of change and forgetting, until we have found all the exploded pieces of the original truth, and have put them together, and can return to oneness with God.

Families at Christmas

Mimi's prediction came true time and again while she was here. She would get on all fours in front of Hank, who outweighs her by six or eight pounds, and issue the high-pitched command, "Lick my face!" Hank would oblige, grinning, as Mimi exploded into giggles. Ellie, more sophisticated and calm, sought the company of the cats, especially Emmylou, who will absorb attention from any and every source.

Adam and the girls decorated ginger cookies together — people, trees, houses, and moose. This undertaking became an excuse to squeeze as much green and red frosting as possible over the smooth brown shapes. The girls put silver-dragee necklaces on their moose. Adam created houses in flames and road-kill moose streaming blood. He is a thirteen-year-old boy; he did this cheerfully and downed the results with glee.

A few nights before Christmas, we all had dinner at Sarah and Joe's, an easy, friendly evening. I felt like a proud parent, showing off Edie, Sam, and the girls. Sarah worries about her son Jeremy, twenty-three, who is seriously involved with a young woman named Marta. She likes Marta very much but worries that these two are too young to make a commitment. I told her that Edie and Sam have been together since high school. They were science fair rivals; first Sam beat Edie, then Edie beat Sam. They married when Edie was twenty and Sam nineteen. They were parents before they finished college — Edie took Ellie to classes in a backpack. Now they are nearing their tenth anniversary, and their devotion is plain. I think this reassures Sarah.

Adam played with Ellie and Mimi while the adults talked, and he reminded me of Jeremy, who used to entertain Adam. Once, when Jeremy was eleven and Adam a year old, Jeremy kept him happy throughout a six-hour drive while Sarah and I talked and drove. I thought that was extraordinary for a boy Jeremy's age. Another time, when Jeremy and Adam were sixteen and six, they spent an evening playing games to escape the adults. Jeremy happily became a six-year-old himself, and Adam adored him for it. Tonight, as Adam laughed and let himself be teased and abused by two little girls, I thought of how Jeremy has turned out — kind, funny, loving — and I enjoyed the prospect of Adam as a similar kind of man.

The day after our dinner out, it turned bitter cold, but I took a long walk to reoxygenate my brain and clear my lungs of the wood ash in our interior air. All the streams were rapidly freezing over. The water rushed beneath clear and cloudy ice that is sometimes smooth, sometimes built up into fanciful shapes. Here and there it was a thick casing, rucked up like a silvery carpet, showing the white flood beneath and creating crystalline edging, like baubles or sequins, all around. It was wonderful to be outside, away from those I love. The cold is absolutely pure and cleansing; it strips down color, heat, and motion and makes everything simple and slow. When I came back inside, I could feel the blood pulse hot in my face.

Edie and I talked for a while after my walk, leaning against the kitchen counters. She spoke of her mother, Judy, Alan's late wife, a woman ten years older than Alan, gifted and demon-ridden. Edie told me she had learned to value her mother as a friend more than a parent. Judy had seven children but was apparently not skilled at motherhood. I gather that the other six sometimes resent her for that, but Edie — the youngest, the last to live at home, and the only one to receive the full benefit of Alan's presence after his arrival, when she was eleven — has found a way to respect and love her. I admire Edie for this. The same journey took me so much longer, and I think my path was not so steep.

Edie told me how hard Alan worked to keep their changeable family together, fed, and cared for. He worked myriad jobs that she said were miles beneath his abilities. He took what was available. Among other things, he worked for five years on the renovation of a Victorian house that was owned by a pretentious, nit-picking SOB who made his money in dubious ways and as often as not had his workmen undo week-long tasks they had just painstakingly finished. Alan has told me how much he learned about fine craftsmanship on that job. Edie told me how much damage it did to his back. Alan got his gentle revenge, though. He put toilet paper holders right where the SOB, sitting on the pot, would gaze at them and be driven nuts by the fact that every single one was a six-teenth inch off the level.

Over the years, I hope Edie and I will get to know each other well. I like her, and she interests me apart from her relationship to Alan. She asked me, a little dubiously, how I felt about being somewhat in the role of a grandmother. She looked relieved when I said it pleased me completely.

Christmas morning, Alan's and my uneasy sleep in the loft was inter-rupted early by soft squeals of pleasure from Ellie, who was opening her stocking in the window seat as Mimi slept on. I stumbled up and went downstairs to make coffee. Soon everyone was up and we enacted the same scene that was playing out in millions of other houses where this holiday is celebrated. Adam was Santa, handing out gifts and restraining his impatience to rip into his own. Ellie and Mimi, though younger and more susceptible to the overstimulation this holiday can induce, recovered rapidly from any emotional glitches and seemed delighted with their haul. Mimi, whose favorite color is "happy yellow," is a sunny child capable of occasional brief cloudbursts. Ellie is the one with quieter, deeper passions. They accommodate their differences well.

By ten o'clock, the living room was knee-deep in wrappings and the gifts were no longer mysteries. We all sat back in a temporary stupor induced by the morning's burst of sweet greed.

I recently saw a billboard-sized sign on a store near here that said, "Keep the Christ in Christmas." Personally, I would like it better if they took the spiritual pretense away altogether and just let this be a pagan holiday, true to its origins. I would rather, in the fall, near the equinox and the likelier time of Jesus' birth, have a solemn candlelit time of silence and praise, sorrow and rejoicing. No gifts, ginger cookies, trees, carols, or feasts. Save those for the solstice and let them mark the earth's slow turning back to light and warmth.

Perhaps it is that darker side of the holiday, the foreshadowing in myrrh, that tells me children are not the only ones for whom holidays can be too much. Edie, Sam, Ellie, and Mimi left the day after Christmas. We took Adam to the airport the next morning, for his flight to Pittsburgh and a post-Christmas time with his father. He was gone before full light. I was up at 4:45 to shower and get Adam up and all of us in the car for the hour-long drive to Burlington airport. The plane took off at sunrise. It was a perfect flying day, but I was uneasy and felt fragile. I fought tears all the way back to Montpelier and all during breakfast with Alan at the Coffee Corner. I lay back down to sleep when we got home and didn't wake for four hours.

Slow Light

I have written all of this record so far on the computer in the office space that Alan and I share, which is right in the middle of the heaviest traffic pathway in the house. I am very private about what I write, while I am writing it, and I am easily distracted by anyone passing behind me, able to look over my shoulder. Even though I know Alan does not read as I write, I get nervous. He knows this, and has his own version of my jumpiness, so he scoured the *Green Mountain Trader* and the Barre-Montpelier *Times-Argus* and found a used laptop for sale.

We drove to Rutland together to inspect and purchase this machine, which I am now using in the window-seat aerie overlooking our woods. The tracking ball is clumsy and reluctant, but I don't mind; it is such a relief to be able to remove myself, and concentrate. It touches me to realize that Alan thinks of these remedies on his own, that he pays attention and solves problems and is generous. I told him I thought I just ought to get over myself, rather than spend the money for this laptop, but I am grateful that he did not take me up on my resistance.

We had a fine day together. We always like being on the road, watching the scenery and sharing a relaxed, close silence. We talked idly and listened to the new CDs we gave each other for Christmas; otherwise, we simply rode together, quiet and happy. On the way back a wind came up, and it began to snow. Nothing much accumulated, but the fine, powdery snow reduced visibility as it spun like cobwebs across the road and windshield. It wasn't hazardous, just a swirling reminder of where we live now.

We left the dogs outside while we were gone. They had food, and they can get under the house for shelter. I worried a little, because we have never left them for so long. They don't tend to roam, and indeed they were fine. They turned themselves inside out with pure canine joy when we came home, making our return just that much greater a pleasure. The dogs know in their bones what people find so hard to learn — that the deepest joy is in our going out and coming home, in loving someone else, in showing our delight.

Alan and I needed the quiet journey together after the more emotional ride of the holidays. I like the peace at this time of year, this New Year's lull between the dark and light, the old year and the new, the things we want to forget or do differently, the things we hope to keep and cherish. But Alan and I feel no need to mark the moment of transition together. We will go to bed well before midnight on New Year's Eve, two old farts. Alan will sleep and I will read and struggle to stay awake to observe a ritual I began two years ago.

On New Year's Eve, 1996, which marked the end of the year in which I left my marriage and moved into the Arts and Crafts house with Adam, I went to a party in my new neighborhood. There, chatting with the hostess, I learned about putting coins face down on a window sill and turning them face up at the stroke of midnight. The coins stay in place all year, their faces turned to the turning stars, collecting good fortune. Something about this appealed to me, and I went home in time to try it out. Within a few weeks, Alan and I had begun our correspondence.

Until then — or just about then — my faith had tended to go about disguised as superstition, questions, or doubt. That New Year's Eve before Alan, I put more of a prayer into those coins than I admitted even to myself. I realize now that I did so because my shaky faith had already worked wonders, finding the online information I needed about children and divorce, helping me understand and allay old fears and hopeless struggles, leading me to the house that crystallized my desire for freedom. It would still be a month before my uncertain faith brought me Alan, but that was little enough time to wait.

Faith, it seems, can flourish on almost no nourishment, yielding a crop of miracles from almost total neglect. It reminds me of the deer tick, which, I once read, can survive on the tip of a twig for ten, a dozen, fifteen years, waiting for a warm-blooded creature to pass. And then, sensing heat, it makes its leap. My tick-sized, patient faith languished on the outermost branches of my life until Alan appeared as words on my computer screen — and then it leapt, changing everything.

WINTER

The snow
began here
this morning and all day
continued, its white
rhetoric everywhere
calling us back to why, how,
whence *such beauty and* what
the meaning; . . .

Mary Oliver, *First Snow*

January

Cold

Last night, the first of January, we went to Burlington to meet Adam's eleven o'clock flight at the airport. We left under a clear sky and full moon, passed through some blowing heavy snow (and attendant anxieties about planes in high-altitude winds), and then saw stars winking through a light cloud cover as we exited the interstate. The plane was on time, Adam full of glad reports about his visit to Pittsburgh, and the trip home uneventful except for our awareness of the iron, subzero cold through which we followed our headlights.

This morning I spent a couple of hours in the living room, as close to the kerosene heater as I could get, reading Jane Smiley's *The All-True Travels and Adventures of Lidie Newton*. This is the story of a young nineteenth-century Illinois woman who marries a quiet New England abolitionist and heads to Kansas Territory with him. As I warmed myself in the pale sun and kerosene heat, I read:

> I wish I could say that I savored and appreciated each of those quiet days in the fall, but I cannot. When the wind ripped my [wall]papers and the cold air crept into the cabin, when the stove went out and refused to light again, when my hunting was poor or my husband preoccupied, I felt prickles of dissatisfaction.

I felt so much like Lidie Newton! I realize I am not a pioneer. I have a washer, dryer, dishwasher, wiring, plumbing, and an income. But unrelated conveniences fade when the cold has gripped your house and land, when winter becomes an implacable presence, almost a being outside your thin walls and windows.

We have our chinks, too. We have been struggling hard to stay warm, and fighting with the wood stove all the way. The firebox is too small, and half the wood left by Sandra and Harriet is too long for it. The stove heats best when it is half full of old coals, which never do burn all the way to ash the way they're supposed to. Just as we get the stove cranked up good and hot, it's time to empty the coals to make more room. This releases clouds of soot that then settle gently onto the piano, into the laser printer, down among the computer keys, and onto the windowsill, books, plants, and telephone. Then it takes two more hours to get the fire hot again, and the cycle repeats itself. Alan gets up once or twice every night to put more logs on, and even with that the fire is often out in the morning.

Nevertheless, because Alan and I are nearer a pioneer way of life than we were a year ago, we are oddly more secure, at least in view of weather emergencies and power outages. We have enough wood for this winter and next. If we buy a generator, as we plan to do, we'll have just enough electricity for short spells of light and occasional use of the pump that draws our water from our well. We already have shelves of canned goods, because Alan can't resist the red-dot specials at the Grand Union.

We should probably stock up on a few more canned goods and some first-aid supplies, medications, and household necessities. But the most important thing is community. Already, I have heard stories of people pitching in during last winter's ice storm, which coated the world in a thick, deadly glaze, shut down power, isolated shut-ins, and made transportation more than usually hazardous.

They say we are in for an ice storm this very night. The weather report predicts deep cold, heavy snow, and, later, freezing rain and sleet. The power could go out for hours or days. We have no generator yet, just plenty of kerosene lamps and ranks of gallon jugs filled with water.

We have stocked the wood room to the ceiling. We have plenty of food, our stove uses propane, and our fridge, in this frigid season, is a convenience but not a necessity. We are fortunate and safe, but still, as I sit here on the bedroom window seat, with many pillows, two cats, and a pot of tea, I have only to look to my right, through the window and down into the woods, to realize I am just inches away from wildness and lethal cold. The thing I forgot, all those years in cities, is that that is true of all of us in winter.

Snow

Last week's ice storm did little of its work around here, but today, at last, we have real snow! It started with some freezing rain this morning, and now, in midafternoon, it is snowing heavily, steadily, and purely. Already, there is a foot of fresh powder on the ground, with more to come.

Adam, who is too sedentary during the warm seasons, loves sledding, and now that he has seen my new snowshoes (from Alan, for Christmas, as I had hoped), he is eyeing them speculatively. He is a cold-weather boy — walks the mile from his bus stop in shirt sleeves if it is above forty degrees, brags to his Pittsburgh friends that he can see his breath when he wakes up in the mornings, adores the snow, and considers today's storm too little too late.

I am more sensitive to the cold than Adam, but I love it anyway. As long as it is above zero, I will bundle up and walk. All the clichés are real to me — the cold is pure, a tonic, an invigorating elixir. It blows the mental and emotional cobwebs away, along with the stink of too much self. When I am in love with the cold, heat seems overstuffed with scents, dust, pollutants. The cold air, on my face and in my lungs, seems unadulterated and perfectly clear. It is like breathing ice. I envision bacteria dying in my system — I want to think the cold will not let them breed.

I think this notion comes from when the stream that runs along our property, beside the road, first began to freeze. One day last week, I stopped and gazed down into it, through its cover of clear ice, and saw the waters still running, air bubbles trapped at the surface, the whole image like one of those blown-up views of capillaries and corpuscles. Water is the blood of the planet, slowed by cold, pure and ceaseless. Even now, when the streams are no longer visible beneath their coverings of thick ice and heavy snow, you can hear the water flowing. It doesn't sound like water at all, more like a muffled thudding, a distant heartbeat against frozen ribs. As I stood beside the stream during my walk, an image popped into my mind — my own body a refrigerator, housing the cold, and all my inner organs slowly seizing like meat in the freezer. This made me laugh. It also sent me indoors to get warm.

Snow Again

Alan and I went to Meeting with Sarah this week. I felt tranquil, looking out of our silence at the silent trees and snow. I feel that same way, sometimes, when I look down into our woods from the window seat where I write. I realize there are just three things to see — hardwoods, conifers, and snow. The patterns they make are intricate, and the colors of bark, boughs, and a few dead leaves still clinging to the beeches are subtle and surprisingly varied. Yet the scene is utterly simple. I am drawn more and more to spareness. I want few decorations around. I like the feeling of space, mental and emotional as well as physical. I like looking through the clear air and seeing only three things.

This afternoon, I put on my snowshoes and went out for three quarters of an hour, just long enough to test my stride and get a feel for this unfamiliar action in the deep new powder. Kathy, next door, had already broken a trail through the woods, so I followed where she had plowed through. I found myself amid the three things that I see from our windows, and the combination of that tranquillity and the heart-pounding exertion of walking and climbing through the deep snow comes as close to bliss as I can imagine. I stood where Kathy's trail bent to the right, up a steep hill, and then I walked forward, into untouched snow, and with my one ski pole I scribbled "thank you"— for the day, the freshly broken

trail, the health with which to enjoy the trek. The new snow had probably covered my scrawl before I reached the next flat space on the trail.

A few days later, I went out again on my snowshoes, for an hour or
more this time, following Kathy's trail farther into the woods and up
steeper inclines. I was glad for my ski pole, which keeps me stable while
I climb in a foot and a half of snow.

The snowshoes themselves are nothing like the traditional kind made
of leather and wood. These have frames made of anodized aluminum,
which deflects snow and ice. The weight-bearing surfaces are vinyl,
lashed to the frame, and the bindings are also vinyl, with nylon webbing
for strapping your feet in tight. There's a toothed rocker panel at the ball
of the foot and another set of teeth farther back, so your feet grip on
slick surfaces and hills. Best of all, it is possible to move along with a
nearly normal walking gait instead of lifting your feet straight up like a
crane in a swamp. On level parts of the trail, I glide along as if hiking.
On steep uphill and downhill sections, I dig my ski pole in and either pull
myself up with it or keep myself from going into a steep slide as I
descend. One of these days I'll just let go and butt-ski down the hills.

This recent snow is settling into itself, growing denser as the days
go by and the air that has kept it as lofty as down escapes. The snow has
somehow gone still; it has more weight. The smell of it is sharp and clean.
Snow is a pure stuff, a source of light, and winter a season of peace.

Cold Again

When Alan got up at six this morning, it was twelve below zero. The car
wouldn't start, so Adam had to hitch a ride with Kathy's family — her
husband, Steve, and their sons, Max and Carter. Carter is one of Adam's
good friends here, the first he has ever had who lives within walking
distance.

When I got up, at about seven-thirty, the temperature had dropped to
twenty below. There isn't much to say about extreme cold, at least for
me, at least in the midst of it. It numbs language, along with everything

else. It inspires great activity, as long as the activity is directly related to generating warmth. We stoke and poke at the woodstove endlessly. We bundle ourselves in several layers of cotton and wool. Alan deals with the car, recharging the battery and rigging a heater for the engine, then takes a hot bath.

Otherwise, we are stock still. We read, write, surf the Internet, make coffee or tea — and feel grateful for this quiet time.

Light

Every season since we have been here — summer, fall, and now winter — has been atypical, thanks to El Niño. Now they are saying his sister, La Niña, may keep the trend going, though perhaps in a different direction. Last summer was wetter than any on record. Fall was warm and also wet, and the foliage never truly blazed until just before the leaves fell. Winter held off and held off, the weather staying warm and snowless until the ski resorts grew desperate.

These past few days, though, this season has thrown just about its whole box of goods at us. Since Thursday, we have had extreme cold, snow, freezing rain, sleet, and ice. Yesterday I went snowshoeing in the most recent trail that Kathy and Steve had broken through a mile or so of ice-encrusted snow topped by a couple of inches of soft powder — a stratified record of our recent weather. But today the sun is out, the sky a clear intense blue that deepens eternally the higher you look. It is warm, almost sixty degrees, and the shadows on the snow are as blue as the deepest cobalt overhead. We have ascended through almost eighty degrees Fahrenheit in a matter of days.

I realized, while walking today, that the direct unfiltered sunlight is a fourth thing in the scene around me — a more compelling component than the evergreens, hardwoods, and snow alone because it casts them all into high relief. It forms shadows that add depth to the flat landscape, and it calls forth colors that otherwise go unseen, a varied subtle palette of grays, browns, mauves, reds, and especially greens — greens tinged with olive, gray, blue, brown, red, and yellow against that crystalline sky. The hills, especially the ones packed tight with conifers, look much closer than they do under the uniform shadowless light of a cloudy day.

Someone in Meeting this morning, after watching the light reflect off the snow and onto the ceiling of the room in which we sat, commented that when you photograph outdoors on an overcast day, the entire dome of the sky is your source of light. Then she added that we receive light in countless forms, all of which have special illuminating effects. This day's light is strong, and it chops the world up into brightly contrasting shadow and brilliance. This light does exactly what Alan says it does — it energizes, it draws a sweet euphoric sap up out of my bones.

This mix of Meeting, light, warmth, and energy constitutes an experience of God that I would not have recognized in days when I thought God must make Himself known in unmistakable, annunciatory ways — as a voice, a scintillating presence, a vibration in the air. Now, I believe joy is the presence of God, the best evidence that a part of God resides in each of us.

This is what I was thinking about during the silence this morning, my occasionally maverick beliefs, which arise from my core — my conviction that God is love, that God does not exile or punish, that God would have us seek knowledge and love diversity, that God does not condemn us for our weaknesses. George Fox, according to his wife, once said,

> The Scriptures were the prophets' words and Christ's and the apostles' words, and what as they spoke they enjoyed and possessed and had it from the Lord. . . . Then what had any to do with the Scriptures, but as they came to the Spirit that gave them forth. You will say, "Christ saith this, and the apostles say this;" but what canst thou say?

This question — *what canst thou say?* — is sometimes more than I can handle, even though it is also the reason I am a Quaker. If each of us really carries God within, really can apprehend God's voice as an echo inside us, then that gives us great power and frightening, but also liberating, responsibility.

What canst thou say? challenges every authority, religious or secular, for if each of us can experience God for ourselves, we can surely think independently about human institutions. For many people, that leads readily to social and political action — known by Quakers and other like-minded folks as "speaking truth to power." It was that way for the earliest Friends, and it is the source of all Quaker testimony on equity, non-violence, pacifism, simplicity, social justice, and truth telling.

At the heart of Fox's question is a challenge that I am just beginning to understand. To answer his question, to know what *I* can say — about God, human dealings, good, evil, politics, action, and anything else for which I might seek guidance — I need to choose deliberately between love and fear. Through much of my life I have been guided by fear, a shape shifter that has come as shyness, self-doubt, a desire for security, anxiety over the opinions of others, a too-trusting naïveté, an inability to stand up to exploitation or insult — in short, a thousand forms of powerlessness and retreat.

In recent years, without quite realizing it, I have more often pushed through fear to choose love — of life, self, Adam, Alan, nature, God, truth. Fear doesn't permit much truth to enter. Abandoning fear means stepping off the edge of the abyss, and that takes faith.

I can't really say when I first stepped fully onto the bridge. It might have been when I learned to love my mother unconditionally. It might have been when I had Adam and had to learn how to absorb new lessons of love every day. I think, though, that those experiences prepared me for the bridge and kept my first steps from being blind ones, even though I could not "see" with my habitual and rational apparatus where the steps would lead. Instead I saw with the inner light, which loving Adam and my mother had caused to shine more brightly, and that light led me onto the bridge. My first steps took me out of the marriage I had held onto not out of love but out of fear. With every step since, the stone bridge has constructed itself just ahead of my footfalls. Precarious as that might sound, I have never walked a safer path.

I am a Quaker because I believe the light that arises inside us and calls out to us from others is the only true authority in spiritual matters. It comes directly from the source. Nothing else can form my faith for me.

Faith cannot be taught, prescribed, conferred, or insisted upon, not even by Gospel, not even by others with direct experience of God, and especially not by force or through fear. Fear casts out love and so denies or casts out God. If we try to make ourselves believe because we fear the consequences of no belief, our faith will not be faith but intimidation.

I can see no pathway to faith except the perfect freedom not to believe and not to suffer consequences if we don't, or can't. If I follow this line of thought far enough, it leads me to believe there is no death, for the light within us is eternal, is that of God. This helps me to understand why my mother did not believe in hell, for if every soul is saved by the light — which she would call Jesus — as she believed it must be, then who would occupy that dread territory? Hell is born of our own fears, and in perfect faith, a thing beyond our human reach but worth aspiring to, there is no room for fear.

Work

I have met with Vermont's commissioner and deputy commissioner of education about the possibility of working for them as either a freelance writer or a part-time staff member. I was given the name of the deputy commissioner by a woman I know in Washington, but I did not get in touch until Alan and I looked hard at our budget and realized it was time to bring in more income.

I spoke with the commissioner and deputy commissioner for more than an hour and am still shaking my head, trying to jog a new reality into place. My work life for the past ten years or so has been surrounded on all sides by bad management, big egos, jealous hierarchical thinking, the theft of ideas, and the deliberate use of intimidation to prod more output.

I have seen a widely known education reformer and university administrator routinely hang subordinates out to dry, giving them more responsibility than they could handle because she herself had lost interest in doing her own part. I have seen researchers, driven by the massive fear that they might never have another worthwhile idea, scheme and jostle for attention like toddlers. I have seen researchers with Ph.D.s in science scorn other researchers who rose up from the ranks of classroom teachers, and I have seen staff—no matter how senior, how long-tenured, how loyal, or how skilled—treated as interchangeable and readily replaceable parts. I have seen them publicly blamed for the errors of management, a deep injustice in itself but a worse one in view of the fact that most staff had no reward from their work—not status, high salaries, creative autonomy, or self-defined challenges—except the satisfaction of doing it well, a consequence of their own integrity.

I was a writer in this setting, which made me professional staff—neither fish (a scientist) nor fowl (administrative staff) but a kind of fish with feathers. I generally found that I had more in common with staff than with scientists. Although some of the people doing research on learning and cognition became friends or treated me as a colleague, more were skeptical, resentful, uncooperative, or simply dismissive. I often thought that this was because my job was to represent their work intelligibly to broad audiences, when their own view was that only other Ph.D.s in their various fields—psychology, computer science, sociology—could understand it.

Now I have had a foreshadowing of something unfamiliar to me. The commissioner, a slight, graying, blade-thin man with a soft voice, stood up and greeted me with obvious warmth and pleasure. He had read some of my articles and reports, and he said my writing could be "a dream come true" for his department. In almost ten years at the university, no one at the top ever came close to wholehearted praise for my editing and writing, even though classroom teachers liked my work, the U.S. Department of Education published some of it, and every now and again it helped bring in millions in funding for further research.

The commissioner and his deputy, a tall, direct, athletic-looking woman radiating energy, have made it plain that they want to hire me for as many hours a week as I want to give, and they are more than happy for me to work from home, send drafts in by e-mail, and present myself in person only for meetings and substantive orientations to new work.

These two speak knowledgeably about what it takes to convey technical, political, complex material in a straightforward way. They promise to bend over backward to accommodate me, at least within the low pay structures of a poor state's bureaucracy.

Still, I am wary of work. Even in a sick workplace, I always felt I should be more productive, should override the conditions that gnawed at me. I couldn't manage that, and so I always struggled with guilt, resentment, and resistance. These corroded my work ethic so badly, I am not sure that even an ideal situation can mend it.

What I hope is that I might move gradually into a new set of attitudes about work, made possible both by a more humane environment and by the fact that the love, home, and faith for which I have searched, haphazardly and half in denial, are now in place. Add solitude to these. I am more of a loner than I ever knew. I am able to love company, whether that of co-workers or friends, to the extent that I have fed my soul enough time for reflection.

Now that I recognize how completely my work life has lacked reward, respect, camaraderie, and fruitful solitude, I no longer count it as a mark against my integrity that I could not work to capacity under bad conditions. Those conditions exacerbated my worst qualities, making me stressed and bitter. One's best work seldom comes out of the perpetual struggle to quell such emotions.

I can see also that my professional work has seldom drawn on real commitment or passion. I have always been a good and conscientious editor and writer, but I have rarely loved these tasks when I have done them for a paycheck. The work I have really loved in my life, whether writing or some other kind of effort, has always related to my cherished trio of values — love, home, and spirit — and it has often been conducted in solitude, my fourth necessity. When I write about these essentials, I love writing. When I tend these essentials, I become lost in the work, I am one with it, it is myself. I can find this wholeness in gardening, mothering, cooking, Meeting for Worship, designing our new living spaces, feeding the animals — even, on rare occasions, housecleaning.

To imagine that this confirms some gender stereotype would be a pretty thin take on things. I think the desire to cultivate one's garden is simply in the blood of some people. My brother Steve, according to his wife, Rita, is "a domestic genius." Though he has been a photographer, newspaper writer, cab driver, and bookstore manager and is now building a clientele for his art-framing business, he is most deeply content when he is tending home and family. Alan, too, is nourished in his soul by physical labor, especially outdoors, especially in the sun. He says that the value comes from working on what is dear to him — a living space, a workshop, a view through the woods. This is true for me, too.

Here's an interesting aside: It occurs to me, as I write about Alan and Steve, that the two of them might come as close to being male counterparts of me as I will ever know, and I am amazed by my good fortune in them both. This does not surprise me about Alan, of course, but there is a certain irony in my feeling this way about Steve. When we were children, we fought passionately and perpetually. My mother told us later that she used to be afraid to leave us alone together. Even my rare moments of warmth toward this little brother could be misinterpreted. I remember one such moment, when Steve was about six and I was about nine. He was suffering miserably, his head and chest congested, his nose dripping, his eyes hot. He was lying on the living-room couch, and I sat near his outstretched feet with our ginger tomcat on my lap. Compassion welled up in me without warning, and, confused by this unfamiliar and to some degree unwelcome heat inside, I picked up the cat and dropped it onto Steve saying, "Here, have a cat." Steve promptly burst out crying, and I promptly got into trouble.

I really did intend the cat to be a source of furry comfort for my ailing brother. I just had no idea how to make my gesture convincingly or with any overt warmth. It went against our pattern together. I was embarrassed by my tender lapse.

As adults, we have had our touchy times as well, but we also have many traits and tendencies in common. We agree about values and politics. We share the same painful resistance to the workaday life. Our sons present us with similar challenges and delights. We have done nearly the same amount of pinballing in our lives, bounding and rebounding from one place or job to another, scarcely thinking about what was next. I see now that Steve has a spirit as restless as my own. We are as much alike as we are made different by gender and our separate interests — Steve, for instance, is a sports fan, and I most definitely am not. I'm a gardener; Steve isn't. We both like to cook, and especially to bake bread and pies.

I can understand how domestic passions in the blood might lead one to focus only on personal matters and family concerns. I see nothing wrong with this unless it somehow treads on others' rights. Done well, by men or women, alone or together, the making of a home in which love and spirit can thrive is a priceless gift to the larger society. It may be that my work for the department of education will give me a chance to contribute something else of value to my new community and state. It may be that other avenues will open through Friends, friends, and other connections.

Whatever my service to the larger good, I know now that it has to come from the long time it has taken me to know who I am and what I want. This helps me to understand at last why I so ill fit the times in which I lived as a young woman, times of action in which I did not act. I believed passionately in equal rights for women, gays, lesbians, handicapped people, people of color, poor people, all people; but I wondered why I didn't do much *except* believe. I accused myself of hypocrisy, vacuity. I thought I should be acting on, and writing about, the issues of my time.

Instead, my words blew smoke between me and the world I lived in. I was in love with the music in language and the rhythms in syntax; I did not see that these had become ends in themselves.

Now my time and circumstances have changed completely. I try not to judge or accuse myself. I ask what my soul requires. I have partnered with a man for whom the distance between the inner life and outward action is about half an inch. The dialogue we began in cyberspace has translated into more action in a shorter time than I could have imagined — Alan's move from the West Coast to Pittsburgh, our move from Pittsburgh to Vermont, and the attendant thorough changes in living and lifestyle.

I now have what I never had before — love, home, faith, and a friend with whom to share them. I am ready to reach out, through work, words, acts, commitment. It has taken me a very long time to reach this point. I less often ask why. I trust it was all necessary.

House

I have become a breeding ground for viruses or bacteria, a hostile host but one they love regardless. Apparently the echinacea and vitamin C I have been swallowing are no match for the microbial colonization taking place in my body. So much for breathing the cold to kill the invaders. I fight, but I sense it is a losing battle. Alan has been sick for two weeks, and my sore throat tells me I'm next.

But as long as I can stay upright, I spend my time measuring and cutting cardboard, building a model of our house as it is now and as we want it to be. The want-it-to-be aspects are tricky. I keep reviewing interior and exterior measurements that we took in the fall. I have already drawn floor plans and have cut a small model out of graph paper, just to see how the angles that are already here fit together. But the additions we need just don't want to take on reasonable proportions.

The part of the house that Sandra built is a two-story rectangular box — our bedroom atop kitchen, bath, and laundry — with what is now the small living room stuck onto a corner of the first story at a forty-five-degree angle. That asymmetry creates design problems downstairs, and the window seat, which juts out from the bedroom, creates difficulties at the upper level. Add to these challenges a terrain that drops away from the existing house — gradually in one direction, steeply in another. Then add the fact that every new piece of roof has to be able to shed snow without letting it collect in any troughs.

I have cleared a section of kitchen counter for my project. I stand amid slivers, triangles, and strips of cardboard, and my work surface is littered with X-acto knives, tape measures, rulers, tape, scissors, and pencils. I am forever in search of some tool or other. I envision, then I cut, then I attach a possible addition — then I add a roof. Then Alan tells me why it won't work. Then I try again.

I rarely get frustrated. I wake up in the mornings with a new scheme, and I start measuring and cutting before I have poured my first cup of coffee.

And all I am trying to do is design this year's construction. This year, Alan will add a larger living room (making our current small one a dining room), an upstairs bath, and more utility space — for a furnace, dog quarters, wood, and a bigger laundry area. Next year, he will enlarge Adam's room downstairs and raise the loft roof, adding dormers and creating a spacious office for the two of us. Some year, he will also build a deck around the living room and dining room; it will hang over a steep ledge, suspending us high above the forest floor, nearly halfway up the trunks of tall trees.

This is why I do not get frustrated. I can envision this place as it will be a few years from now, and although I anticipate these outcomes with delight, I am not impatient for them. I love the process. I crave change; it is my drug. But small changes, and the large effects they make, are enough to satisfy me. I do not want them to happen all at once, because each needs to be savored fully.

Word Games

I have given in to the viral invaders and spent the day in bed. I have been reading Barbara Kingsolver's *The Poisonwood Bible,* in which there is a character, Adah, a disabled fourteen-year-old who drags her lame foot, and does not speak, but who uses her internal language in sophisticated, ironic, and playful ways, creating anagrams and palindromes while also observing acutely and sometimes cynically the foibles of her family.

I like Adah's wordplay immensely. It is in my own family's genes to read words back to front and turn them inside out. It is a twist of mind I share with both brothers, and it comes directly from my mother. I remember once, sitting in a restaurant with Steve and my mother, talking about an acquaintance who had named himself Elad because he hated his given name. "Oh, Dale," said my mother and brother in the same breath, without even a pause to think.

I am fond of anagrams and palindromes, like Adah. A palindrome that I wrote myself — *Eros, misuse divides us, I'm sore* — went some distance toward winning Alan's heart. I am puffed up over that palindrome, both for its humor and for the fact that it actually makes complete sense, a rare thing within the tight, pushme-pullyou limits of the form. Alan's response to it delighted me. He told me he laughed his ass off, and then he said, "I do enjoy the way your mind works."

Once, I tried to come up with a palindromic name for palindromes. First I messed around with "oroboros," which is the word for a snake with its tail in its mouth — the right kind of image — but it is a singular noun and would have to be a plural in order for the singular, "oroboro," to work as a perfect front-to-back match. I had a similar problem with a word I made up, "mirrorrim," which, given the Hebrew-type ending, would have to be the plural form but suggests no suitable singular. I guess this would be a problem with any such word. It would have to be declared both the singular and the plural form. I could do that, couldn't I? All right, then. Palindromes henceforward shall be known as mirrorrim!

Wordplay is a close cousin to the image-making impulse, and both reflect the way my mind works. I could no more forgo them than I could change the order in which my bones are strung together. When I question my relationship to language, and wonder about the source of my urge to construct analogies and metaphors, it does not dilute my huge pleasure in verbal games and challenges nor does it reflect any doubt about the value of expression. Rather, it is because I want to know what else is available to me: Can I have my words and swallow them, too? Can I enter silence fully, extending it all the way into my mind? Can I infer and apprehend, suggest and not have to say? I am learning more all the time about the riches to be mined from the ground beneath language, no matter how dazzled and delighted I might also be by the verbal gems to be dug from overlying strata.

One Way to Die

I have been trying to call Sarah and have been getting only the answering machine. Finally I reached Joe, who told me Sarah's mother, Alice, has had a stroke and is in the hospital in Burlington. Sarah has been there around the clock. Her father is confused, her mother scarcely able to speak and totally unable to walk. She was probably "stroking" for several days before seeking help.

Sarah has been an attentive and reliable daughter. Her only sibling, an older brother, was killed nearly twenty years ago in a car accident. Her parents appreciate what she does for them, but they also nit-pick and complain — about Joe, for whom they would have come up with different design specs, and money, though they have lots of it, and Sarah's haircuts, which haven't been their business for forty-some years. Sarah walks a careful line with them, not willing to take mistreatment but not wanting to spark it, either.

As her parents age and loathe aging, as they fear death and deny it can happen to them, the patterns of their lives and relationships become exaggerated. Alice and her husband, Luke, are both concerned with Luke's welfare above all else. Luke, meanwhile, drinks too much, is losing memory and mental acuity, burns bacon at three in the morning, and sets off the smoke alarm, which brings their retirement community's security personnel out to check on things. He does not grasp what is happening to him at any level, neither in regard to burning the bacon nor to his wife's health nor to his failing body and mind.

People tell Sarah how "cute" her parents are, for being so devoted. Behind the scenes they can be hard to get along with. Mainly, they are old, failing, afraid, and entirely unable to confront their fears, talk about anything real, or take comfort in their daughter. That seems to me the saddest possible way to leave a life and loved ones.

My own hope — easy enough to describe from the vantage point of health and energy — is to open myself to truths that the thinning of life's

membranes might reveal, if only dimly. I am glad Alan and I came together at this time of life. It seems an appropriate period in which to
meet a soul mate. I believe we can help each other discover the lessons of
aging, the wisdom to be found by continuing the search for patterns and
meaning, the courage we'll need in the face of our bodies' infirmities.

Rooflines

More model building. It is taking shape. I am working on a scale of half
an inch to a foot, which lets me picture just enough detail. I wish I could
model the terrain first, because this cardboard house I am building sits
on a flat surface, whereas the real house will follow several slopes and
irregularities that my measurements must take into account. By the time
the actual house is finished, there will be two or three stairs from almost
every room into the next. But I like sensing the lay of the land beneath
my feet indoors. I like knowing that the shape of our house will continue
to conform to the shape of the terrain on which it sits.

When you come up our driveway and over the hump at the top, you
see the various roofs and dormers of the house, which nestles below that
hump. The existing house covers at least three levels of earth; the new
part will be built yet another level lower, where the land gradually
declines toward a sheer ten-foot drop (which the outer edge of the deck
will parallel). The final roof patterns and angles will indeed be complicated, but we think we have figured them out. On every drive we take
now, for errands or pleasure, we examine the rooflines of houses and are
comforted to know that ours will not be the strangest.

Tapestry

Today, January 28, is the anniversary of the first message Alan sent me
two years ago. I still catch my breath when I think about the cosmic coincidences that caused our orbits to intersect. It all seems about as likely as

floating a message in a bottle and having it reach the right person walking at the right moment on a distant shore.

An old friend, a former Jesuit brother, once said to me (quoting Boethius, I think) that everything is pattern but we are on the underside, where we cannot see the way the warp and woof intersect to form a coherent design. It occurs to me that what we call coincidence might take place at moments when we can peer over the edge of the tapestry and briefly discern the whole stunning fabric of existence. We dismiss these moments, we say they are "just" coincidences. Why, then, do we recount them with such amazement? Why are we so fascinated?

My decision to post a profile on the Web, and Alan's discovery of it through some odd, even willful, computer behavior, brought together two people of the same age who have the same spiritual beliefs, politics, social values, skin-eye-and-hair color, broad gene pool, childhood geographical landmarks, sense of humor, attachment to nature, propensity for solitude, taste in music, and longing for God. And that's "just a coincidence"? It looks like design to me.

February

Meaning

Reminding myself of the remarkable coincidences that brought Alan and me together is a way of staying focused on spirit in the midst of our daily life — eternity in a grain of sand. It has convinced me that my soul is always at work, whether I pay attention or not. Paying attention, though, yields better outcomes.

What I pay attention to lately connects to that old matter of specificity, the riddle that so troubled me at eighteen: Why this, not that? Why here, not somewhere else? To which, now, I would add: Why this series of purposeful accidents? Coming at this time of my life, and urging me as they do to examine all the years that preceded this love and these radical changes, the questions now have to do with the meaning of life, the improbable fact of my own, or anyone's, existence. We are all products of incredible coincidence, pinpoint timing.

Suppose every conception in human biological history had taken place a month later. Who would populate this planet? What would the world look like? Would the centuries tell any of the same stories? Intriguing puzzles, but the fact remains that out of billions of possible combinations of forebears and genes, a few precisely particular ones gave rise to all of us. Why us? What are we to do with this minute exactitude? The notion of specificity echoes in a different space now than it did when I was young. It insists to me that our being here, against all odds, either means something for all of us or nothing for anyone.

We are apparently hardwired to search for meaning. It would be a nasty twist if our human nature were at odds with the rest of nature, if our urge to find meaning were just a fluke in a meaningless universe. Where, in such a case, would that persistent fluke have come from, flowing down uncountable generations to this moment? On the other hand, if we are born to search for meaning, and there is meaning to be found, why haven't all those generations made more sense of things?

It isn't because our predecessors have failed to put great wisdom before us. Look at the millennia of writings and works of art, the myriad disciplines through which the passionately curious have examined our world and the human condition. Look also at how few of the wise or their works we heed or study in our busy lives. Our human progress is eternally slow, despite the wisdom of the ages, and I think it is because answers, even simple ones, can't just be handed over. If meaning were bequeathed to us like a trust fund, free for the taking, it would turn quicksilver, it would elude our grasp. We need, each of us, to uncover the truth of our lives on our own.

We can get a lot of help from thinkers and artists, to be sure, but we have to know what to ask them. And they can give us only what we have made ourselves ready to receive. I realize now, after writing about so many personal, lifelong questions, that I can make myself ready only by consulting that of God within me. If I can't passively receive meaning and answers, then I need to find them in active cooperation with soul, intuition, imagination — anything that takes me beyond my five senses and my habits of thought and reaction. Meaning infuses the commonplace stuff of my life, but it originates in some realm beyond. To find it, I need to transcend what I can actually know; I need to take the leap of faith. In leaping, I have found the stone bridge over the chasm of my fears, and failures.

I need to make that leap almost daily. I am forever stepping off the bridge and back into the compelling, distracting habits of the here and now. I forget the bridge or mistrust my knowledge of its safety. I have never made it even halfway to the middle. So I repeatedly set myself the task of remembering what I have experienced and trusting the inner light to lead me again and again to faith and insight. I succeed best when I consciously open myself to this light in every act and experience, knowing they all connect, knowing they form a larger image than I can see. This task — this trusting, remembering, opening — is now, for me, the major enterprise of life. It is the ultimate act of love. It enlarges every relationship I have, every piece of work I do.

That Mother, This Daughter

My thoughts on specificity and meaning often come down to the dynamic between my mother and me — two people out of billions, two generations out of all those that have ever been. Our complicated, often sad connection has been a first and guiding instance for decoding the patterns in my life and finding their hints of meaning.

My past resentments toward my mother arose from her abandonment of life's knotted, confusing stuff — the way she would hole up in her bedroom with her annotated Bible and tracts called *Unsearchable Riches;* the way she would carry on intense correspondences with like-minded distant others while scarcely talking to us, her family; the way she would visit and speak tenderly to a sweet, doddering shut-in by the name of Mrs. Kaiser, whom she called "sister," while I wondered in silent surprise why she never spoke to me in that same soft voice.

What is the point of this extravagant world if it is only, as my mother seemed to think, a riot of temptation, a great test we are supposed to pass by passing it by? What a waste, to turn our backs on the beauty, the struggle, the love to be found, the help to be given, the work to be done, the surpassing pleasures of nature, the body, the heart, and the mind. Surely, that would mean turning our backs on spirit, too, which is alive everywhere and hums its counterpoint melody right in the middle of life's great clamor.

I learned from my mother, who did not know what she was teaching me, that we need to live fully in this world but listen for echoes from another. We need to go about our business with our eye to the immediate, and we need also to contemplate unreachable, unknowable mysteries. We need both our limits and a vision of limitlessness — and we need to connect the two, which is what that stone bridge does for me. Meaning flows over it like two-way traffic, like blood to and from the heart.

My mother's willingness to forgo this world for the sake of the next, and my childhood feelings of responsibility for my mother's unhappiness, made for decades of continued denial and sacrifice on my part, which in turn made for resentment and frustration. Sacrifice did not resemble generosity; it did not teach or nurture anyone; it did not let love in.

My mother's sacrifices brought her no joy, perhaps because she did not come to know any person or thing, except Scripture, deeply and with passion. I think she gradually came to see that Scripture — ancient, largely untraceable, variously translated and endlessly debated — is the product of humans like the rest of us, part mud, part light, who opened themselves to their piece of the truth and then passed their vision down with all its flaws and glory. I am afraid, though, that my mother's rejection of this world prevented her from finding her own truth here, because it prevented her from loving wholly and openly — herself first, and others as a consequence. She became a sad, remote woman, though now and then capable of connection and humor.

My childhood sacrifices for the sake of my mother — my doomed attempts to take care of her and cheer her, my fears of displeasing her, my many small betrayals of my own nature aimed at somehow lightening hers — likewise bore their seasons of stunted fruit. Yet I am more fortunate than she was, because those fruits carried in them the seeds of a flourishing crop that now sustains me — a crop that includes, perhaps foremost, the unconditional love I came to feel for my mother in her long decline. That love revived the first love of my life and makes all other loves richer.

Much of the joy in my life today unfolds from earlier resentments in a way no one could ever have planned or foreseen. It has arisen from exactly who my mother was and who I am. She could not demonstrate love, but I came to understand that it lived somewhere inside her, and I reached that understanding through the very sorrows that her mothering created. Every lesson I have needed in life and in loving has come down to me from the numberless and unlikely generations before me, and those lessons spill over, again.

Fish in a Barrel

For much of my adult life, when I have looked back at my younger self, the figure in the rearview mirror has seemed an idiot girl, a weak, insubstantial person ready to dissolve and blow away. Gradually, such judgments have softened, until, as I write this, I realize they are largely gone. So many questions arise in these pages: Where did my early fearfulness come from? Which crossroads in my life have led me to this place, now? What has made me ready? How do my actions and attitudes affect others? These mysteries braid like a stream, become a river, spill into an ocean of simple humanity. I am less than a drop in this ocean, yet I am still myself, distinguishable, reflecting light in patterns unique to me. That light is finally a purposeful beam, which I find I can aim consciously on my puzzles and doubts.

The idiot girl appeared first during my marriage to Ned. Until then, though I had more insecurities and anxieties than many young women my age — which must explain how readily I hooked up with Ned, whom I characterized from the start as a judge, a dark figure wreathed in cigarette smoke — I had as well a certain groundedness, an awareness that I possessed at least some skills and insights. I was smart, quick, pretty. I could summon wit and humor. I was generous. I suppose, though, that I felt I wasn't enough of any of those things; I wasn't perfect and thus perfectly safe. Or else those desirable qualities did not quite belong to me. Perhaps they visited impersonally and could leave without saying goodbye. Who knows? I am just aware that I never felt stupid until Ned.

I married him at nineteen, less than two years after I had left my parents' house—for Colby College, in Maine, but also, I think, in search of a place in which to belong, a person to belong to. I did not yet belong to myself, and so of course things went wrong. I assumed they were my fault. Ned made dismissive, often vicious remarks about me, which I believed. He took advantage of my better qualities. He did less than his share of everything except drinking. I kept assuming I could "fix" things, just as I had long ago assumed I could make my mother happy. My efforts to understand and forgive made me a dupe and a target. Ned even said once, to a friend in Toronto, that it was no fun being mean to me because it was like shooting fish in a barrel. That friend, as I recall, said, "Well, Ned, if that's your sport. . . "

Still, nothing is all one thing, unmixed. When I saw only the negatives—myself as an idiot girl, Ned as the purest bastard—I perpetuated the harm Ned did, which I unwittingly allowed him to do. This is the danger of a perfectionist streak, of harsh self-judgment. Not only did I later on give myself no credit for the love and generosity that had impelled my loyalty to Ned, I also, in thinking ill of myself and being on the defensive, set myself up for further hurt and then spread the hurt around to others. I persisted in taking bullets throughout the years in California, but this time I also shot back. Too often, as with Rich, the lover I mentioned many pages back, I hit the wrong target. My sights were anything but clear and straight.

Now, after two failed marriages, two all-but-lost friendships, and a sharper picture of my combined strengths and weaknesses in each relationship, I remember what a friend of mine in Pittsburgh used to say: First, do no harm—unless you mean to. Her addendum says it all. So much harm in relationships is willy-nilly, like Ned's, like mine with Rich. I think Ned never set out to harm me, though he apparently came to enjoy it. I had a hard time believing this, so I kept putting up with it in the name of patience and understanding, out of a misguided sense that love suffers all and remains kind. What I did not understand, and what made me for a while a blind carrier of further injury—an emotional Typhoid Mary—was that respect, for self and others, is the only vaccine, and that sometimes it stings.

Respect is a mindful thing. Quakers try to exercise respect in all dealings, but never without intently assessing a situation. Respect is deliberate, aware, evaluative. It relies on the truth of a person or circumstance. Applied to the self, respect protects against harm from others; applied to others, it protects them against harm from oneself. Now and then, it requires that a certain kind of harm be done. My mistakes with Ned were functions of my good impulses, which were not enough. Had I added self-respect to the love and patience I was willing to supply, it would have required me to turn around and hurt what needed to be hurt in Ned — his overblown ego, his prickly defenses, his sarcasm. All the things that spurred him to do hurt would have had to be hurt — that is, brought down, refused, dismissed.

First do no harm — unless you mean to. It is a mystery to me that some people understand this very young and almost by instinct. The success of Sam and Edie's marriage must owe a debt to their innate respect for self and other, whereas my own young marriage foundered on the absence of this quality. It has taken me so long to absorb the lessons of respect, and the costs to me and others have been so high, that I think I will always have to be deliberate about it — ever alert for the need, ever conscious in summoning the toughness and discipline that respect can require.

But there is joy in this effort, for now I can look at the young woman who was married to Ned, and I can respect her refusal to return cruelty for cruelty. Some peacemaking impulse prevented all-out war with Ned, and so it prevented the harm between us from escalating. This true, inward thing was not fully formed then, and I did not recognize or own up to it — I called myself an idiot girl, instead. Later, I went on to hurt others, not knowing my own strength. I did harm without meaning to.

That is the willy-nilly part, and the genius in my friend's dictum. It is not so easy, balancing respect for oneself with respect for others. It is not easy to look for the truth about oneself, all of it, both good and bad, and then to act on that truth. I am best able to do this if I don't berate myself, if I don't succumb to the idea that I am an idiot girl or a bitch or a victim or any other negative thing. I am only human, and sometimes it is my flaws that keep me that way, that help me connect with other flawed and struggling people and respect us all.

Soul Love

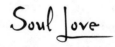

We had no grand show of sentimental affection on Valentine's Day, though I bought Alan and Adam big mugs full of chocolates and jelly beans and gave them cards. Alan, likewise, bought me some small gifts and a card with a message about souls in love. It is in the day-to-day that the deepest love plays out, the unconditional love I discovered first through Adam and my mother, and now through Alan. That discovery colors all the other loves of my life, either deepening them or showing me the limits of my ability to care.

These unconditional loves belong to the soul, not to romance. Romance idealizes — lovers, children, mothers, friends — and then is crushed by reality. But the soul seeks the truth of each person and loves the frailty and failures along with the glory.

That has not been possible — yet, or again — with Emma and Ellen. Right now they can't love me because, I believe, they feel I have betrayed them. I cannot love their flaws and sharp edges because I have been hurt by them. Time might live up to its reputation and heal these wounds, but for now we judge each other from a polite distance.

In this I do not live up to my own beliefs. I know that each soul has its own pathway and agenda, imperceptible from the outside. We are all unknowable to each other, except at the soul level, and most of us don't get that close. We can never just tell each other who we are or how we have come to our choices, because to do that we would have to say everything we have ever thought and describe every incident and setting in our lives. Even then, we would be speaking to someone not us, some-one different. We are left to guess each other through outward acts, intuition, the risk of trusting, and the apprehension of the light behind another's eyes. Even Alan remains mysterious to me, though I feel he is someone I have always known, even in other lifetimes or on other planes.

I think every relationship is a soul connection, whether we allow it to go deep or not. I think it follows, therefore, that every relationship must be as much unknown and left alone as seen directly. It shines more brightly that way, just as a faint star is more visible when you look slightly to the side of it. So my soul mate is also a stranger, and so is every other person I know. That keeps the mystery alive and growing; it is reason enough both to love and to hope for love in return.

Somehow, Emma and Ellen and I have limited ourselves to straight-on scrutiny, a literal viewing of each other's lives that diminishes their mystery and richness. In the events that have strained our friendships, we seem to look only at the surface, without faith in each other, without the deeper knowledge that our souls are no doubt true whatever our mistakes. This could be the whole nature of the rift between us. We cannot see each other with the eyes of love and imagination.

How We Love Is How We Live Is How We Die

This is a stale, sluggish season. Energy has ebbed out of reach, flu symptoms hang on just enough to hamper action, the wood pile is dwindling too rapidly, and the indoor air is close and gritty with wood ash. Alan surfs the Internet, looking for political news, entertainment, and information on any issue that arises in our lives — homeopathy, orthodontia, cardiovascular health. Alan is itching for spring, and the moment when he can start building. Meanwhile, he considers roofline variations, siding choices, trim colors, and our rough terrain, which is tough to visualize beneath the snow.

I spend my time reading, writing, e-mailing, or zoning out on the

Internet. I am eager for more work, having finished my first assignment for the Department of Education, a short article on Vermont's recently implemented education assessments and how various schools and districts have fared in this. I have done no drawing this winter, which disappoints me. I have made no quilts with Sarah, because of her mother's stroke. In fact, I see little of Sarah, who has been driving to Burlington almost daily for several weeks to tend to the needs of both parents, Luke and Alice.

The aftermath of the stroke is hardest on Luke, eighty-five, who has not yet been able to comprehend that his wife will not return to their retirement-community apartment any time soon, if at all. Although she is in the community's rehabilitation center, he worries about who will care for her when he goes off on his next business trip, which he still does, every spring and fall, in preparation for flower-bulb seasons. He has sold flowers all his life. He travels to California to pack and ship the bulbs. He still has a higher annual income than Sarah does. He wonders who will drive him to the airport and pick him up again, now that Alice is barely ambulatory and can use only one arm. He tells Sarah, "People can drive one-handed." When she explains that Alice will not be one of them, he thinks about taking up driving again himself, despite his near blindness.

I think about Luke and Alice when I feel the effects of this deep-freeze time of year and contemplate the weeks of bad weather still facing us. I remind myself that lassitude in February will lead to fruitfulness in a warmer season. We need the slow times. We need even the sad and frustrating times when our will is not strong enough to engage our energies. The land is sleeping, so why shouldn't we? What matters is using my limited energies well, knowing when to resist the melancholy of this month and when to relax into the cycles of the seasons and my own soul. I do this so that I will not become like Luke and Alice, consumed by a terror of dying and yet unable to utter a word of truth about either the dying or the fear. The seasons and every other cycle of sadness and joy, dread and exhilaration, prepare us for the immense cycles of our own mortality. We can either fear mortality or know that we share it with everyone else. It can divide or unite us. We can, in the end, die wrapped up in our pain or let ourselves be comforted by those we love, who will miss us.

Someone in Meeting, a person who is becoming a friend, is fond of a Cherokee proverb that goes something like this: When we are born, we cry and the world rejoices. We must live our lives so that when we die, we rejoice and the world cries.

Much as I wish to live up to this notion myself, I realize how hard it is to sustain the reaching out and cherishing that it requires. Nothing isolates us like pain or sorrow, and I am ripe for the blues in this cold season. Especially, I am haunted by lost friends and the failure of love. These things enter my sleep and my waking thoughts. I have conjured them deliberately but am shaken by the fervor of their response.

On Sunday I went to Meeting alone and sat amid a smaller group than usual and brought the faces of Ellen and Emma before my inner eye and asked for the light to shine on my feelings of resentment, sadness, and bewilderment. I wanted to remember the things that once loomed so much larger than this recent tension. I wanted to recall the times when I felt easy and companionable with one or both, when we laughed together, when they and I alike behaved the way friends just do behave — offering support, defending each other, listening sympathetically, going to movies or concerts, sharing milestones, family news, or insights on our own and each other's work. All of these strands once wove our connection.

I think my reflections on friendship were prompted by a recent e-mail from another woman, much younger than the rest of us, who became a volatile sort of friend when we worked together at the university. Her name is Liz, and we enjoyed each other's company a lot. We also, on occasion, burst into arguments that flared hotly and then subsided the next instant. We fought mainly about work, sometimes about more personal issues. We lost touch when she left her job as an editor for one of the senior researchers. Now, I am happy to be back in touch with her.

But Liz, because she was absent from my life for a time, enters my thoughts of Emma and Ellen. On Sunday, as I sat in Meeting, I tried simply to let go of my analyses of friendship and feelings of confusion. I tried to make room for insight and intuition to do their work.

They have been working very hard. They have sent me a deep blue mood during the day. It feels like grief. They have sent me dreams about an Alan figure — actually a set of strangers bearing his name, all of whom betray me in some way. And then, in these dreams, I believe I can win back my friends if I admit defeat.

In the midst of this haunting comes another lost friend, by happenstance. Adam had a dentist appointment yesterday, and we arrived early only to find the dentist herself running late. So we got back into the car and headed for Bear Pond Books. While Adam went in search of his favorite authors, I scanned the rack of magazines and reviews. I opened the current issue of the *Utne Reader,* and there was an essay by Nora Gallagher, a woman I knew in California twenty-five years ago. She and I had met at work also, and for a while we shared a brief, tight friendship. It ended abruptly, and I was never sure why. I think she dumped me.

Nora's essay in the *Utne Reader* is the first chapter in her book, *Things Seen and Unseen: A Year Lived in Faith*. In the essay, she describes the death of a friend from AIDS and the struggle of her brother with cancer. Liz, too, is in mourning, for her father, who died a year or so ago, and for a brother who was mugged and murdered in September, not so far from where Nora now lives.

I thought to myself, these things might not converge randomly — tragic e-mail from lost Liz and a searching essay by lost Nora appearing in the same week, even as I am mourning the apparent loss of Emma and Ellen.

Now I am dwelling with anxiety and sadness on the question of my role in these losses. I ask myself if there is something about me — something aloof or selfish — that drives friends off. I face the secret fear that I think we all harbor: If someone gets too close to me, they will find out what I am really like, and they won't like me. In these emotions I become a child again, vulnerable and hungry for love.

I think I can take any criticism from a friend if it comes with evidence of love. But when no caring shows through the complaint, and when the whole basis for working out problems therefore seems buried or crumbling, then I clench up and grow angry and thin-skinned.

With some people the love is palpable even when they find fault and pick bones with us. Such connections serve the soul, allowing us to be fully ourselves, to risk errors and anger, to follow through and trust in the strength of the bond that love forges.

In the early days of our friendship, Sarah was one of my best teachers in this regard. I remember once, twenty-some years ago, when she turned on me angrily for some thoughtless behavior, some failure to consider others in the household we shared with various roommates in San Francisco. I have forgotten or suppressed the details, but I was guilty and knew it. I was shocked at my own blindness. Why had I not seen this error for myself? I felt threatened and ashamed. But Sarah was able to hear what I had to say, and she did not stay angry — especially once I told her that her anger set up so much emotional noise in me that I could not hear her message. I felt I would not run out of chances with her. Our friendship could withstand such tests.

So, I learned, could my connection with my brother Steve. On two long-past occasions, he became mystifyingly furious with me, accusing me of not having time for him, not thinking well of him, judging his life. I believe I considered his charges honestly, but I never did feel guilty of what he described, except perhaps the time squeeze. I thought it possible that his anger rose from inward troubles he had not yet confronted. I also never doubted, though I was hurt and puzzled, that Steve would grow, and so would I, and we would survive with our love and kinship stronger, even if we had to apply patches and glue. Today, the people I turn to, in self-doubt, crisis, or celebration, are Sarah, Steve, and Steve's wife, Rita.

I also have friends whose reactions to Alan and my life with him carry only openness and trust. I spoke with one such friend this weekend. Her name is Pat, and she works a thankless, stressful job managing the life and schedule of an arrogant, selfish boss. She has worked in the same terrible place for at least twenty-five years. She is almost sixty-three. She has never gone elsewhere because she has reached a salary level no other employer could match. She has also needed the security. She raised three daughters on her own — racially mixed offspring of her early marriage to a black musician. One daughter is a surgeon, another is a nonpracticing attorney, and the third is an addict trying to get her life on track. This third daughter's daughter has lived with Pat for the past several years. This granddaughter is about to turn thirteen, so Pat is raising her fourth teenager, and she feels too old and ill for the task.

Pat is the original crusty-old-broad-with-heart-of-gold. She has a mouth like George Carlin, drinks more than is good for her, has smoked for forty-five years, and will never quit despite emphysema, osteoporosis, and the risk of much worse.

I used to talk with Pat about her life, my life, our dysfunctional workplaces, and our two children — Adam, and Pat's granddaughter, about the same age. I came to see immense generosity and compassion behind the smokescreen — a heart too tender to be worn on a sleeve, exposed to the elements. When I told her I was moving away, she locked eyes with me, said "shitfuckpisscunt," then started to cry.

We talked on the phone Sunday, and Pat said, "I can't tell you how I miss you. I never pass your office without saying, That fucking bitch, why'd she have to leave!" Pat swears and blows smoke so she won't give too much away. She curses me and then in the next breath says, "I am so happy for you. You just can't imagine."

I know Pat means this. She doesn't begrudge me a moment of joy in this new life, even though she is sad that I am gone, even though her own life is fraught with anxiety, stress, ill treatment, and ill health. This is real love. And this is why I love Pat — because she refuses to isolate herself in her pain.

I don't understand why my thoughts of Pat should lead me here, but suddenly I remember two things about the end of my friendship with Nora — that she was angry with me for being defensive about something, and that she told me if our friendship ended it would be my loss. I took her to mean that she herself wouldn't lose anything, that I represented nothing of much importance to her, and I could not ride that out. Did I dump her? Did she want me to?

What have I learned in twenty-five years, since then? I have learned that comments like Nora's are not to be taken literally, that they arise out of hurt feelings, insecurities, doubt. I wish I had grasped that before I lost Nora. Nora herself said in her essay, " Being faithful to God means being faithful to others, in sickness and in health, for better or for worse."

Sometimes, though, to be faithful to others requires that we break faith with ourselves. That is how I have sometimes done it. That is how I have sustained relationships that I should have let go of. Love is the only good faith there is, and I am worried that Emma, Ellen, and I have lost love, or only thought we had it, or buried it beneath our defenses. We have let our pain isolate us from each other. In time, perhaps, we will let love rise back to the top, and we will forget the ill feeling we have recently stirred up.

Distances

In the meantime, Emma never writes at all, not since a terse birthday greeting. I sent a quick reply—a warm one, I thought—but I never heard anything more. Perhaps the geographic distance between us confounds any affection she might still have for me. She said to me, before I left, "I'm still mad at Delia for moving to Mt. Lebanon!" Delia was another close friend; Mt. Lebanon is a suburb of Pittsburgh. Vermont must seem like the moon.

This puzzles me, because I find it natural and easy to maintain long-distance friendships. I have been friends for seven years with Tori, a woman in Massachusetts whom I have met only three times in person but with whom I have carried on a rich, supportive, sometimes searching and often funny e-mail correspondence. And, of course, I fell in love long distance.

I stay in touch with Ellen in a superficial way. I don't know whether anything entirely honest is left for us, but I am not willing to cut the line that she now and then tosses into my waters. I throw it back to her, bearing small fish, or I bait my own string and take idle initiative. I suppose we will keep trolling, perhaps until something surprising rises up and tests our connection again. We apparently care just enough to wait and see.

The whole matter is filled with a kind of pain no insights can soothe. I was in tears about it several times yesterday. I sometimes think I need to apply Alan's bless-and-release formula. I need to remember my friends' faces at their truest and most open moments, value the lessons we learned from each other, rejoice in the sweet times shared, and bless these good things and release them to history — a history that will thereby stay alive for me and bless me in return.

This morning I settled into Meeting amid considerable bustle. An older woman entered with a cane and was helped to her seat. A half dozen small children stayed in the room, as usual, for ten or fifteen minutes before going downstairs to First Day School. A few latecomers entered. Parents shushed their children. One child proclaimed in a loud whisper, "I don't like the silence!"

There is always noise and rustling before Meeting truly "centers down." This morning the process was different for me. Instead of trying to shut the noises out, I invited them in with a strong sense of God in all the sounds of seekers entering and leaving the room. There was so much life there. I couldn't help thinking of Pittsburgh Meeting, where so many Friends are so vexed by anything that breaks the deep silence of the gathered Meeting, even, sometimes, the ministry of other Friends. It is a relief to be free of that tension. Increasingly, I feel God is in everything, every willful childish utterance or late entry or chair scrape; the sounds and distractions are not separate from the experience of Meeting for Worship but very much a part of it, whether as a challenge to our discipline or a reminder that we are all together — and altogether human, flawed, aspiring.

Sometimes the Plainfield Meeting remains silent for the whole hour of worship. This morning, out of fifteen or twenty adults, five gave ministry.

The thread that ran through all the messages was the need to act faithfully on our Quaker beliefs. One person spoke about the struggle of Lucretia Mott, an early Quaker, to discern her own truth when Friends split dramatically and emotionally into opposing factions. Another person told the Purim story, in which Esther saves the life of Mordechai by risking her own. Other speakers mentioned directly personal matters.

If I could transcribe every word of this ministry from memory, I know its power would not come through. The words themselves, conveyed outside the context of spiritual readiness and humming expectation that the silence can produce, would fall flat, seem unremarkable. At the time, under the spell of each voice and the counterpoint of silence, the ministry swelled and echoed, growing much larger than the words or the people who delivered them.

There is no controlling or orchestrating this process. Sometimes it happens and sometimes it doesn't. Sometimes it happens for just one or a few people in the room; sometimes for most, or none. Readiness, attentiveness, discipline — all of these play a part, but they are no guarantee that that of God will rise up, as it did for me this morning through the cumulative energy of all the messages.

This unpredictable, unprogrammable dynamic is why Meetings like ours do not have ministers. No prepared sermon on a topic chosen in our behalf and written by one person, however wise, however faithful to Quaker practice, could have the same capacity to magnify the light as those messages did for me. The inner light is our only true authority, as it was Lucretia Mott's, and yet the portion of light that belongs to each of us is often more likely to illuminate to full capacity in a group. When we come together to wait patiently for God to speak to us, and through us, and when our inner promptings yield ministry that is rich and well ordered, as it was today, then it feels as if God has served as divine editor of the whole process and that everyone's truth has grown as a result.

The inner light gainsays, for me, the poet Rilke's comment that we are all, "at bottom, unutterably alone." This light requires us to look within for guidance, and it reminds us that the opinions, dicta, and dogma of others, whether institutions or individuals, are restricted by their human fallibility and worldliness and not worthy of our full faith and obedience. And yet the inner light is magnified when we seek to share it. Our individual portions grow, like the multiplied loaves and fishes, until the inner light of everyone together becomes the one and only eternal, reliable antidote to our aloneness.

March

Hoo and Hah

Alan's and my e-mail exchange is where I began to examine in depth the intuitions and beliefs that were coalescing after a lifetime of seeking, resisting, forgetting, and seeking again. Not long into our exchange, I sensed I had found a sympathetic soul, a traveler whose path resembled my own. Quakers, like many other seekers, have a saying to this effect: There is only one mountain, but there are many pathways to the peak. Neither Alan nor I believed in any straight and narrow route. We had each been meandering for a long time. In fact, just after we described to each other where we had lived and traveled in our lives, he wrote:

> Sounds like the road to where you are was not a straight-shot superhighway either. Have been to, through, or lived in all of the places you mention. It all began when I read Kerouac in high school when I was supposed to be doing Thomas Hardy. Probably have done a coast-to-coaster in or on just about anything that has wheels (and a motor — no bikes or skates): trains, buses — both Greyhound and psychedelic VW's — BIG TRUCKS, and once by motorcycle. Visions of Iowa, giant corn tunnel w/ aroma of pigshit shoved up your nose at 70 mph . . . Happy-to-have-done-it, but NO MAS. It would require many hours on a meetinghouse bench to collect an ass that sore.

Our conversation about faith, spirit, seeking, and discovering drew much from our personal experiences and also from books we shared or talked about. After Alan's first questions about Quakerism, the dialogue resumed in an indirect way. Alan mentioned a profound mistrust of mainstream medicine, which had served him poorly when a scaffolding fell on him around 1965 and broke four sacral vertebrae. He discovered chiropractic therapy after a repeat injury in the mid-eighties, and that has helped him more than the drugs, bed rest, and gritting of teeth prescribed by physicians at the time.

I responded to Alan's story with Shari's. She is a friend and hero of mine, a young woman I hired as a communications specialist at the university about five years before I met Alan online. Shari suffers from a constellation of respiratory and neuromuscular problems severe enough to put her in a wheelchair and require her to carry oxygen and adrenaline wherever she goes. No one in the medical profession can tell her definitively what is wrong. No one can do anything more than allay her symptoms and treat them topically.

Alan knew a lot about conditions like Shari's, because he had done intensive research for a friend of his own with the very same symptoms. Included in some of the things that had helped his friend — along with spinal adjustment, acupressure, and deep tissue massage — were herbal infusions.

> There are probably 20 to 30 different essential oils, floral and herbal, that can be applied, depending on the need. Lotsa books available on essentials — usually in the "New Age" section of the bookstore. (Ever notice how much "New Age" resembles old wisdoms — when you remove the part about the fool and his money?)

I answered, referring not only to the foregoing message but also to a string of related others:

> Must confess I don't know a lot about New Age because I lumped it in with hoo-hah just like you. (By the way, I thought hoo-hah was *my* word.) But instinctively I sense wisdom beneath the pop manifestations.

And I have benefited in the past from some chiro visits and especially from trigger-point myotherapy, which hurts like hell but does wonders for rocklike knotted neck muscles.

We decided to share "hoo-hah." I would use the "hah," and Alan would use the "hoo." We ranged through some New Age readings and beyond. I was reading — or trying to plow through — Harold Bloom's *Omens of Millennium,* and I tried to describe to Alan some of Bloom's wrestling with the problem of evil:

Bloom can't reconcile a benevolent God with human evil, the Holocaust being his sticking point. He does experience the divine, the "God within," which sounds very Quakerish until he goes on to say that that experience also involves a sense of the "Fall of the Godhead" (an inner fall, I gather, as well as a divine one). He seems to conclude that the God who made the universe botched it and slunk off in embarrassment, leaving behind human yearnings for and experience of (the remnants of?) the divine. I tend more to the idea that even if we lived in paradise we wouldn't know it without the counterexample of suffering. So I guess I think God created a world of paradox and contrast so that through enlightenment we can come to grasp what is sacred.

In another message, after quoting some of Bloom's more abstruse language to Alan, I said: "Now there's a man who couldn't say hoo-hah if a New Age snake bit his ass."

Alan replied: "Now *here's* a man who can't either (a friend is playing w/his hah at present)."

Alan always nudged me away from being too serious, even as he made very plain what his own beliefs are and how deep they go. His view of occult and mystical phenomena was "always one of bemused tolerance: 'Yeah, that's neat — call me when you're gonna bend some spoons, I wanna watch.'" Increasingly, though, he took more notice of some New Age, new spirit, ancient wisdom messengers:

I started becoming aware that a lot of the stuff I read dunlopped [Alan's word for the way things interconnect and overlap with one another] over into some of the religious-philosophical stuff I was pursuing. Somewhere a fascination w/ science is woven through all this—fascination without the discipline. Just tell me your theorem or hypothesis, don't give a damn about the formulas that got you there, wouldn't understand them anyway, got one of those brains that was totally lost in algebra while A-ing in geometry. Throw in an interest in things ecologic, find out that there is this scientific-academic field here—ecopsychology, which dunlops into the medical field 'cause they're using this stuff to *heal* people. Interesting, 'cause during 30-something years as a country boy have had many guests—frapped-out city folks who come to spend some time. Always noticed how after a few days they seem to mellow out, stress vanishes.

"Dunlop" comes from an old joke about a fat man whose gut "dun lopped" right over his belt; or another about a fat woman on a bus, whose girth "dun lopped" onto the next seat.

Although Alan now refuses to be too serious, he has confessed to me that he once overthought things, suffered from deep com-/perplexity. Long ago he drank too much, too, like many of the men in my life. Then he took to heart the twelve-step slogan "Keep It Simple." He still, almost thirty years later, relies on the Serenity Prayer daily. He sets out with deliberation to cut through formulas, justifications, and arduous intellectual slogging to experience directly the natural world, the God who made it, and the possibility of love.

Alan and I both saw power in the natural world, which is why he had lived in the country for so long and why I had always longed to be there myself. (Had I sought simplicity, like Alan, I too would already have been there by the time we met.) We suspected power in natural remedies. We believed in every person's in-born natural source of divine power. We believed in a benevolent God and saw Bloom's so-called "fall" as deriving from the myriad ways in which human beings depart from God and venture passionately into the not-God, fool-and-his-money, complexifying world of getting, spending, rationalizing, and discovering the world's secrets without asking how to use them to serve God—that is, to generate love, mercy, compassion, tolerance, intuition, and a connection with spirit everywhere.

We read and shared books on soul and love and soul-love. We read Thomas Moore, James Hillman, John Welwood, David Abram, Clarissa Pinkola Estes (every last one of them a Jungian). Alan sent me Neale Donald Walsch's *Conversations with God*, which at one time would have failed my hoo-hah test altogether — but in which I now found clarity, faith, simplicity, serenity. I had no problem with the idea that Walsch conversed with God. Quakers do that all the time, as do seekers of every faith. I was skeptical about Walsch's claim that his book was a literal transcription of God's own words. Then I let go of my skepticism and simply appreciated the messages.

Whiteness That Is Not Snow

I finally went for a walk for the first time in six weeks or so, since the onset of the flu. It wasn't much of a walk, but it did get my thick blood flowing. Kathy and I covered the mile or so to the end of our road to meet our boys at the bus. They ignored us, naturally, but we could see pleasure through their affected disregard. And anyway, we had more than enough things to talk about, having seen each other so little for so long. So we walked back alone, deep in a discussion of bigotry.

Kathy's adopted sons, Max and Carter, are African American. Kathy and Steve are white. Most of Vermont is white. That is changing, but slowly, and with the usual growing pains. I asked Kathy about neighbors at the top of our road who began flying a Confederate flag late last summer. She groaned. "Sometimes I am tempted to confront them," she said. "But they would be shocked. They love Carter and Max. They have no idea how that flag comes across." Kathy has decided that leaving the issue alone — letting her sons see both the flag and the warmth its owners have for them personally — better illustrates life's complexities and ironies than calling on those neighbors to declare themselves one thing or another.

We moved on to discussions of prejudices in our midst. We both have relatives or acquaintances who find it necessary to sort people into the acceptable and the unacceptable, the saved and the damned. She worries about Carter and Max as teenagers in a place where there are not many other children of color. Will interracial dating be all right with the parents of her sons' classmates? Will the boys experience real bias for the first time when they reach that juncture?

African American social workers in the out-of-state adoption agency Kathy and Steve worked with objected when they adopted Max and Carter. The social workers did not want black children raised by white parents. In the abstract, they might have a point, but in reality, there were no black families looking to adopt a pair of brothers at that time. Kathy and Steve believed love, nurturing, and stability were more important than anything else to the boys' development.

Now, in mainly white Vermont, their beliefs are about to be tested at school dances and sporting events. It is probably inevitable that someone will object when one of Kathy's boys asks a white girl out on a date. It is probably inevitable that Carter and Max will sometimes feel sad at their estrangement from the community into which they were born. They are black children raised white, no matter how many African American friends they find here or how conscientiously Kathy and Steve bring them into contact with African American art, movies, music, and writing. Even in our broad and diversifying culture, mixed-race children, whatever their genes, still have no place to feel at home. A friend in Pittsburgh, a black woman married to a white man, has the same worries about her son that Kathy has about Max and Carter.

My money is on the boys, who are ahead of our time. Having been raised with devoted attention and respect, they are better able to withstand what ignorance can dish out than the ignorant can withstand what they represent, which is the kind of love that sees deeply into our humanity and finally becomes blind to the color of skin.

Winter in Retreat

We had a foot or more of snow yesterday. Today, the sun is out, the sky a perfect chambray blue with high white clouds like bleached spots. This won't be our last snow, and yet there are subtle signs of spring. The days, of course, are much longer; it is no longer pitch dark when we get up at six, let alone when one of us takes Adam to the bus stop at seven. The sun doesn't go down below the highest ridge until almost five in the afternoon now, more than an hour later than it did in late December, and it sinks several degrees north of its earlier goodnight spot.

The animals know the change is coming. Yesterday's fresh white blanket is quilted with the tracks of large and small creatures on the move. We are seeing many more deer these days, including a pregnant doe out by the mailbox and a small herd of five in front of my headlights the other night. Two days ago, Kathy and I followed moose tracks right down our road — huge ones, six feet apart. And night before last, at three in the morning, I heard the yipping and singing of what I am told are coy-dogs, offspring of domestic dogs and coyotes. This is their mating season, and they set up quite a chorus. I lay awake and worried about Annie and Hank, who often want to go out as early as five in the morning, while it is still dark. What if they mix it up with the coys? I have read that coyotes seldom weigh more than about thirty-five pounds, and Hank is almost double that by now, with Annie trailing him at fifty-some pounds. But the coy-dogs have wildness and numbers on their side. I hope they are not as close as they sound in the dark.

People, too, are beginning to stir outside their winter patterns. Alan and I both sense new opportunities for meeting people, reaching out. We are interested in the Progressive Coalition, a group of activists who may be on the verge of becoming a third party in Vermont. We have been getting to know more about the Friends at Meeting, and I know some women who are interested in starting a readers' group. Through the summer, I think our circle of acquaintances and friends will begin to grow, bit by bit.

The surest sign of spring's slow approach, though, is Alan's restlessness. He is wearier of winter than I am and is seriously impatient to start building the additions to this house. I have had more to do, from snowshoeing to writing this journal to working for the education commissioners, and so the waiting has been easier for me. Alan has been housebound, unable to finish felling trees and cutting them, unable to work on interior projects because his shop is unheated and he can't easily get to its tools and materials for the layers of ice and snow in the way. But he recently bought himself a snowplow with an unregistered, unroadworthy, but still functional '72 Chevy truck attached. So next winter he can prepare better. He can begin from the beginning to push the snow out of his way, no longer relying on hired guys who put it where they think it should go. And he can set himself up to finish the structures that he will get framed and weather-tight during our short warm season. Next winter, with more friends, better preparations, and larger living spaces, we should feel even more at home here.

Passion

I have been assigned to write a report on the Vermont Teacher Forum, which took place today at the Capitol Plaza Hotel in Montpelier. I stayed for the whole daylong event, which provided an opportunity for about 140 selected teachers to give the commissioners and policy makers an earful. Because the state of Vermont has in recent years adopted new academic standards, the teachers are all expected to meet higher and higher demands and to raise student performance along with their own, with limited resources and often with seriously limited skills and knowledge of the subjects they teach.

This is true everywhere, not just in Vermont.

As I walked into the conference area this morning and began shedding boots and coat, I chatted with one of the teachers. "I have no idea what I'm doing here," she said with good-humored exasperation.

What she was doing there was meeting with teachers from across the state to talk about what *they're* doing, and what they still need to do to meet the higher expectations placed on them by the state. After the discussions, which took place in small groups, they were invited to turn around and tell the state — meaning the commissioners, the state board, and elected state and federal representatives — what they require in order to do this daunting job. Above all, they concluded, they need time. One teacher said, "We can't fix the airplane and fly it at the same time."

It was a high-energy day in general, but the highest energy of all came from the keynote speaker, a former national Teacher of the Year. She was a well-dressed, well-coifed, very blonde, heavy-set woman in her fifties who spoke in the flat accents of the flat Midwest — and yet she delivered her speech with the fiery style and the roller-coaster cadences of a Jesse Jackson or a Martin Luther King, Jr. What a show!

She talked about passion, of all things. No wonder she sounded as though she had borrowed from black preachers. Middle-aged white women, especially schoolteachers, are not supposed to be passionate!

This woman didn't know that. I am dead certain she has been told, both straight out and roundabout, but she has obviously never listened. In a voice that sometimes rang, sometimes pleaded, sometimes dropped to a hoarse, emotional whisper, she dared her audience to take risks, reach out, grab their students' hearts along with their attention, and let themselves be hurt if need be. She told stories about her own students, and she made it clear that she had been moved, challenged, shaken up, delighted, and infuriated by them. In other words, she loved them.

It must be love when a person can speak about her own thirty-year career and keep the focus on the work and on the students, not on herself. It must be love when she can address an audience of struggling, unrecognized colleagues without even a hint of zealotry, self-righteousness, or *I-made-it-and-so-can-you* formulas for success. It must be love when, without a false note or any hyperbole, she tells them repeatedly that they do "the most important job in the world." And if it's love, in all these instances, it draws directly on that of God. I know nothing about this teacher's spiritual life, or whether she would say she has one. It doesn't matter. The inner light beams straight out through her eyes.

This teacher used her breath not to puff herself up but to inspire — literally, to breathe life into — her audience. They could tell she was the real thing, a colleague, a friend, an example, and they cheered her as she left the room. She wiped away tears as she grinned and waved.

William Butler Yeats wrote, in his poem "The Second Coming": "The best lack all conviction; the worst are filled with passionate intensity." I have seen some of the best lose conviction. They either run screaming from the mainstream, as Alan did, or they slide into a quiet current and let the major players set the course and sail on by. A scientist I used to work with did this, for reasons as principled as Alan's. I guess I did it, too, having no stomach for jousting and careerism. The major players too often are in the game just to win fame, rewards, perks, promotions. Many of them become intense and self-congratulatory, but not what I would call passionate.

Simple, genuine passion, without overstatement or posturing, is rare. I have seen it firsthand in one psychotherapist, one school superintend-ent, one or two research scientists, a great many parents, a few teachers in my own school years, some gardeners and crafters, and occasional writers, musicians, and artists. I am pretty sure it fuels the vision of Ver-mont's education commissioners.

The ego gratification of doing good work is important. But from what I have seen in the education world, there needs also to be an ele-ment of selflessness, an ability to put the work itself first. This is love. To love any job as today's keynote speaker loves hers is to *make* it the most important job in the world.

Time Travels

I have heard that time is another human construct, like religion or morality — that God and the cosmos are beyond and outside of time and that truth, ultimately, is simply what it is, without reference to our ideas of right or wrong. Alexander Pope's long poem "Essay on Man" declares, "Whatever is, is right." I thought that ridiculous in my twenties, but now I begin to see sense in it.

In any case, if time is not sequential, if every moment exists simultaneously with every other moment, and everything that ever has happened or will happen is happening now, then that might explain why I sometimes look at Alan or Adam with surprise, as if they had materialized just this instant before my eyes, arriving from thin air. In some part of my mind, or in my soul, I must still live in the time or space before I knew them.

I have been looking over the e-mail messages that Alan and I were exchanging two years ago, when we had known each other only about six weeks. The trust and intimacy that sprang up so fast between us makes me think that at that time we somehow, also, intuited this one, where it has all turned out so well. There were hints and foreshadowings in our correspondence, pointers to the life we live now. We were obedient to the script that began with Alan's bemoaning his lack of Marthaness followed by my admission that I had that but lacked tool-guy skills. Naturally, every couple tests the waters of fantasy, values, goals, and longings, hoping to find them mutually inviting. We just keep being surprised by how dissimilar we are outwardly, in personality, style, and manner, and yet how entirely at one in sympathies, faith, and trust. Virtually every single thing we ventured to discuss has found a solution or realization since we have been together.

For example, I wrote to Alan that my work was the area of greatest dissatisfaction in my life, the most in need of change. I could not yet see my way clear to another way of surviving, and yet I felt a deep stirring that promised change:

> The light shining into the box in which I've been living—it makes me think the tasks I face in responding to it are nothing less than reordering, rearranging, rethinking almost everything, from where I work to where I live to how to honor my own best promptings, long dismissed or denied.

Meanwhile, we talked about Vermont — about Sarah and Joe, about Vermont's only congressman, Bernie Sanders, about my puzzlement as to why I had never followed my heart to the North Country. We talked about the importance of "place" in one's life. Alan traveled all over the country in the aftermath of Judy's death, and he ended up back where he had begun, finally choosing the place freely. He liked where he lived. I felt stuck:

> I can't pursue the need for place right now, so I make my house and garden my place. The longing for natural surroundings never goes away, so I sit on my bed and look above the houses across the street (they're a story lower than mine) and watch the small view of the hills beyond. It's one of the things I love about my house, that view. I know it's not the same as a redwood grove or Vermont panorama, but it serves.

Amid my constraints — mortgage, job, city life, boxed-in view of hills — I clung to the Quaker notion that if something is right, "way will open." I was staying open, making way. That was my frequent incantation at that time, "Stay open, make way." In this time, right now, when I sit writing in the window seat, I imagine my struggling, earlier self cocking an ear, listening quizzically to this very message as she sits on her bed and gazes at too-small, too-distant hills.

Alan and I moved around in time, or in some medium from which each of us plucked important parts of ourselves and our stories and held them up for the other's inspection. We returned to the James Dean–Natalie Wood theme of adolescent sexuality as if we knew that coming to terms with that ancient angst would help us be together. I confessed my prim, shy discomfort with boys, my fear that if I loosened up and let anything real shine through, a boy might think I "liked" him. I confessed the times later on when I "teased and flirted, with no intention to follow through, just because I needed to get someone to look at me." I admitted the fear of being exploited, being thought fast, being used or hurt, not valued for anything but the outside, whitebread, pretty-girl self (which at the time was about all I valued myself). I told Alan that the

mysterious Natalie Wood, in *Rebel Without a Cause,* "craved an emotional, affectionate, fraternal, deeply inquisitive search for intimacy and
acceptance."

Alan answered:

You got any idea how much HE craved those things? But he had been
taught that these were not manly things — and the *worst* thing anyone
could call you was "queer." I can't quite fathom why it seems important
to me now to go back 30 to 40 years into my life to resolve these very old
conflicts. Maybe need to understand the *then* before can understand the
now. This is helping.

Our dialogue helped me, too. I told Alan:

I think we need to see the pattern whole, integrated, accepted — the
then-and-now woven together. Only recently can I look at my younger
selves and feel about them (sometimes) the way I feel about Adam: compassionate, clear-eyed, not judging but understanding.

Self-love of just this kind was another theme to which we paid attention, sharing the realization that it was at the heart of every other kind of
love. I had been reading Patricia Raybon's *My First White Friend,* in
which she tells the story of her decision to put away hatred, especially
race hatred, and deliberately seek to love. I told Alan about it:

First chapter or two is full of language about love that moves me — how
love of self ends up permitting selflessness, how love is full of risk, how
she keeps saying God-help-me as she talks about pursuing love with
deliberation.

Alan replied:

Big hurdle here — love of self — w/its egocentric-narcissistic-negative
connotations. The God-help-me part elevates the concept of love to a
higher dimension — first you got to have it yourself before you can give
it away.

Whereas Raybon sought to reconcile a lifetime of mistrust toward
white people, Alan and I sought to divest ourselves of mistrust for the
opposite sex. I concluded:

If men and women and boys and girls exercised their good imaginations and spirits in order to re-create each other's reality, in order to respect the Other instead of seeking gratification or power there, there would be room for the tenderness to enter, for sexual love to partake of every other kind, for male and female to be equal partners in passion.

Alan responded with "a squib from somewhere in the land of hoo":

"I honor the place in you in which the entire universe dwells. I honor the place in you which is of love, of truth, of light, of peace. When you are in that place in you, and I am in that place in me, we are one."

And we are. Mostly, Alan and I are one because we choose to be. Looking back, I can see that we were in the process of choosing each other from the very first e-mail, looking always for each other's light and truth and being deliberate in our search. We still do that. I don't think a day goes by that I don't look at Alan and choose him all over again. I focus on that place of truth and love in him and I create him in me according to that image. Just as I came to love my mother unconditionally by "reenvisioning" her as another woman, a sister, a child, I "envision" Alan as a soul accessible to my own soul, a being with whom I have found love at an unprecedented level. Nothing else that happens between us can rock this bedrock. We disagree, we become irritable, we miscommunicate about surface matters. But we never yell, are never bitter, do not try to change each other, and do not undermine or attack.

This is possible for me because of Alan's commitment to truth, his search for what makes sense to him. The stories he told in his e-mails gradually showed him to be incorruptible, uniquely pure of heart despite disappointments, skepticism, and impatience with most other humans on the planet. When he found the light in another, it thrilled him.

An example. Exactly two years ago, Alan was working on his place in Cave Junction, renovating it, building a redwood deck, and preparing his land for cultivation by downing some trees and having them skidded out.

Interesting morning, this one that started out on BIG CAT feet. Awakened at six-thirty to the roar of many big diesel engines in the yard — loggers' body clocks are stuck in the middle of summer, when the heat and fire danger have you out of the woods by 2 P.M. BIG tractor-trailer rig carrying BIG bulldozer (that Cat), BIG autoloader. Skidding logs out of anywhere makes a mess, but these guys' focus is on minimizing the impact (could digress here and go on a long rant about how the most environmentally conscious people I've ever met are the ones who make their living cutting down trees — how if you want to preserve the forest, the first place to start is by nuking the Sierra Club — RRRAAAHHHH!!! Oops, not going to do that, not now anyway).

Anyway, we figure out the best route for the skid trail — all machines fired up and roaring. Work commences. And the noise all stops. Catman is down on his knees in front of the bulldozer, poking around in the grass. Little patch of daffodils poking through the soil right in the middle of the trail. No way around 'em and w/several tons of logs on a chain behind you, you don't back up. And he ain't gonna run over 'em. Trying to get my eyes to focus through the A.M.'s first cuppa, watching Big Catman, Big Trucker, Big Logger digging up this little patch of flowers and trans-planting them to a safe place. Little bit of buttafry in that Caterpillar man. But *I'm* not going to tell him that — not to nobody who looks like he eats barbed wire sandwiches for lunch . . . not me.

For all Alan knew, the Catman, like so many others in the northwest woods — and in Vermont, too — might have been a physicist or pianist or refugee from a Ph.D. program. His card read, "Cat Man Do." He probably would not have minded if Alan had pointed out his "buttafry" qualities.

Alan was a refugee, too, of course, and I think that has been both cause and effect of his completely independent take on the world. In his sympathies, he is about as left-wing as they come. He is entirely for the little guy, skeptical of authority, suspicious of prepackaged thought, on the lookout for corruption and conspiracy, willing to believe the best of individuals and the worst of institutions. He takes nothing and no one at face value. His only knee-jerk reflex seems to be his compulsion to shout "That man's naked!!" when the emperor walks by wearing only his lies or denial.

For instance, Alan began snarling about Bill Clinton — for whom he had voted twice — even before the Monica Lewinsky scandal broke, and he did so largely because he reads every source he can find, especially on the Internet, that claims to have a piece of the truth that no one else has reported. Then he triangulates, coordinates, culls, and dissects what they have to say and builds for himself a "take" that rings true, however sour the note. This is the only holdover from his long-ago days as a journalist — he researches everything and stays impartial until the evidence sways him one way or another. He may be the most independent-minded person I know.

Here is just some of what Alan sent me after his mini-rant had made me curious about his thoughts on the Sierra Club:

First hint is that the Sierra Club headquarters is in downtown San Francisco. Nada lotta trees to hug nearby. Most members are Marin County types who sip margaritas in their redwood hot-tubs on their redwood decks and holler: "Don't cut the trees." Well-meaning folks, but badly misinformed. Their ecological philosophy is right on — trees are important to maintain an environmental balance — trees are the lungs of the planet. But policies they have inspired — for example, no human use at all, which for some reason leaves forests more susceptible to fire — can end up killing more of the forest than they're saving, not to mention devastating rural economies, trashing families.

Maybe it's not the Sierra Club's fault, except that they don't protest, but today, vast quantities of land in the western states are "owned" by the federal government. A lot more is "owned" by multinational corporations. At present the vast majority of the timber cut in the West is sold as raw logs to Japan, while our mills close because they can't get the timber to process. We've had a regional effort to attract secondary wood-product industries to the area — furniture, cabinetry, millwork — but can't get access to materials because they're getting shipped overseas. This is all junked in w/some international trade agreement that lets us sell car parts in Japan.

"Workin' in the woods" is a way of life in this part of the country — nobody that earns their livelihood from the forest wants to destroy it. They want to nurture it and make it grow. "Workin' in the woods" is more than cutting timber. Just cleaning and culling provided income for many; thinning produced fence material; culling dead cedar produced shakes and shingles; cleaning up dead-and-down wood produced fire-wood, brush for chips, and so on. All the injunctions have done is cut off access for everybody.

Somewhere in here you throw in the Audubon Society folks, who like to wade into freezing marshes in Maryland to catch a glimpse of the scarlet pimpernel or the wax-winged dooflingy. Which is neat. I like birds. Got lotsa feeders around. Don't wanna see any species disappear because of something I did, either. Even spotted owls.

Trouble is, the Maryland dooflingy folks don't know squat about spotted owls. Yup, owls nest in trees. They would rather nest in your barn, but there seems to be fewer of those around as the small farms disappear. Current forest policy is every time somebody spots a spotted owl, they draw a two-mile radius around it and that's off limits. All you gotta do is see one, once. Nobody checks a while later to see if the owl is still there.

Funny thing about spotted owls — they build really flimsy, crummy nests. Why? Because they don't tend to stay in them very long. They eat the little rodentia that live around there. They eat a lot. Once they have scarfed the population, they move on to another place. Meantime hundreds of thousands of acres are off limits for any activity because an owl used to live there.

Summing up — would value the politics of the Sierra Club more if their HQ was a log cabin in the middle of the Klamath National Forest rather than a see-ment monolith on Market Street, San Francisco.

As Alan later told me, he applauds the Sierra Club's stated goals, but he worries that the organization has become so cumbersome and corporate that its main concerns are now its own image and its inner politics. He also suspects that many of its members never get close enough to the ecologies and creatures they lobby for to understand subtleties that could cause well-meant policies to backfire.

Not surprisingly, Alan ends up in strange company as he ponders the claims, evidence, power grabs, and posturing of advocacy groups, politicians, and others. He may agree with Pat Buchanan about this, Jesse Jackson about that, and both about a third matter. He shakes his head, talks back to the news, and sits at his computer scanning political Web sites and muttering, "*Jeez-us!*" He finds echoes of his own mind in unlikely places, but he always recognizes kindred thinking because he knows what he thinks and values himself. This is one reason I have always felt Alan is instinctively a Quaker. He is willing to take truth wherever he finds it, regardless of whether it is politically correct, whether the source is someone he otherwise admires or dislikes, whether the pieces all add up or need time to steep.

I saw or sensed all of this in the messages Alan sent me, and his sense of humor was a huge bonus. I still cherish and laugh at the image he painted so well with his words — the Catman and his Big pals transplanting daffodils.

The Ground Beneath My Feet

Yesterday, I went for a walk on our thawing road, which was rutted almost axle-deep in many places. I balanced, arms akimbo, on mounds between the ruts, which were filled with puddles filled with sky. The streams are thawing, too, and the river is rushing, singing a very loud psalm to spring. I saw a redwing blackbird and two robins, all adding their notes to the music. Halfway between our house and the end of our road, I came upon a deep hole, not just in the road but through it. A fast stream roared along underneath, where a culvert had given way. Someone had come along and placed a stick with an orange flag into the hole as a warning to cars. Once I saw this startling break, I began noticing hairline cracks over other culverts. I wonder how common it is for whole dirt roads to collapse into the air and water below them. It is a surprising notion; somehow I have always thought of roads as even more solid than other ground.

Solidity is always an illusion, of course. We walk on the earth and take from it a sense of permanence that extends even to ourselves in our frail bodies. We rely on our five senses, which render everything indisputably, in-your-face real, forgetting about the predominating space between and within atoms and molecules, forgetting that everything is mostly air, including us — where we are not water. I like these elemental illusions. I like the paradoxes — how real our temporary, physical state is to us and how airy and elusive our eternal spirits. That suits me right down to the unstable ground I walk on.

Vernal Equinox

We have survived the winter and made it to another equinox. This time, when the neck-and-neck moment is past, the light will have overtaken the darkness and will stay in the lead for the next six months. The light will melt the snow, draw forth buds, blossoms, and leaves, and warm our days until we complain about summer's heat.

In the meantime, we have mud season, which could last for weeks. Last year, it never entirely left. Our drainage ditch had at least a trickle in it right up until it froze. Soon, it will be a fast-flowing stream, when the snows from ledges above us begin melting in earnest.

This slow transition to spring invites Vermonters both to rush the coming season and dare the departing one. They shed their coats if the thermometer nears fifty. They open their car windows. They turn their faces to the sun as if they were in Florida. They also keep sledding down slopes that show bare earth and grass. They ride their snowmobiles over slushy, thawing trails. They go pond skimming — skiing down a patchy incline next to a lake and out onto the melting ice, taking bets on how far they can make it before they splash through. And they play a defiant game with pickup trucks and ice.

Yesterday, when Adam and I drove north to East Craftsbury for his piano lesson, we passed Lake Elmore, as we always do. All winter we have watched skiers, snowmobilers, and ice fishers enjoying the frozen surface. But it has been warm enough these past few days to melt a lot of ice, and still we saw three or four trucks parked well away from shore, out near the middle of the lake. This is risky. The local TV news has shots almost weekly of trucks sinking slowly through the ice of one or another lake or river, sometimes with injuries or death to the driver, sometimes not. Adam and I made our usual stop for snacks at the Elmore Store, right next to the lake, and I said to the woman at the counter, "It makes me nervous, seeing those trucks out on the ice. Maybe they know how to tell if it's thick enough to hold them." She raised her eyebrows and said, "You won't see *me* out there." Maybe it's a guy thing.

Subverting Youth

I just finished my third or fourth assignment for the education commissioners, with another one waiting. This recent one was an op-ed piece responding to criticism of the department's use of a standard margin of error in determining, from statewide assessments, which schools are most in need of technical assistance from the state to improve their performance. The assessments reflect Vermont's "Framework of Standards and Learning Opportunities," a document that specifies in eye-glazing, bureaucratic, and also inspiring detail exactly what knowledge and skills students should have at certain grade levels and what they should be able to do with these raw materials.

Standards, though they represent an enormous challenge to everyone in education and can be abused in the wrong hands, are not a fly-by-night education whim brought to us in the same flimsy wrapping as open classrooms, Skinner boxes, new math, and whole-word reading instruction. Standards, at least the ones adopted in Vermont, are the outcome of about thirty years of research on learning and a decade or so of collaboration between researchers and education practitioners. This has been a dicey relationship, full of the predictable snobbery of some researchers and the insecurity or defensiveness of some teachers, but it is a crucial partnership, however rocky. No skilled and self-respecting teacher will buy a research-based reform that does not consider the daily complexities that real children raise — *rooms* full of real children, who come from different backgrounds, may speak different first languages, and have different abilities, personalities, attitudes, and levels of interest in any schooling at all.

Diversity and differences notwithstanding, standards aim to raise achievement levels for every kid, turning out students who can wrestle with concepts, articulate their own thinking, solve problems, and demonstrate strong literacy, math, and reasoning skills. This can be a very hard sell, since many people believe intelligence levels are locked in at birth and some kids are just too dumb to learn much beyond what they can memorize, spit back on exams, and then promptly forget. But the fact is, just about everyone can learn, and successful schools and districts have shown this time and again, pulling unprecedented performance from students who would traditionally have been tracked at low levels and left there.

Good standards, well applied, are equity insurance. They require every child to demonstrate the same substantial knowledge and skills, and so they demand instruction that can get them there. Some students will reach the standards faster than others, and some will go way beyond them, but all will be treated like learners and taught how to achieve.

Naturally, this presupposes support from communities, voters, policy makers, parents — groups understandably wary of yet more education reforms. But if it is true that — barring serious mental disability, injury, abuse, or other trauma — every child is capable of learning to a pretty high set of standards, then we have to change everything we have ever thought about education. Not only will we have to change our tendency to group children according to perceived differences in ability, but, even more radically, we will have no choice but to teach them to think critically and clearly about every written or spoken authority, including our own. How else can we turn them into skilled thinkers and independent learners?

We can either educate our children to their highest capacity and let them fly on the wings that come with that, or we can tell them what to think and how to think it and thereby keep them grounded. But if we clip their wings, we can't expect them to meet the ever-rising demands of work and citizenship. If we clip their wings, we can kiss democracy good-bye, because we will have no educated citizenry, no voters capable of thinking their way into or out of a polling booth. We are already dangerously close to that condition. We will have to turn that around in order to ensure that government of, by, and for the people can proceed.

Of course, democracy depends as much on respect for individual voters as on their level of education, and high educational standards likewise presuppose respect and responsible communication. Classrooms must be places in which it is safe for students to speak up, experiment, fail, start over again, risk exposure. Becoming a learner and thinker requires lots of interaction and, through that, a sense of confidence. Our kids need to pump up some intellectual and imaginative muscle, and they need to engage with other students doing likewise. This process is best served by diversity and difference; it allows emotion to be expressed; it builds community — and it therefore makes school violence, gangs, and vicious cliques a little less likely. It promises empowerment, as all true learning does.

All the things we say we want — good jobs for our children, an equal chance for all, a strong showing in the global marketplace, a high standard of living — now depend on something many people have tended *not* to want, which is young people who know their own minds, who develop their own beliefs and values instead of adopting their elders', who can express and justify their thinking, and who work toward a coherent personal ethos that can guide their politics and practices in every arena.

I just love this pickle. I only hope we are not setting such standards too late.

I almost do not want to write about the beauty of everything that good, high standards imply, the way travel writers don't want to spread word of an unspoiled vacation paradise. If I call too much attention to what is happening here, it might just get ruined — by the religious right, who don't want their children or ours to think anything but what they are told is gospel, or by parents who have had bad experiences in school themselves, or by stakeholders in power who would not want young upstarts scrutinizing their means or methods too closely.

Standards are unlikely to go away, though, and the more they are implemented and attained, the more those who attain them will feel their power. Year by year, they will be more deeply entrenched, until we just might end up a citizenry educated not by rote and not through fear of failure but by deep curiosity and a passionate drive for understanding.

One can always hope.

Birds

All winter I have hardly seen a bird except for crows and jays. In February we finally put up two birdfeeders, one outside the living-room window, facing west, and the other—fitted with suction cups so it sticks right to the window itself—attached to the northwest-facing window where I sit and write.

The birds ignored our black oil sunflower seed for weeks. Kathy said I should move the window-seat feeder because it doesn't get enough sun, but I was reluctant to give up my image of finches and chickadees as my northwoods muses.

Suddenly, birds are everywhere. We hear the chickadee's sweet two-or-three-note whistle first thing in the morning. I have seen downy woodpeckers, redwing blackbirds, and even a pair of northern mockingbirds in the woods and alongside our road. Purple finches and chickadees at last are visiting our feeders. They fly in one at a time, landing long enough to snatch a seed before swooping away to eat it while another bird darts in. I have my muses now, as long as I keep the cats away from the window seat, where they are likely to try leaping at the birds through the glass.

Death and Resurrection

It was during this same week in March two years ago, after deepening our discussions of God, faith, and the primary themes in our lives, that Alan and I started edging emotionally closer as well. I confided in him the grief I experienced when a member of our Meeting attacked the woman he lived with, who was also a member. I told him more about my marriages than I ever had before. I talked about my brothers, Br'er Mike and Bro' Steve, and Alan instantly understood which one had become a born-again southerner and which one still clung to his Yankee identity after twenty years in North Carolina. I also sent Alan a highly personal article I had published on abortion, and he sent me a story he had written and photographed with a colleague roughly thirty years earlier, a piece of work that someone believed should cost him his life.

Alan was living in New Hampshire at the time, taking classes at the University of New Hampshire, and running a small public relations business with a partner. They were hired by the university to study and report on hunger throughout the state. This was in the days before New Hampshire had food stamps, when surplus food was distributed by the state to poor families and individuals. The state wanted to know how the program was working and asked the university to find out.

Alan and his partner interviewed the recipients of the surplus food, and Alan photographed many of them. His haunting black-and-white images verified the desperate poverty in which so many residents of New Hampshire lived. Children gazed at the camera with feral eyes, adults with empty ones. Those who spoke with Alan and his partner described their humiliation at the hands of the state workers who distributed the food; they were treated as lazy, dirty, stupid, less than human, undeserving. They also dropped hints about program personnel profiting illicitly. Alan and his friend uncovered proof, and they wrote about it. They described exactly how the state police commander himself was diverting railroad cars filled with butter, which he then sold on the black market.

The hunger study, called "The Curse That Lingers," came out in the summer of 1969, and it caused a bigger stink than anyone could have predicted. The *New York Times* picked it up. Alan wrote:

> Dunno if it was a slow news day or what, but excerpts got feature space in their Sunday magazine, along w/ a double truck blow-up of my best Dorothea Lange imitation (waifs around a woodstove). Pieces of it got put out over AP and sorta ran all over the place — even as far as *Reader's Digest*. Got itself to some of the "good guys" in D.C. Partner and self

were invited to participate in the White House Conference on Food, Nutrition, and Health (the very same one in which Tricky Dick gave his neat-o cottage cheese and ketchup speech to show everyone how well he related to tough times around the dinner table).

Sharing a dais w/the likes of George McGovern, Jake Javits, Gene McCarthy, and Jesse Jackson (when Jesse were still a pup) was pretty heady stuff for a lad in his twenties (maybe his 15 minutes). Sitting three feet from Barbara Jordan and Fannie Lou Hamer, both wound up to full tilt boogie, *was* heady — still get goosebumps at the thought of the power they emitted.

Meanwhile, back in NH, the shit was really hitting the fan. The infamous *Manchester Union Leader* featured us as the subject of front-page editorials for a solid week — not once attacking the factuality of anything. Attacking us as carpetbagging, pinko, hippie do-gooders. Many things learned in this process — relevance of stuff like "killing the messenger," getting "hung out to dry," "twisting in the wind." The UNH academics who wanted their names and pedigree placed prominently on the title page all of a sudden didn't know who the hell we were — jerked my fellowship, along w/degree and employment . . . and it went on. Followed constantly by state police, thrown in jail for a cracked tail-light lens.

My house was torched at 3 A.M. with six people inside it. Message pretty clear because the gasoline cans were left around the perimeter. Thank God everyone got out — not sure we were supposed to. Two days later the barn was torched . . . whoever did it didn't have the decency to open the door and let the animals out first.

When I read the hunger study for myself, and saw the photographs, I caught a glimpse of an Alan I had not met before, a dead-serious campaigner for fairness and human dignity, a person capable of being outraged and heartbroken by the consequences of greed. Now, he says, "Most efforts of mine for the 'greater good' tend to be locally oriented and, whenever possible, very anonymous."

In retrospect, probably not too different a scenario from what happened to civil rights workers in the South. Just sort of a pattern that kept repeating itself through my "career" — trying to do Good Things, running into lotsa Bad Guys dressed up like good guys . . . just came to an abrupt end at the point where the bean counters were trying to "cost effective" their way out of screening bad blood.

Right now, Alan is cultivating his garden, building our house, seeing what unfolds in our life here. He is not used to civic inaction, but knowing what to do and how and with whom will take time.

By the end of that March and beginning of April two years ago, Alan and I had progressed from sharing our long-past passionate writings to confiding more immediate matters. He told me about numerous cross-country drives to visit his father, who was dying of cancer in Georgia. He described the tender silence in which he would sit at his father's bedside, hoping for some overt expression of love that never came. I told him about an extraordinary event in my sister-in-law Rita's life, which I attended in North Carolina during that same early-spring period. This involved some well-orchestrated role-playing therapy, an attempt to replay and thereby illuminate some traumatic and crippling occurrences in Rita's early childhood. I played her father, a nonbeliever friend was God, a lay therapist was Rita's mother, and various others were a grandfather, a teacher, a few other central characters.

This psychodrama took place on a Wednesday near the end of that March. It was a sunny spring day, but we all faced it with trepidation. The replaying of Rita's younger years took most of the morning and afternoon, following an introduction by her therapist and the laying out of an annotated family tree by Reet. In every generation there had been suicides, tragedies, early deaths, depression, illness, and losses. Rita's early life had been a hard one.

Once I would have suspected this therapeutic occasion was yet another form of hoo-hah, but I had begun to learn that anything — therapy, art, work, family, self — can become what we envision, and if our envisioning is rich and our struggle to make peace is authentic, then miracles can happen.

What happened to Reet that day looked like a miracle to me. Close to Easter, it looked like a resurrection. I watched a woman recreate herself, surrounded by people she loved and trusted in the roles of other people who had betrayed or injured her. The spiritual alchemy succeeded, and the lead casing of sorrow and self-hatred that had coffined Rita cracked open and fell apart, letting her spirit shine.

My drive to North Carolina for Rita's "reconstruction" (her therapist's term) had an anticipatory air of miracles about it. Perhaps I sensed what was coming, or perhaps it was just that in driving south I entered spring. I remember noticing that the undergrowth in the woods greened up before the trees did. Mother Nature got dressed like the rest of us, undies first. All along, I felt Alan's presence, a powerful connection to my family, and the burgeoning of faith. I knew I was in the middle of an extraordinary adventure, and I relished it. I listened to jazz, opera, rock and roll, country, and gospel music — especially the Blind Boys of Alabama, who sang about a beat that can "move you, when you don't wanna move." I was moved, and I was moving, and my life was not going to stay put anytime soon.

With Reet's permission, I had described the purpose of the psychodrama to Alan. I had told him I would be away for a few days, and why. I asked him to hold us all in the light, especially on that Wednesday, the day of Reet's deep remaking.

Tuesday night, while I was uneasily asleep at Steve and Rita's, Alan received a phone call from his brother Don, saying their father's condition had worsened. Recovery was out of the question, yet Don could not bring himself to pray for an end to his father's life. As Alan wrote, in a welcome-home message I received that Friday:

I had gone through that same kind of agony with Judy. At that point I could only say, "Please, God, care for her." Together, we did the same for our father. Wednesday morning, woke with the first light of day. Living-room windows face east, and it is my habit to open the blinds and watch the sun break over the foothills and through the giant fir tree in the front yard. Greet the day/meditate/pray/have moments of silence. This day, I was sending thoughts/prayers/light to you and your family, and to my family — bundled them together and attached them to that stream of sunlight that was coming from the east, and as the sun is still a bit in the Southern Hemisphere — an entirely appropriate direction.

About this time the phone rang. My stepmother had arisen that morning, gone in and sat beside my father, held his hand, and asked God to please care for him. He sighed once, closed his eyes, and left us for a place of peace without pain.

Death and resurrection took place on the same day and in answer to the same prayer — that God might care for those we loved. Alan's father died just before Rita began rising from the ashes of her painful childhood and youth. Sorrow and grief attended each event, James's death and Rita's resurrection, but beyond the sorrow in each case was the joy of spiritual release and the love of friends and family.

This coincidence, this powerful confluence of themes in our separate lives, brought Alan and me closer than we had so far dared to be. Over the next two months, at a rapidly accelerating pace, we grew more intimate, more gleeful, more daring, and more playful with one another. We began discussing when and how to meet. Alan never had been concerned about the geographical distance between us. Even in our earliest messages, when I told him I was happy to make friends even a continent away, he said, "What continent?" and told me about his Road Warrior persona, his love of following his windshield across the country and watching the scenery play out before his eyes. He, too, traveled to music.

After telling Alan about Reet's resurrection, I said:

It all keeps playing out, through dinner that night, through the next morning before I leave. Steve goes to work, Reet and I sit and have coffee, breakfast, conversation. Just before I get in the car, I ask her what she will do, if she will be all right. She says she might plant the butterfly bush her older sister gave her, thinking it was dead. We laugh hysterically at this gift, this dead gift from the dead family, which turns out not to be dead after all. We both cry while laughing, and Reet goes in before I pull away. I wonder if she shares my superstition: Never watch someone you love go fully out of sight.

Alan, meanwhile, was out of my sight for a few days — that is, he was outside the realm we had started referring to as "the space between," a territory larger than cyberspace, filled with spirit, coincidence, shared themes, inside jokes, probing questions, and growing affection. He had decided to spend the Easter holiday with family in Ashland, Oregon, but first he planned on some time alone on his drive up the coast — time in which he would say farewell to his father.

On his return, he described an unexpected aspect of his healing:

This day, from the corner of my eye, I caught sight of a little side road that I'd never seen before. Followed it to its end, parked, and walked down a winding trail to where the Smith River meets the sea. Don't think I have the wordpower to describe the awesome magnificence of the panorama spread out before me. Fresh water rushing down from the hills, meeting salty surf. The waters swirl together, intermingle, create a frothy foam that is lifted by the wind into the blue of the sky.

Incoming tide had left just a narrow peninsula of beach — walked along this finger of land toward a promontory of rock that jutted out into the ocean, pitted and pocked, worn down by the wind and the waves. Climbed to the top, which turned out to contain a large bowl-like meadow of thick soft grasses and a profusion of wildflowers. Surf crashing into the rocks, exploding, rainbows in the spray, salty mist blowing into the wind. At the edge of the bluff, 60 or so feet above the sand, was a little pool of water trapped in the rock. In the pool, no more than 18 inches in diameter, were a million little plants, tiny swimming things with swishing tails, little crablike creatures crawling on the bottom. Could not guess how they got there, unless tossed aloft on a storm-spawned wave.

Microcosm of life in this tiny pool — macrocosm of infinity in this place where the forest ends, the earth meets the sea, the sea meets the sky at that point on the horizon where the sun has painted the water a shimmering gold.

Probably be room here for a zillion analogies: waves, of water and emotion; salt, of water and tears; beginnings and endings and the place where they converge. Many thoughts, feelings, and some insights, small ones and great big ones. Flashbacks to all the happy good times in this much-interrupted life-with-father. Find this piece of father's soul that intermingles with my own . . . peaceful release.

and . . .

                            then . . .

SPLATTT!
dis Jewish boid (Seigel) done shat
upon the very place
on which he sat . . .

which sort of interrupted this Richard Bach-analia of cosmic soaring metaphor . . . begins the giggles . . . giggles to guffaws to rolling-on-the-ground belly-busters . . . tears of a different flavor . . . and a lotta stuff seems right with the world again.

When Alan returned from his Easter trip, our conversation in the space between kept deepening. We began to acknowledge our abstract but very real sexual curiosity about each other, even as we knew there was nothing immediate to be done about it. It made us nervous; it delighted us; we were content to experience it fully and then just let it be. We knew that something beyond words was going on between us. Alan wrote: "Words have never carried so much heart, soul, care."

He described to me his reasons for wanting to send me his first gift, a redwood bowl:

By the way — I have this gnarly old piece of redwood-root-turned-bowl that needs a place to be. Every once in a while, a chunk turns up that has some special quality that binds itself to me in a holding pattern that says: "Wait for special person, special place." This was a chunk ripped from a riverbank, swept out to sea, pounded by the waves, and thrown back on the beach to bleach in the sun. The "soulness" in this old chunk of wood spoke to me so much in the manner of our dialogue, including the river-ocean symbology.

At that time Alan was reading Thomas Moore's *Reenchantment of Everday Life*. He said:

Then in this chapter on Talking Trees comes: " 'Cleave a piece of wood,' says Jesus in the Gospel of Thomas, 'I am there.' "

Raised a bunch o' them goose-willies, more so in light of the Easter season, and, in this case, this old chunk of wood might have just been living on the planet at the same time.

So, with your permission (I don't fling stuff over transoms or through milkboxes-turned-mailboxes without asking first), I would like very much to forward this chunk to you.

From the beginning, Alan and I felt we spoke to each other through much more than our words. The space between was the geography that separated us physically, the meaningful air between the lines that we wrote, some plane on which our souls were in control and our minds and flying fingers on keyboards just servants of our deepest selves.

For me, the space between became a wellspring of faith, a realm in which it was possible to glimpse the tapestry of existence through the series of coincidences that kept flowing in like a tide. I could never list them all, but they had somehow linked Alan and me since earliest childhood—both fathers in the Navy and then largely or entirely absent, both mothers somehow unreachable, both young childhoods in neighboring towns in Ohio, both families tended by Dr. Sam Sheppard or his brother. Our coincidental near misses continued through our later years, when we both lived in New England at the same time, in California at the same time, in Pennsylvania for at least one overlapping year. More than that, we were the same internally—we saw the patterns of life similarly, we believed the same things about God, we trusted intuition and apprehension more than our five senses alone, we liked the same songs by the same artists (Paul Desmond's "Skylark," Ella Fitzgerald's "Don't Fence Me In" and "Love for Sale"), we made each other laugh, we were honest even when it was not easy to be.

The more I trusted what passed between Alan and me, the more possibilities life seemed to hold—whether we ever ended up together or not. I understood that my faith was growing just through our conversations about faith. I was beginning to see why faith the size of a mustard seed is enough to transform a life: Faith will do more of the work than we know or can even believe. Given any room at all, it will fill that space and create more room for itself.

Selves

I am more than ever aware of the comings and goings of people in my life, wishing I could see the stage directions. Finding a soul mate in Alan has spirited me away from two friendships I had thought were sound. Now, perhaps, it has revived one or two older connections.

Yesterday I drove to Burlington, then north to Grand Isle, where I took a ferry across a skinny bit of Lake Champlain to Plattsburgh, New York. I went there to visit an old friend, Ann Tracy, whom I had not seen face to face for about twenty-five years. Ann teaches at the State University of New York in Plattsburgh, where she is a senior member of the English department. She went to Colby College, in Waterville, Maine, as I did, but she graduated the year before I arrived. We met in Toronto, in 1967, after I had finished at Colby and my then husband, Ned, recognized Ann in a graduate seminar he was taking at the University of Toronto.

In those days, Ann was unlike any other woman I knew. I was twenty-three, unsteadily married, naïve, conventional, and without ambition. She would never dream of following any such banal ways. She was the first feminist I ever knew, and she had apparently been one since birth. She had stuck a toe into the world of dating and sexual games and traditional expectations for women, but she had found the waters unappealing and had withdrawn from them. She found sex boring. She said that for her it was more important to cultivate friends than to marry or start a family. She was in her late twenties then, and dying to turn thirty so that she would finally command some respect in her chosen world.

Ann's dissertation was on the gothic novel, and she herself adopted a gothic style that, with variations and additions, she still maintains. Her apartment in Toronto had heavy carved furniture, some velvet and gilt, and a gargoyle before gargoyles became trendy. Over the sofa she had hung a hand-calligraphed quotation from Sir Francis Bacon — "There is no great beauty without some strangeness in the proportion."

Ann looked the part she had assumed. She had wild dark hair, black shadows — real ones, not kohl — around her eyes, a kind of turn-of-the-century Gibson-Girl-meets-Morticia strangeness in her own proportions, and a light and laughing manner of speech in which she could deliver both barbs and straight talk without giving offense. She had been born and raised in rural Maine, the daughter of a schoolteacher and an aging headmaster.

That part of the North Country can be especially dark, spooky, and bleak, and it made Ann deeply susceptible to the Canadian Indian story of the ice-bellied, cannibalistic Windigo, a myth told to her by her anthropologist brother, Bill. Ann made potent and hilarious feminist art out of this tale in her first novel, *Winter Hunger*, which the Canadian novelist Margaret Atwood admired enough to discuss in one of her 1991 Clarendon lectures at Oxford. (Ann is now on sabbatical, working on her third novel, this one about a flood of molasses that drowned parts of Boston's North End in January 1919.)

When I arrived at Ann's, we hugged and beamed at each other and then stood a bit awkwardly, not quite knowing how to proceed from the first effusive burst. Her entire house is well suited to such moments; it invites inspection and comment. Her front entrance hall, a small area maybe seven by ten feet, is painted bright yellow and illustrated with cats and naked women in wild array, striped and contoured in purple, green, pink, blue. The window frames are red, with white script winding around them. The first quotation, from somebody named Haldane, says, " The universe is not only queerer than we suppose, it is queerer than we *can* suppose." The second, by an obscure Burnet, reads, "I readily believe that there are more invisible than visible Natures in the Universe."

The living room, also yellow, is the most formally arranged area on the first floor, but still it is occupied everywhere by paintings, drawings, bits of sculpture, embroidered pillows, framed photographs, books, plants, mementos — and bats, everywhere, in drawings and in three-dimensional media. Ann is known in town as the person to call if a bat gets into your house. She goes with her ladder and heavy gloves and picks the poor thing up and releases it. Her car window sports a small circular sticker that says, "Bat Protection Squad."

Surveying Ann's lavish array is an oil portrait of Ann herself wearing black academic robes and rather a quizzical expression. The portrait, painted by a friend, captures her well — it has great, benign presence.

Ann is in her late fifties now and has, as she puts it herself, "grown fat and lame." She has rheumatoid arthritis, which, with her weight, gives her a rocking gait. Her hair, still long and thick, is streaked with gray.

She wears mostly loose and flowing garments in gray and black. She coddles her cat, Guido, who, like Ann, is fat, gray-black, longhaired, and gimpy. He too rocks when he walks; he uses first his right legs and then his left — the oddest manner of locomotion I have ever seen in a four-legged animal.

Ann's voice and laugh are entirely unchanged.

We talked a great deal, ranging over many recollections and events in our lives. We compared notes about people we both know. We compared styles and the way they reflect us. Ann's abundance — her books, memorabilia, and overflowing rooms — reveal so much about her. My own tendency is toward light, spare, airy spaces. I think they would not put a stranger or an old friend as quickly at ease as Ann's territory does.

But Ann confessed that she once studied the styles of mentors and friends to find one she could adapt for herself. One professor liked Danish modern furniture and kept her house immaculately tidy. Another was more Eastern European. I think Ann simply stuck with what I saw in its early form in Toronto, modifying it through various moves and changes. I always did think she was born knowing herself. I see impressive consistency in her life — not a bland sameness, not with her inventive capacities and her legions of friends, students, and families of waifs she has rescued over the years — but a consistency that gives clarity and vision to a life.

I seek this myself. I wondered out loud to Ann that she should have been so much herself and so certain of her identity, while I have imagined myself anew in every marriage and circumstance. I told her my experience recalled that old saying about carving an elephant: You just chip away at everything that doesn't look like an elephant — that is, a self. Or it was like Michelangelo's prisoner escaping from the marble, the stone that wouldn't quite release the figure. Ann herself admits that she has not had much chipping to do; she has simply grown increasingly herself as she has grown older.

I suspect Ann's consistency of self has been possible in part because she never bought into the programmed culture that aims to get us by the throat and make us in its image instead of our own. She never did want what she was told to want, and so she never lost touch with her nature, her soul. Some of us have to chip away at stone for decades to find what we have buried; we learn what comes naturally only through unnatural compromises and surrenders.

I have ended up with what I want, nonetheless. Until recently, my life has been a seat-of-the-pants enterprise, but satisfying, now that I gain perspective. I look at Adam, and feel drunk with love. He grows more kind, knowing, and easy every day; he keeps his counsel, and like Ann he will be true to himself. I look at Alan, still, in wonder at our meeting and our life. I see his effect on Adam, and on me, and I know I lucked out.

Maybe, if one has a talent for joy and a strong enough urge to love, those will rescue a person even from herself.

Another good thing: When I returned from Ann's, I found e-mail from Nora. I had tracked her down to congratulate her on her book, which I was probably passing on to Ann even as Nora was responding to me. Nora's book — the first chapter of which is the essay that appeared in the *Utne Reader* — is about the renewal of her faith through an Episcopalian community. She reflects on the church calendar, on its religious seasons and holidays from Advent to Pentecost, and she connects them to parallel seasons and themes in her daily life, which she calls ordinary time. Ann, too, is Episcopalian, and I believe I have caught another tiny glimpse of the tapestry in connecting with these two women, two writers, two who live their faith. I believe there is pattern and purpose in this, whether I can see it or not, whether the relationships progress further or not.

Clouds of Glory

Recently, Adam told me that he thinks reincarnation makes sense, and that in each life we have the same identity — that is, the same soul — but no memory of having existed before. Each life, he said, is a giant case of amnesia.

This morning, in Meeting, I recalled from Wordsworth's poem "Intimations of Immortality from Recollections of Early Childhood" the line "Our birth is but a sleep and a forgetting." Perhaps the spiritual challenge of our life is to wake, and to remember.

Whether we have one life or several on earth, I think we enter with distinct memories of God and the world of spirit. We arrive, as Wordsworth says in the same poem, "trailing clouds of glory." We come from a vast place bearing vast awareness, and the moment we squeeze through the birth canal into this narrower existence, we begin to forget where we have been. With each word we learn, step we take, task we complete, our amnesia deepens, until, in many cases, we even believe God impossible, dead, imaginary, an opiate for weaklings.

The silence at the beginning of Meeting today was among the deepest I have ever experienced. The room, holding twenty or so adults and a few children, was absolutely still. I sank with gratitude into that stillness and stared into the light behind my eyelids, which seemed to illuminate a large space. When the surface of the quiet was broken by latecomers — among them some noisily whispering children — it seemed to me that the silence flowed over and around the sounds in the room, embracing them and making them a part of itself. It was not that I could not hear the sounds. I was even briefly disturbed by them. It was more that, with a renewed and steady focus on the light and the distances within me, I could bring the sounds into oneness with the state of worship.

More and more, that state is one in which I seek wordlessness. I stare at the inner light, I choose a point behind my eyelids, I hold my body still, I regulate my breathing. I turn off language and open myself to direct experience, to an apprehension of God and the immensity from which we all arise.

I think about David Abram's book, *The Spell of the Sensuous,* and his idea that we have cut ourselves off from the living, spirit-filled world around us through our overreliance on language. I think about what my friend Ann said in one of our conversations Thursday night — that once you write about an experience, it loses its impact, it is crystallized, it is no longer flowing and able to embrace and inform other events, as the silence this morning embraced sound and changed it.

I think, also, about Alan and his slowness to speech, seeing it as part of his spirituality, his focus on direct experiences of this life and memories of his origins. For example, Alan refuses to describe, beyond the single paragraph he sent me in e-mail, the moment of his wife Judy's death, the dance their souls did before separating. I understand his resistance, now. Should he capture that moment in language he would cage it, tame it, rob it of its power.

Silence and wordlessness. They represent to me a way to awaken from our sleep and our forgetting. They allow spirit to reveal itself, to speak, to move us beyond our habits of mind and into reminders of immortality.

I like this idea of reminders. It seems to me that faith revives memories of glory. The more I concentrate on spirit, the more I intuit the vast world we leave behind when we squeeze into this life.

Since I have been in Vermont, and especially since I have begun writing about the recent and old events that have led me to this place, I have been able to concentrate on spirit more intently than at any other time. This is both cause and effect of extraordinary changes in my life. One begets the next and they all loop around to my origins, to my past, to the lessons I can gain by paying attention to patterns of character, desire, circumstance, and action that grow a little clearer all the time.

When I write about the moments in which I apprehend a larger realm — moments in Meeting, on walks, with Alan or Adam, or here at this keyboard — I am nearly always surprised at what emerges. I know that many people who create, whatever the medium, feel this energy, this sense of being connected to a source beyond themselves. My personal experience of it confirms for me a lifelong intuition that our daily life and five senses deliver only a fraction of reality. It also assures me that we have access to worlds beyond our habitual ways of knowing.

Still, my daily life and five senses contain most of my immediate existence. They are familiar, comforting territory, and it always feels risky to venture beyond them. Maybe this is as it should be. I saw in my mother someone who preferred prayer to people, contemplation to experience, the next world to this tangled and compellingly beautiful one, and I do not want to be like her. I want, somehow, for my intimations of eternity to bring light into all my dealings with this tangible, persistently present world so that I can give everything its due instead of avoiding or ignoring life in the name of far-off, otherworldly spirit.

Last week a Pittsburgh friend, Gillian, called me to say thanks for a birthday gift I had sent and to relay the latest in her plans to move away with Dave, the new man in her life — perhaps even to Vermont, after other things fall into place. Gillian and Dave paid us a brief visit in February, both to see our place and to look around this part of Vermont.

In our phone conversation, Gillian left me with a disturbing story about Emma, whom she encountered at a coffee shop near Pittsburgh's Carnegie Museum of Art. Gillian chatted pleasantly with her, and then said, "Oh, I saw Kate in Vermont." Emma's expression did not change. She did not show any particular interest. But Gillian persisted, and described our house and life and "rugged terrain." Emma said, "I can see Alan there, but not Kate."

I think I have indeed stepped too far outside Emma's frame of expectations. I think I have become invisible to her, which is very sad.

SPRING

To turn and to turn will be our delight
Until turning, turning, we come round right.

From the Shaker hymn, "Simple Gifts"

April

Son Shine

Adam has shown his native resilience recently, both in adapting to awkward, orthodontic "appliances" and in taking responsibility for cranking them to new settings at frequent intervals. Last Thursday, before I went to Ann's, I picked Adam up during his lunch hour and took him to the orthodontist to have the second of these two contraptions fitted. Both are expanders. They will gradually widen the arc of his upper and lower jaw to accommodate all his teeth. Braces will follow, once the expanders have done their work. The bottom expander was installed two weeks ago, and that one gave Adam no problems at all. The top one went in on Thursday and proved a whole different story.

I stayed in the waiting room while the fitting took place, and then Adam came to get me so I could see what had been done and learn about the care it would require. He stood in front of me and looked stricken. Then he spoke, and the hissing and lisping that went with that formerly simple process were dramatic. He was miserable, humiliated. My heart seized up, and I followed him mutely into the torture chamber.

There I watched Adam's moral and emotional stature take on new proportions. (Expanders, indeed!) Little by little, as the technician showed me how to work the tiny key that turns the screw on this new mouth-rack, Adam responded to our carefully low-key commentary by taking charge. He learned how to turn the key himself and took that every-other-day job as his own. Even more, he found his sense of humor. By the time we got in the car, he had discovered which sounds were hardest for him to make, and he exaggerated them, falling into fits of laughter. I know he was preparing for his return to school by taking the initiative away from any would-be tormentors. Who could get any satisfaction out of teasing him if he's already bent double laughing at himself?

I drove him back to school in a state of pure, delighted awe. Relief, too, of course.

Adam no longer has much noticeable impediment in his speech. He had mastered most sounds by the time he got home from school that first day. So far, he never forgets to turn the key when he needs to. For a kid who was mortally dreading his orthodontic trials, he has brought this one down with a slingshot.

Kosovo

Over and over the television reporters and pundits remind us that Good Friday is the most solemn day in the Christian calendar, and then in appropriately somber tones they describe the day's NATO bombing runs against Belgrade. We — the Western allies — are fighting the mainly Christian Serbs, who want the mainly Muslim ethnic Albanians out of their territory. The bombing runs indeed have let loose a flood of emigrants, hundreds of thousands of Albanians fleeing to nearby Montenegro, Macedonia, and Albania. So perhaps we are doing the Serbs a favor, even as we bomb them.

Good Friday commemorates a brutal and violent execution, and countless wars have perpetuated further destruction in the name of the one who died — or in the name of some other saint or holy one, some tenet or dogma.

If people truly believed that God does not punish and is not violent, it seems to me there would be no war. If we understood God to be love, compassion, mercy, and patience, how — especially in God's name — could any of us do grisly and vicious harm to other children of God?

Maybe it is difficult to believe in something so simple and singular because of the complexity into which God has plunged us, having had no choice in creating but to create all and everything, including the illusory not-God stuff such as fear, greed, hatred, violence. As I have already said, I feel in my bones that it was beyond God's power to do less than everything — omnipotence bears the seed of powerlessness right in its very heart.

The one thing I believe God did not create, though, is any possibility that a single soul can be lost, damned, or given to torment beyond what we encounter in the shadows where we live our earthly lives. That would violate the merciful logic of Creation, which says that until we find our way back to the sacred we must live amid fragments and dichotomies. If love exists so must hatred, if good then evil, if peace then war. To doom a person who does evil is to punish necessity, and that I believe God would not do, even though humans sometimes have to.

If we are evolving, if we are making our way to God generation by slow generation, then by infinitesimal degrees we will wean ourselves from war, evil, and violence. The pathway to this freedom is to discern light from shadow, that of God from that which is not-God. This is what free will means to me. Not that we can fully control our individual fates or natures, not that we will be punished if we fail to do so, but that we can think, grow, and choose with what we have. We can decide to search for the light and follow it. The alternative is to consent to darkness.

Moose

All winter Adam and I have been hoping to see a moose on one of our Saturday drives to Craftsbury. We have been told our route takes us right through moose territory, and sure enough the highways are marked

at intervals with signs saying "Moose, next 2,000 [or 500 or 4,000] feet."
On one section of Route 12, a sign on the southbound side says "Moose
next 2200 feet," but on the northbound side it says "Moose next 4 miles."
Jokingly, we have wondered whether the moose read the road signs. Do
they stay dutifully in the northbound lane for four miles and enter the
southbound lane only where it is marked? How else do the moose know
where they are supposed to cross? Now, having watched the trails of
deer on our road and in our woods, I can see that they follow the same
runs over and over. Presumably, moose do this too, though that still does
not explain the discrepancy in the signs on Route 12.

Finally, today, as Adam and I rounded a bend on another secondary
road, Route 14, we saw ahead of us not one but two moose, covering
both lanes of the road. I think they were females, but this being the time
of year before the males grow their racks, I could be wrong. A car was
stopped in the southbound lane, facing us. We stopped, too. The moose
looked us up and down at their leisure. They ambled left, they ambled
right. They stood higher than horses on their rangy legs, which they used
as if they had recently experienced a sudden, adolescent growth spurt.
Soon they sauntered off into the wetland beside the road. If moose could
speak they would sound like Goofy. They are gawky, enormous creatures. We were thrilled to see them.

When we got to Mary Anthony's, and Adam told her of our close
encounter, she told us moose are dangerous to night drivers because
their eyes do not reflect light. Deer, raccoons, and just about anything
else you might see on roads at night will throw your headlights right
back at you, their eyes shining like flashlights. Moose eyes give no such
warning — or could it be that moose are too tall, their eyes above reflection range? Except for this hazard, the giant animals are apparently
benign, at least when it is not rutting season.

And how many children in the world see moose on their way to piano
lessons?

Action and Reflection

We had Easter dinner at Sarah and Joe's yesterday, a last-minute plan designed to give Sarah a break from her parents' needs and querulousness. She and Joe and other family members had had a brief early holiday meal with Alice and Luke yesterday at their retirement home. Then they escaped with guilty delight instead of inviting the two old people to return with them. The second holiday meal, cooked by Joe and supplemented by the rest of us, was for friends only. The absence of her parents somewhat bothered Sarah, but not for long. It was a hilarious event, and even Sarah laughed — real, raucous, belly laughter — for the first time in recent memory.

The other guests, besides the three of us, were two women, the teenage daughter of one of them, and a couple who are dedicated activists, involved in several advocacy groups, including a brigade to Nicaragua that recently has aided hurricane survivors. These two have an energy and air of conviction that I remember well from the sixties and early seventies, an air that somehow mystified, attracted, and repelled me all at once — probably because it was something I couldn't imagine ever sharing. I was too shy, and I didn't trust that my thinking would hold up under pressure. Word person or not, I feared language would desert me the moment I was challenged, the moment I had to argue my position on the fly. I avoided activism for the same reason I avoided graduate school — insecurity. The thought of speaking out in a seminar, defending a thesis, or articulating a passion for peace or equity — it was all beyond me.

When I was in my last year of college, married to Ned and preparing to support him while he worked on a master's degree at the University of Toronto, I learned a thing that surprised me. Ned went for a walk one spring night, a few weeks before my graduation, and encountered my classics professor. He was working in his garden and asked Ned about our plans for the next year. Ned told him, and Professor Westervelt shook his head and said, "Your wife should be going to graduate school." Ned reported this to me with a certain condescension that was typical of him at the time, but I was grateful regardless. It had never crossed my mind that anyone could hold it — my mind, that is — in high esteem.

It also never crossed my mind that I could have served social and political justice by *not* engaging in argument. Some arguments are a distraction — they run counter to the core purpose of action. I could just have said: War is wrong, oppression is wrong, racial inequity is wrong. The need to argue and defend is like a war in miniature. It is adversarial, it distracts from constructive action. When I bought in to a need for argument, it kept faith out of reach. It kept me from trusting my purest convictions. It opened them up to attack.

I still prefer to be a behind-the-scenes person. I would rather make my contributions anonymously. I dislike being out front and visible, and I think I would truly hate being famous, unless I never had to show my face anywhere or speak ad lib, unless I could be like J. D. Salinger or Thomas Pynchon or Emily Dickinson. That's just a matter of personality, but it raises the question, Why do I write? Why am I writing *this?* The answer varies. Sometimes it is an older Adam who sits at my shoulder, perhaps a middle-aged man wanting to know more about his dead or doddering mother, whom he can no longer ask directly. Sometimes I am my only audience, and I write for the sake of what I can learn, or I write because I am so in love with my family, friends, dogs, cats, life, and ten acres.

But of course, like most writers, I wonder how it would be to have strangers hear in my voice their own half-wakened thoughts, struck like a gong, echoing and growing. That would validate the struggle to know myself, to seek God, to articulate values, to assess my reality; it would eliminate any compulsion to grieve the long time it has taken to begin making sense of my life. I would no longer have to wonder whether the time has been wasted.

The activists of this world — at least the ones who act out of compassion and not out of an arrogance of ideas or a dividing self-righteousness — do make a measurable difference, ease suffering, communicate their passions through direct, unambiguous deeds. I used to wish I were more like them. I often wonder what I am supposed to do instead, from the wings of the great play. But way will open, and I will find out.

Discerning a Gift

My father would be eighty-four today, April 6, if he were alive. He died at seventy, a couple of months before Adam was born. I have been thinking about him lately, realizing how little of this journal or my reflections he has occupied.

James Hillman, in *The Soul's Code,* propounds an "acorn theory," which holds that we all are accompanied into our lives by a daimon or spirit or nature that has chosen our parents and many of our life challenges for us. In other words, we contain within us the seed of what we are meant to become. Whether we become it or not, I infer, depends on whether we learn to heed the voice of our daimon and whether we can get along with that entity. Hillman says most cultures hold some such belief in a daimon, developed Western cultures being virtually the only ones to reject or ignore it.

I love this theory. As Hillman explains, it takes away from parents the tragic almightiness that our psycho-laden century has placed on them, and it takes away from children the sense of powerlessness that comes from so-called accidents of birth and family and circumstance. There are no accidents of birth. Wordsworth was right — the clouds of glory that trail us into this life, and then dissipate so rapidly, are memories of God and cosmic patterns of intent.

So I ask myself, why would I, or my daimon, have chosen this father? I had relatively little to do with him as either a child or an adult. Over the years, I came to see him as a decent man made weak by a bullying father, a timid mother, and a fearful, sensitive, if unimaginative, nature. He was sentimental — perhaps because he could not be forthright and truthful about his emotions. He was self-righteous — perhaps because he could not or would not think thorny issues through for himself. He was reflexively patriotic—perhaps because he was afraid to question much. He was ingratiating with his bosses, who failed to respect him. He compensated by being rude to telephone operators, plumbers, waitresses. He spoke in clichés and pretended things were better than they were—at home, at work, in his heart.

I dread sentimentality, groveling, and pretense. I see too much of my father in me—in my own past conventionality, my nervous adolescent naïveté, my earlier drive to shrink and befriend difficult emotions, a tendency to take things and people at face value in order to avoid confrontation, difficult honesty, or maybe rudeness. I am suspicious of my own nature when the sight of a red bird against a blue sky, flying across the ghost of a moon and above the roar of spring rivers, can almost bring me to my knees. Am I sentimental, like my father?

I want to think I am not. I want to believe that powerful emotion is an outlet to eternity, a pressure valve from our tiny lives to a bigger realm, and that emotion dilutes to bland sentimentality only when it is habitually suppressed, pretended to, or denied. Sentimentality simulates emotion; it is not the real thing.

If I, or my daimon, chose my father, I believe it was for his emotional nature, not for his refusal and fear of it. It was for the raw material of passion, which, with my mother's more analytical, more spiritual, more imaginative coolness, has made it possible for me to become whole while also recognizing and accommodating multiple aspects of myself. This is a gift of such magnitude and grace that I can begin, slowly, to feel for my father a hint of the same unconditional love that I learned for my mother.

Coyotes

I have been misinformed about coy-dogs and coyotes. I always did wonder why people seemed so sure that the night-time yipping and singing in our woods comes from a coyote-domestic hybrid. Wouldn't that mean there had to be actual coyotes?

Now I have learned that the eerie, sometimes keening sounds we hear do come from coyotes, but not from the more solitary, thirty-to-thirty-five-pound canids of the American West. These eastern coyotes live in packs, and the males can reach seventy pounds or more. It is thought that the eastern coyote, during its migration from the Midwest into our northern woods, might have mated with timber wolves, which would explain both its larger size and its closer-knit packs. So, of course, would the notion that the coyotes had bred with large domestic dogs like German shepherds. Probably some of each theory is true. The *National Audubon Society Field Guide to North American Mammals* lists coy-dogs but does not mention any interbreeding between coyotes and timber wolves.

In any case, the western coyote was able to migrate across a large area because its habitat was contiguous, not severed by roads, buildings, neighborhoods, shopping malls, and industrial so-called parks. Many wildlife species are now threatened by the fragmentation of their habitat, which isolates them in areas too small to permit the broad gene pools and ecodiversity that keep these species robust.

This, and much more, was part of a presentation that Alan and Kathy and I attended, a slide show and talk by a naturalist named Susan Morse, a Vermonter who travels all over the country and the world on behalf of wildlife and wild habitats. She is the founder of a group called Keeping Track, and her talk was in part a recruitment effort, a search for people wanting to learn tracking and data recording techniques so that four times a year they can monitor critical sites and report on the wildlife making use of them.

Kathy and I signed up. If we are selected, we'll take six training sessions over the next year or so. We'll learn not only to identify the tracks of bobcat, mink, otter, fisher, porcupine, pine marten, lynx, bear, moose, deer, coyote, and other creatures but, even more, to recognize other signs of their presence — their bedding sites, nests, scat, claw marks, tooth marks, and the remains of prey. It would appease some long hunger in me to enter in a knowing way the secret world that thrives out of sight, to be able to walk in the woods and see with intelligent eyes patterns of life and death that now I pass right by.

I think that what we truly know we love and protect. When we are ignorant of the natural world its members can die and we don't mourn or even notice. What we don't know may not hurt us until it is too late. Our ignorance allows cancers of our own making to bloom darkly, eating away at healthy natural systems until they can no longer sustain the lives of important species on whose well-being the health of others, including humans, depends utterly.

Mud Season—A Time Between

This is the first gray, chill day we have had for a while. A few small snowflakes drift idly past my window. It is only in the forties outside, and it feels colder. Recently, though, we have had enough spring weather that virtually all the snow is gone, and its mud wake is deep wherever we step outside. Birdsong proliferates in the mornings. Instead of the chickadee solos of recent weeks we now have a full chorus. The jays add their catcalls, the robins their *cheer-cheer-cheer*. All around is the soft music of warblers I can't yet identify. And the phoebe says her name again and again, first as a question, then as an answer, as if she has to remind herself daily who she is — and who hasn't had to do this, some days?

Behind the house, Alan has cut up and split dozens of the trees he felled and has cleared the brush away into towering heaps that will dry to tinder and eventually be torched. I have tossed split logs onto separate heaps, bending and throwing until my back and arms are as stiff as the wood that got them that way. At last, though, there is a broad clear path back there, banked by brush and wood, able to accommodate Alan's truck and its loads of supplies. Construction is about to begin!

Yesterday and today Alan wore himself out digging holes for the concrete footers that will support our new living room and utility space. Unless he hits solid rock first, he digs the holes three to four feet deep, inserts a cylindrical form made of thick, hard cardboard, and fills it with cement. The ground slopes away a good six feet from where the new room will join old walls, so, to accommodate the uneven terrain and ensure level floors, the footers must vary considerably in height. Some of them are flush with the ground; others rise up to four feet higher than ground level. Heavy posts — six-by-sixes — will be bracketed onto the footers, and atop them the immense weight of beams, walls, floors, windows, and roof will keep it all stable.

The entire area surrounding the house, front and back, is a boot-sucking muddy chaos. The snow has gone away and left us to deal with a winter's worth of dog turds and debris. Sandra and Harriet left building supplies, old canvas chairs, shoes, and God-knows-what beneath the mudroom and cottage room. Annie and Hank, in their teething frenzy, have hauled it all out for blissful mastication. They have lovely teeth! But in front, the trash and turds are strewn amid a horizontal forest, twenty or so felled trees that still need to be cut, split, and cleared away. Behind, the mess is liberally augmented by lumber, wheel barrow, cement mixer, post-hole digger, bags of cement, and ranks of tall ugly stumps like tombstones.

Little by little, we will clean it all up. It's very simple. People often say to Alan, "I can't imagine building a house; it's so complicated." He insists it isn't; it's just one hole, one board, one nail at a time. Likewise with my gardens-to-be. Alan jokes that I plan to landscape the wilderness.

I suppose I do — at least the part of it that is our clearing. I envision our rocky hillside, now shrouded in black plastic and littered with the carcasses of trees, blooming everywhere with white clover and ground-cover roses, with flowering shrubs and bulbs tucked into hollows and around outcroppings of rock. I see large mowable areas, right up to the edge of the woods, along which I will sow daisies, black-eyed susans, coneflower, bee balm, phlox, asters, and a thousand other zone 3 to zone 4 perennials — perhaps Oriental and Asiatic lilies, too, if I can keep them protected from deer and chipmunks. I see a rock-edged hillock bearing shrubs, small fruit trees, lilacs, sweet woodruff, and ferns. I see clematis clambering up trees, roses climbing the shop, a vegetable garden near where we will one day have a deck. I even see, in a flat sunny spot on the other side of our one-room cabin, below the shop, an organic labyrinth formed by fragrant and decorative herbs lining curvilinear pathways.

This notion comes straight from Nora's book, in which she describes the ancient contemplative practice of walking a labyrinth as a form of prayer, a way to center the soul.

These gardens will occupy me for the rest of my life — winters for planning and design, springs for cleanup and planting, summers for enjoyment and caretaking, autumns for more planting, and for pruning and putting to bed the things I grow.

Yesterday was Emma's birthday. In light of Gillian's tale, I sent no message. I thought honesty would be unwelcome and anything short of that too false. It made me uneasy not to acknowledge the occasion at all, but I could think of no way to do so that would not exacerbate my discomfort.

Last night, I dreamed vividly about Emma, and this morning I woke up knowing what to say to her. I felt I could keep faith with both of us if I described to her what my subconscious had done without my conscious responsibility. Here is the e-mail message I sent:

> I thought of you on your birthday yesterday, even though I could not compose any message that felt right.
>
> Then, last night, I had the following dream: I was in a small, crowded gallery/curio shop/coffee house, and people were milling about. You sat at a table, beneath a painting I had bought for your birthday — it was sort of an impressionist scene of trees, meadow, and sky. The painting suddenly burst into live, three-dimensional bloom, right over your head. Someone asked me why I had given it to you, since we did not seem to be friends anymore, and I answered, "Because I love her."
>
> I am not sure what to make of this, but I suspect, beneath the bewilderment, anger, and hurt we have both felt this past year, there still exists a well of affection from which such images arise. What do you think? Is the well accessible, outside of dreams?

I had thought I was finished with Emma, but my deeper self apparently thinks otherwise. I suppose it is that of God in me that resists my giving up. I hope it is that of God in Emma who opens her e-mail. If this effort goes awry, I tell myself I will not try again. I just don't know whether I believe that.

Gardens

It is no surprise to me that images of natural scenes and gardens appear in my dreams. Gardens are both real and profoundly symbolic to me — they represent both paradise and paradise lost. I became a gardener at thirty-eight, after ending a pregnancy because I had learned that my child would in all likelihood be profoundly disabled, deformed, and ill, if she survived at all.

That pregnancy had been a joyous surprise. I had not thought I could conceive. For the first four months, my life narrowed down to the simple, miraculous state of being pregnant. I was single-minded. I thought only about my changing body and the life inside it, but I felt larger in spirit than I ever had before. Then came shattering news.

I was scheduled for amniocentesis at sixteen weeks, but the technicians could not withdraw enough fluid for genetic analysis. I went in again at eighteen weeks, and although the fluid was withdrawn at last, I was told the baby was smaller than it should be. About a month later, results showed a partial trisomy 2 — extraneous genetic material on one arm of one of the second chromosomes. It took two more weeks and a worldwide literature search to find another case in which the location and amount of anomalous material had been the same, or almost. In that one case, the pregnancy went full term, but the child died at two weeks old of devastating multiple abnormalities.

That was all I had to go on. I was twenty-five weeks pregnant by then, beyond the legal cutoff for abortion. My doctors said to me, to calm my panic, "No one is going to force you to give birth to a child that is probably fatally deformed. And anyway, the baby is small for its dates. You might not be as far along as you have thought."

Some situations in life offer no hope of a right choice. They force us to weigh evils, to base our actions on whatever slight differences we can discern among our appalling options. My options, which to this day feel unbearable to me, were to have my child and thereby, if she lived, choose for her the strong possibility of a life without health, learning, aware-ness, or flourishing, a life perhaps consumed by pain — or to consent to a saline injection that would cause her to die inside my body. That is what I did. I contained her death, assimilated it, bore it within me. Then I went through labor to deliver my dead daughter. I took drugs to stop the flow of my milk. I went home from the hospital with a lap full of flowers covering the tomb that my belly had become.

That was in late May. All summer long, during the season of growth and light, I buried myself in dark grief. I could not live without my child. I could not let my child live. And I could not let go of the joy I had lost or the pain of its ending.

As I faced my late-September due date with no baby on the way, I suddenly began tearing out overgrown vines and neglected shrubs, beefing up soil, planting bulbs, picturing spring. I had never done such a thing before. I worked possessed but did not make the connection between planting and healing until later. In spring, when the green tips emerged, and bloom followed, and I was drawn out every morning to see what else had come up, I understood what a determination we have for life, what energy to create. I learned that one thing is not another — a garden is not a child — but love will seek its level.

Had I planned my garden in order to heal, and had I set out to map love's level, I doubt my efforts would have succeeded. There was some-thing essential in my unconsciousness, in simply doing.

Now, because I simply did what I did almost sixteen years ago, I can always find healing in the garden, a deep spiritual renewal that comes partly from solitude (since I have always, until Alan, gardened alone) and partly from close involvement with natural processes, cycles, scents, and soil. Gardening teaches patience — one learns to think in years, even decades. It teaches balance and proportion — one has to consider each plant in relation to all the others in a garden, to coordinate colors, heights, growing conditions, bloom times, textures, and shapes. And it teaches the folly of too much planning. No matter how carefully you calculate the design of groupings in one corner of your garden, you can be sure that some accidental combination in another will put forth something lovelier, that you never would have thought of.

When I remember the agonies of having to act, but having insufficient light to see my way, and when I still, after all these years, feel the weight of doubt bear down on me and renew the deepest moral fear I have ever known, I look at Adam. I presume nothing about cosmic purposes. I presume only that he would not exist if it were not for his sister's brief, watery, beloved life. Her small sojourn inside me created circumstances that made it possible for Adam to be. He thrives, he is a blessing, he has a sweet soul. Together, Adam and his sister have taught me much of what I know about love, death, terror, and our desperate need for light. I draw on those lessons every day.

And the lessons deepen. I have always affirmed my decision about that abortion, have always said I would do the same thing again. For the first time, I am reviewing that habit of thought, not because my convictions about the necessity of reproductive choice have in any way diminished, but because my internal life has changed.

In recent years, my life has proceeded by celestial navigation — I steer by the light, and the light steers me. From the moment I returned to Meeting in January 1996, I have felt the tug of a surprising satellite controlling my inner tides of faith, emotion, awareness. I took one step, back into the meetinghouse, and this gravitational pull guided me straight to the others. From that first Meeting, my path turned, and on the new one I found a liberating, humane divorce, a new life, a new love, a new home, and a return to half-buried parts of me that experience God, love, and joy directly. These parts, which apprehend my being and the ground of my being, are the source of my new reflections on my choice.

Had I known in 1983 what I know now about the power of love and the way we continuously recreate one another through our empathetic imaginations — as I recreated my mother during her final years and came to love her purely and completely — I wonder if that power might have led me to continue my pregnancy, if only to let my daughter's fate play itself out, without my intervention. Might I have let my daughter live, as I let my mother die her long death, without acting as her agent, without forcing any issues? Perhaps I would have found a kind of strength I thought I lacked, right in the midst of what would test it. Truly, I have no way of knowing. It is equally possible that my intervention was a necessary part of my daughter's fate, that it wasn't entirely my choice at all.

I do know, because something incontrovertible tells me, that Adam is meant to be here, is meant to be my son, has a fate of his own to fulfill. He once told me, when he was between two and three years old and still trailing clouds of glory, that I was the mommy he had "picked out at the people store." Consider that in the light of Hillman's acorn theory, and it is more than a cute toddler fantasy. I believe his soul truly did choose me, as I believe mine chose him. I believe the pronouncement scripted around my friend Ann's window — "The world is not only queerer than we suppose but queerer than we *can* suppose."

Had my daughter been born, I don't see how Adam could have been. Had she lived, my life would have been bound up entirely with her care. Had she died, and had I then conceived another child, the biological complexities that engendered Adam would have been different, and Adam some other baby. Or not. Who knows? Perhaps those complexities would have waited for him. Perhaps every soul waiting to be born gets born, and the others — the aborted, the stillborn, the miscarried — entirely fulfill their purposeful interactions with our own souls during the mothlike span of their lives. My daughter's fluttering presence inside my body, her small swimmer's kicks and strokes, filled me to my whole capacity for love and grief at that time. Once she was gone, I went fallow until that fall, until that first garden. Gardens nourished me until Adam came along. Together, Adam and gardens have opened me further, calling out to that of God in me and causing it to rise. The rising, finally, has brought me Alan and brought me home. It all takes time, it all has purpose. This is what I am learning, as I live and as I write it all down.

Pacifism

Last night Alan and I went to a Simple Supper at the meetinghouse, a bread-and-soup meal put on by Friends to raise money for the Albanian refugees from Kosovo. The proceeds will be sent on to the American Friends Service Committee, pooled with funds from across the country and forwarded abroad to Quakers' efforts on the scene.

Quakers always maintain a presence where armed conflict and its attendant tragedies are taking place. We realize we are regarded as quaint by our friendliest critics, unpatriotic, stupid, or traitors by our angriest ones. But we have always, from George Fox's earliest preachings, borne witness against war because it extinguishes the inner light in its victims and dangerously dims it in the planners and perpetrators. It denies the love of God for all people and nations. It feeds hatred and deepens division, mitigating against the unity of all. War serves human greed and perpetuates habits of thought that make enemies of those who differ with us and from us.

Fox said, in a letter to Charles II in 1660:

> Our principle is, and our practices have always been, to seek peace and ensure it and to follow after righteousness and the knowledge of God, seeking the good and welfare and doing that which tends to the peace of all. We know that wars and fightings proceed from the lusts of men, . . . out of which lusts the Lord hath redeemed us, and so out of the occasion of war.

There are so many convincing arguments for war, as many arguments as there are views of a given trouble spot on this ravaged planet. It is harder to devise strong arguments for peace, negotiation, mediation, nonviolent resolution. Given the adversarial nature of both war and argument, this is not surprising. Peace and argument are antithetical, which might make it appear that peace and logic are, too. It is easy to believe that those of us who would resist war are illogical, unrealistic, or deluded. But someone has to honor and speak for ideals regarded by the majority as unrealistic; someone has to make them more and more familiar to the rest of the culture, as John Woolman and others did with the abolitionist ideal. Though Woolman was aware of how dependent world economies were on the labor of slaves, he persisted in his opposition, along with more and more others, and slavery was finally outlawed. In this country, it took a war to put a full stop to slavery and any trade involving human beings, but, as a pacifist, I believe other means would have worked, had they been considered. By the time the Civil War even began, there had long been passionate, steadily growing opposition to the practice of slavery.

Like most idealists, I tend to believe that our culture's insistence on so-called hard-headed realism and argument have boxed us into a dangerous, tight place. I also believe that cultures, like individuals, can break out of their confinement. Woolman's historic example is one of many that keep modern-day struggles going. How long these take is not up to us. How faithful we are to the light *is* our choice.

And anyway, how logical is our involvement in Kosovo? Consider: In Kosovo, we are fighting because the Serbs wish to eject all ethnic Albanians, whom we defend even though they in turn want to oust the Serbs. In fact, ten or so years ago, it was the Albanians who engaged in ethnic cleansing and the Serbs who were the victims. But NATO supports the ethnic Albanians' effort, which is furthered by the Kosovo Liberation Army, despite the evidence — reported by some underground online sources — that Osama bin Laden is connected with the KLA.

Those we claim to protect through our aggression, the ethnic Albanians, are now worse off than they would have been without our so-called help. Civilians are dying, the work of generations is being destroyed, the environment poisoned. But we are told that Slobodan Milosovic is another Hitler, who must be stopped at all costs. Violence is the only language he understands. And the only remedy for six hundred years of violence is more violence.

Meanwhile, we ourselves are peace-loving, humanitarian people who resort to bombs and destruction only because our enemy forces our hand. We are not supposed to notice that this makes us over in our enemy's image. And we cherish our enemy's image as one of horrific inhumanity, seeing in our opposites no reflection of ourselves.

Quakers take it upon themselves to say, as someone did in Meeting just last week, that there is no right way to do a wrong thing. Quakers believe it is heinously illogical to suppose that one can achieve peace through war, safety through murder, nobility through all that is base and divisive in humankind. To be moral, noble, and truly at peace requires a nation or a people to seek the highest paradigms, not stoop to the level of aggressors, terrorists, or militaristic egomaniacs. Suppose we do destroy Slobodan Milosovic? In a region like the Balkans, where hatred and murder have prevailed for centuries, will such a so-called victory reduce the bitterness one iota? Will it dissipate hatred fomented by centuries of outsiders' meddling? Will it allay deep-seated suspicion? Or can mistrust and violence give way only through the arduous and painful work of reconciliation? Wouldn't peaceful measures eventually take away a Milosovic's foundation for aggressive, brutal leadership?

Last week, a Friend rose in Meeting to ask: Who are the neighbors we are supposed to love as ourselves? She did not begrudge the many local efforts to help the Kosovo refugees, but she was appalled that we have no shelters or accommodations in our own area that can meet the needs of mothers and children. She had recently tried to locate such a place, when a family of ten was evicted from their apartment, and she could find no way to help the family stay together. She wondered why we did not sufficiently take care of our own, why we first create desperate circumstances far away and then attempt to support those whose suffering we have, in large part, been the cause of. She wondered why our nearer neighbors do not even know about the plight of desperate people in our own midst.

If every community, from the Balkans to the Middle East to the gritty streets of our own inner cities, decided to focus with sinewy, difficult love and kinship on its nearest neighbors, resolving conflicts and seeking that of God in everyone, no matter how different, demonized, or threatening, then they would experience what George Fox called "that life and power that takes away the occasion for war." What Fox saw as the causes of war — human "lusts" such as greed and the desire for power — by definition elevate some people over others, and this is possible only through a refusal to know one's neighbors, a willed ignorance of their humanity and realities.

Loving one's neighbor instead of hating and suspecting him is perhaps the most difficult thing a person, community, or nation can do — or, rather, it is the second-most difficult thing. Really, war has got to be harder. Love takes only an inward effort, gargantuan as it might be when we are struggling to love what we have been taught to hate and fear. But love does not kill us, leave us homeless, split up our families, starve our children, destroy our heritage and rob our future, poison our water and land, benumb our souls, or drive us mad with horror. Only war does that, and if we want lasting peace, we must give up war. *That* is logical. We might not be strong enough yet as a human family to renounce violence, but a good first step would be to admit that it doesn't make sense. Without first steps we'll never make the journey at all.

Birds

From my window seat today I have seen two pairs of evening grosbeaks and two pairs of American goldfinches. I have watched a male and a female phoebe swoop back and forth from the trees to the mud-and-grass nest they have built in the eaves just outside my window. I have watched the chickadees and purple finches who have been here for weeks, and I have seen a brown-headed cowbird, some hairy woodpeckers, red-breasted nuthatches, white-breasted nuthatches, countless robins, and, farther down in the woods, crows and ravens. I am hoping cardinals will show up, sooner or later — though they might not like our elevation. I am distracted from writing by the frequent need to grab my binoculars and field guide. The distraction is purely a pleasure.

Emma

A message from Emma this morning read, in its entirety:

> My ongoing thread of communication with you, albeit a thin one, has been intended to keep the well open — if you'll pardon the mixed metaphor.

This surprised me, because I had not noticed any thread at all, just a single brief message last October. Still, it seems affection survives, somewhere near the bottom of the well. I just wonder where we put that rope and bucket. If we never find them, if we never regain access to the love that remains, that love will still be there. More and more, I think that will be enough for me.

Hooks

Adam has been in Pittsburgh all this week, and his father has sent me numerous messages celebrating a new presence and confidence he perceives in his son. It has been four months since he has seen Adam, so the changes are striking. But I see them, too. Adam has blossomed this past year.

Ironically, I worry more about having separated father and son now than I did when we planned this move, and I do so for two reasons. One is that we — all the adults — originally thought that Adam would visit Pittsburgh once a month as well as for extended holidays. That has not happened, apparently because both Adam and his father felt the weekend visits every month were too hectic, not satisfying. That was their choice, and Adam has not complained about it.

The other reason is odder, and it surprises me. When we first moved here, Adam's father was still his old self, incapable of lifting his head out of his work for long, and full of frustration about his life and work — a mood that left him unable to change, take responsibility for his condition, or relate very well or deeply to anyone, even Adam.

Now, he seems to be loosening up, a little at a time, and I assume this is in part because of a relationship he began last summer with a woman he had known when she was a graduate student. She has adult children, she believes in God, and she seems to be presenting this man with new ways to regard his life and habits. The surprising part is, the more he does this, the less I resent him for not having done it sooner, to save our marriage and family. That was not the time or circumstance for him.

I even have wondered — thinking of Hillman's acorn theory — whether the only reason for our marriage was to provide Adam's daimon with his chosen parents. If that is so, I believe we all three agreed to the arrangement, among our separate souls. Whatever the reasons behind any of the mysteries, I feel more compassion now than I could before. This father does not have his son in his daily life, and the superficial reason for that is his earlier inability to *be* a father in any active, perceptive, attentive way. Other reasons go deeper, into him and into me.

When we make morally ambiguous choices in our lives, we know that the circumstances under which we choose are not static — we can't foresee the long-range impact of our actions.

I chose to move to Vermont with Alan, and I chose it for both Alan and myself. We wanted the same things, and I could not refuse either of us for the sake of someone else, especially someone I had allowed to constrain my life for far too long. I considered Adam's welfare, using all my emotional and thoughtful capacities. I considered his father, too. But this time I also considered myself. In leaving my ex-husband, in joining with Alan, in moving to Vermont, in nearly severing some long-standing friendships — in every choice and act — I finally learned a simple lesson: It is perfectly all right to let people off the hook, provided we don't dangle from it in their place.

Trying to hold other people specifically accountable for their actions and their treatment of us — that is, trying to change them or to prescribe their behavior — does not put them on the hook. Only they themselves can do that, and only they can climb down. When I stayed with Adam's father for Adam's sake, and when I put up with neglect and disregard, I chose that course of action myself. But the choice meant putting myself on a hook that did not belong to me. It meant trying to save a marriage from troubles I had not, in most cases, created.

When I took myself off that hook and left the marriage, I climbed up onto another hook, this one my own. It had many prongs, representing acts for which I was truly responsible — initiating divorce, loving someone else, leaving Pittsburgh, separating Adam from his father. The latter was difficult, but the alternative was to let Adam's father build a belated father-son relationship at my expense, and Alan's. Given a job I disliked, my changing, waning friendships, and a longing for this north-woods life with Alan, that overdue possibility would have been my main reason for staying. It was not enough.

I would do the same again, even knowing what I know now — that I can feel, for the man I used to love, something more generous than resentment, frustration, and impatience. This newer form of caring has been a struggle, but it is a relief from the cold exasperation that prevailed for years before I could finally leave.

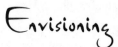

Envisioning

Slowly, the look of our land is changing. Alan and I have spent two days cleaning up. He has cut the last of the downed trees into "bite-sized pieces" that I can remove. I have raked up endless piles of trash, turds, old leaves, and other organic litter. Alan tilled the area in front of the house; I smoothed it and sowed grass seed. I cleared everything my rake could reach from under the mud room and cottage. I even built a small stone retaining wall along an unstable dirt ledge on the little hillside I cleared. It's about three feet long and one foot high, and it resembles other tiny walls that Sandra built here and there to hold a bit of bank in place. Now I need to dig up wild blackberry from that area and begin deciding what will go where amid the ferns that remain.

I become obsessed. I ignore my writing assignments and my arthritic shoulder. I will pay for this. But when the sun is out, the air cool, the light spilling off of every hemlock needle and birch branch, I am simply driven outside. I will be forced to rest my shoulder, which will see to it that my work for the commissioners does not go neglected for long. But as soon as I can move again, I will be outside, moving wood, raking debris, digging the earth, transplanting the perennials I missed last fall, which are sprouting everywhere — irises, especially. Then, when the seeds I have planted indoors sprout and grow, I will move them to the spots I have prepared. There will be hundreds of seedlings, annuals and perennials! Trips to the nursery just north of us, in Elmore, will burden the truck with shrubs, groundcovers, a tree or two. It all blooms in full, three-dimensional color inside my head. One day, I will walk right out our door and into my own vision.

I believe this because other things I picture come true. Adam flew in from Pittsburgh last night, and we picked him up at the airport, as usual. I always create in my mind's eye the image of him stepping out of the long covered corridor from the plane and into the terminal. That is exactly what happens. He emerges smiling, his dark blond hair a shining helmet, his eyes glad and a little shy, as if he's afraid I will make a public display of how crazy I am about him. He carries a duffel bag over his right shoulder, and with his left hand he sketches a little wave when he sees us. I restrain my urge to squeeze him. I say, "I didn't miss you at all, you know." He grins. "I didn't miss you either." What a delicious moment.

Today, Adam seeks Alan out with questions, stories of his visit, things to share. This would not have happened a year ago. They have inched slowly closer — they seem to like each other's company, they make each other laugh. This too is what I have held in my mind and waited for like spring.

Two years ago, near the end of April, Alan sent me a book he had found while browsing the hoo-hah section. *Dancing Moons* is an illustrated compendium of spiritual reflections for each month of the year. April's was on regeneration:

> Now is the time to learn how to breathe all over again. . . . Passing through a time of solitude and introspection makes you realize how precious simple things are. . . . Ask yourself: Is there enough of you to go around? Do people expect too much? Is your work something you want to do? Or have to do? Do you yearn for a new place? A new person with whom to share your life? . . . Regeneration allows you to grow wings. . . . Regeneration means that you can start growing all over again, this time from the inside out. There is time for everything, even that which you thought too late to happen.

The words were an uncanny description of exactly what was happening in Alan's and my separate lives as we gradually came together. The images — the envisionings — we held were images of regeneration, and they were becoming real.

Growing from the inside out means listening to that of God, paying attention to what the inner light illuminates, and engendering from that source a vision of how life can be. We are so much more than we think we are. We are wild creatures, with God inside us, and we have the power to envision and to realize our visions. I have gone from skepticism about this to experiencing it directly. Now I understand that I have always experienced it. I just didn't grasp what was happening — I thought it coincidence, accident.

Prayer is the heart of this creative process. When I was a child, about eight or ten, I prayed for specific things. Twice, when I focused beyond my own interests, my prayers were answered to the letter in a matter of days. The first time, I prayed for a girl my age whom I had never met. She was the daughter of someone my father worked with, and she had contracted bulbar polio. I had no idea then, nor for many years afterward, that "bulbar" referred to the involvement of the medulla oblongata, the part of the brain that controls the body's involuntary functions. Obviously, the child's prognosis was dire. That much I understood, and

I asked God to make her better. I could vividly imagine the pain and delirious terror of severe illness, and I put all that imagining into my petition. Within a week, my father came home and announced that, to the doctors' great surprise, his coworker's daughter was expected to recover, with no permanent effects.

I prayed again, this time for the Korean War to end. I have no clear recollection of why I did this. I did not know anyone in the military, and I was not worried for myself or my family. I think I pictured blood and killing and was so repelled by the images that I dove head first into passionate begging that they would stop. Or perhaps I only imagine myself imagining in this way. Perhaps I was just in training to be called a bleeding-heart liberal. But the war ended.

I don't mean to suggest that my childhood prayers alone cured another child's polio or ended a war. Prayer is mysterious to me — I often feel my prayers are answered, but not literally in most cases. That is why, these days, I don't pray for anything specific unless those I love are in some kind of trouble. I offer gratitude, I heap praise on God for this spectacular world, I ask for a larger heart, I pray for light, patience, courage, and guidance. I keep my senses, all six or seven of them, tuned for cosmic signals. Mostly, I pray: Be with me. Be with us. Show me the way.

The strange, surprising power of imagination and emotion, which to me are components of prayer, is what got me through Alan's and my first phone conversation and an inexplicable terror that followed it.

When Alan sent me the redwood bowl, he also sent a photograph "of him who made it." In this shot, he sits up high in a driftwood tree next to the blue Pacific. He wears sunglasses, a baseball cap, and a full beard. I liked the photo, but it didn't tell me a thing about what Alan looked like.

I realized I would have to send a photo in return. I had none of recent vintage that I could bear for him to see, so I asked both Adam and my friend Gillian to take some snapshots of me. I sent Alan one or two by each of them, and no two looked like they were pictures of the same person. I have a changeable face.

Alan detected my uptightness about being photographed, especially in the ones by Gillian. "What was she pointing at you, a Howitzer?"

Once we had these uninformative photos in our possession, we decided we should speak on the phone. Little by little, we were narrowing the space between, becoming ever more real to each other. I had already invited Alan to visit. He had already accepted and was planning to pull his red truck up to my curb on May 30.

We set our phone date for April 22. We were nervous. We both had the heebie-jeebies. That morning, Alan wrote:

{{{{{{{{{{{{gulp}}}}}}}}}}}}
OK. Will call tonight.

I wrote back:

Not sure when (if?) gonna breathe again.
    If you get recording that says we're on the phone, it just means some doofus has called untimely and I'm tryin' like hell to shut 'em up. K-K-K-Kate

The phone was going to ring at nine-thirty Eastern Time, after Adam was in bed. I lit candles, poured a glass of wine, and sat in the living room, waiting, with the phone on the couch beside me. On the dot, Alan called. I answered on about the third ring, and his first question was, Had I decided in advance how many times I was going to let it ring before picking up?

The conversation was fun, if a little self-conscious on both ends. I don't remember what we talked about, but we talked for an hour or so. All the while, I was aware of Alan's voice, smack inside my head, resonating, insisting. *Alan* did not insist — he was nothing if not gentle and proper. But my mind took insistent hold of him — his presence, his reality, his escape from the computer screen and into the gift he had sent, the unrevealing photograph, the words in my ear, his mouth so close I could just about feel his breath.

I got into bed that night, turned the lights out, and panicked. Over and over I thought, Oh, God, how did this happen, I can't do this, I want out. I don't want Alan, I don't want anyone, ever.

I knew right where I was, a place described vividly by John Welwood in *Journey of the Heart*, a book on intimate relationships that had affected me strongly. I shared it with Alan, who was equally heartened and inspired. Welwood lays out in this book, clearly and eloquently, the need for a new focus in male-female relationships—a focus on soul. To accomplish this, one must sometimes dwell for a while on the razor's edge, a place of terror, a place where one reveals oneself to another. If you tell the truth, there at the razor's edge, it can also be a place of great intimacy and growth, a place where fear gets dispelled and love deepens.

I spent that night trying to sleep on that sharp straight line, but it didn't happen.

There's a huge responsibility in telling the truth, especially to someone you care about. I cared enormously for Alan, and yet I was poised for flight. Why? It wasn't anything he said — he said only funny, kind, or poignant things. It wasn't how he said it — he had a slow, deep voice, and he didn't overstate or exaggerate anything. But his voice was uniquely his own in timbre and pitch, and its individuality made him too close, too real, too ready to follow where our growing intimacy would lead.

I had not been emotionally or physically intimate with anyone for most of a decade. I had never been intimate at a soul level, had never built a relationship on spirit and faith above all. Suddenly I found myself grabbing for my box lid and trying to wrestle it back onto my life. But that impulse was a piece of truth I knew I would not mention to Alan. I would not tell him about my full-blown panic at the prospect of love and joy. Something else, which proved in possession of a stronger truth, would make me very careful.

Soon after we hung up, while I was tossing around in bed, Alan wrote:

All of a sudden time just melts. Heebie-jeebies melt also, becomes peaceful, easy. I like very much the voice that now goes with the face. Warm, good, sleepy feeling this night.

I wrote back and told him I had felt the same easiness and pleasure in our conversation. Then I got to the hard part:

No sleep all night, very strong sense of edge, night of feeling old and deep stuff surfacing. Must tell you about this, because I think it is where I either greet the razor's edge or start rationalizing, pretending, doing old things. This is new territory, need new tools (you the tool guy, right?). I don't understand the agitated feelings except that I think they are connected with having been alone for such a long time. That "stuck" place in which I lived with my ex-husband for nearly a decade had to be, in part, of my own choosing, but I've not understood why I stayed in it for so long.

That stuck place was not at all comfortable for me, was filled with sadness, anger, sense of loss — but not with fear, was too familiar for that. Think I am right now feeling small panic at sudden bursts of speed in my life. Hope you will stay with me, help me slow down dizzy feeling a little.

Alan was calm and reassuring. He seemed to take my attack of nerves in stride. And he confided:

If it is any solace, you are not the only one who had a sleepless night — mine was not last night but the night I brought Welwood's book home and again the night after I read it.

He added, when I said I was grateful for his calm replies:

I am surprised myself at the calmness I feel, although the edge of the razor is probably sharper than it has ever been.

After I had thought further about my "all-night butterflies," I started to get a better sense of their origins:

I've gotten very used to doing everything for myself, being alone, being independent — and also doing without love and intimacy. I can think I am OK with this because, hey, I stay on top of everything, take care of everything, raise Adam, keep house, go to work, see friends, take part in Meeting — have a full life. Except — big hole where love and intimacy remain absent. So how real is self-love if it does not expand outward to embrace, invite another?

Comes into this picture someone who seems to know how to love, to take care, to give, to invite intimacy, and seems willing to accept these in return.

And (same) someone who lives very far away, is messages on a screen and through a milkbox. Very lovely messages, exciting, open, real — but still far away.

And then this someone is a voice — nice, deep, slow voice which sounds very immediate and real and full of care. Reality of this far-off person comes rushing in fast and breaks right on top of all that aloneness. All my habitual ways of being, which have kept me upright for years if not a lifetime, feel suddenly shaky.

All the while, I was feeling split down the middle, sometimes attacked by butterflies-turned-bats and sometimes sure the creatures were illusions bent on putting me back into spaces too small for me. In view of this, Alan could not have replied better than he did:

> Into my life comes also this picture. Although my reality of this far-off person came not last night, but when Welwood came into my home. All-of-a-sudden understanding of *my* habitual ways — very much like my father, strong, stoic, silent on the outside, and inside a heart and soul that cried out to be seen and accepted. This space-between has been the only place in my life where this part of me has been so openly accepted, encouraged, and I will be ever grateful to you for this. You honor me with the trust you have in me to be able to express these thoughts — your daimon — with me.
>
> As much as I understand it, this is Welwood's message. The conflict within *is* the razor's edge — and for any relationship to succeed, to grow, it has to have a place in it where these conflicts and fears can be shared, acknowledged, and honored.
>
> I will tell you my truths in any and all ways that I can. And please, call if you need or want to hear a voice to go with the words — any time. I am here for you.

Now, here is my thought two years later, almost to the day — that as Alan was calming the Kate who suffered butterflies and bats at night, and as that Kate was wrestling with both a longing to meet another soul and a terror at the leap of faith that that would require, this Kate, the one who is writing these words now, was (is) saying: Take the leap, take the leap. And that Kate, then, does.

Perhaps this is how it always works. Perhaps silent messages get passed from our later to our earlier selves. Perhaps if we could hear our later selves better, we would not feel compelled to plan and control our lives so tightly in the present.

I think, with Alan, my imagination refused to let go of the vision that was coming true then and is now the whole shape of our life. I think Alan and I invented each other—we made each other in the image of our fondest desires. We are both different now from the ways we were before. We are larger, we touch our own and each other's souls. We have entered our own imaginings and found each other there.

We also understand that our spiritual and often silent bond is not credible to many who have not experienced it. That, I realize, is another reason I am writing all this—so that someone else might come to believe in the power our souls have to make another person as real and important to us as we ourselves. I have no doubt that the fate of the world rests in the power of our souls and not in our hearts and minds alone. We might as well start with our closest relationships, infusing them with spirit and learning from them how to take spirit with us everywhere.

Hollow Children

Time and *Newsweek* arrived today, both with cover stories about last week's shooting at Columbine High School in Littleton, Colorado. The cover of *Time* bore blown-up photos of the two young killers, surrounded by smaller shots of their victims, with the headline "The Monsters Next Door." I don't know whether this was meant as poignant irony—a way of saying, Look at these innocent, handsome faces; these boys did not look like killers.

Everyone is asking, how could such violence happen? To me, the cover of *Time* reflects a way of thinking that is itself a contributing factor. Regardless of the intended tone of the headline, the implication is that these boys were bad seeds, they were either born evil or readily turned. They gave no obvious clue, they were so canny. How could privileged, bright young men become so angry and cold? The same questions, exactly, were asked about Leopold and Loeb. Our perceptions of evil and our search for antidotes haven't changed much in almost eighty years.

As a Quaker, I think our questions do not look deeply enough into ourselves or the killers. If we really want to know what makes killers of people still in childhood or barely out of it, clues abound in a culture that worships wealth and material success and that continues to believe in the efficacy of violence, the justice of revenge, the exclusive supremacy of the rational mind and five senses — a society that pays little attention to soul and the merest lip service to the challenge of respecting others as ourselves. I am not suggesting here that any kind of formal religion should enter public life but that public life should reflect the best in us, which comes from the promptings of our souls. We can't see the light in others if we don't perceive it in ourselves.

If we all taught our children that they and everyone else have a light inside them, we could change the world. We need not raise them in any particular creed, but we can encourage reflection, empathy, and intuition, qualities that together open the eyes to the light. We can acknowledge their emotions, which are another important pathway to soul, and we can celebrate their imaginations, which are the seat of soulful envisionings and creativity. We can help our kids resist conformity and value diversity. We can help them understand that evil of every kind comes from denying, squelching, wounding, or disrespecting the soulful qualities in ourselves or in others. Those qualities are connectors; they build bridges among people. Denying them divides us from one another.

The jocks in cars who throw beer cans at nerds on bicycles are digging gulfs and bombing bridges. They can't know the effects of their divisive cruelty in advance. They can't know where or how deeply the shrapnel will lodge. When they toss around casual evil, laughing and thinking little of it, they are nevertheless responsible if the consequences breed violence and horror, as they did in Littleton. But if no one teaches children from birth that they are responsible for the outcomes of their actions, and that their actions affect other people, they might never discover these elemental facts of life.

When teenagers can lose their friends and their standing just for wearing the wrong clothes or talking to the wrong person in the lunch room, it means outward symbols and trappings have become everything to them. It means our children have learned emptiness — they have been hollowed out. That is how they become cold enough to jeer and, in the extreme, cold enough to kill both others and themselves. That is how they lose both self-love and the ability to empathize with another person.

The only thing that fills the emptiness, instead of assuaging it briefly with popularity and material goods, is some awareness of their universal humanity — their souls, their higher selves, their inner light — and their interdependence with everyone else in this knotty web of being. When everything our kids encounter, in and out of school, focuses on competition, individuality, material gain, and striving — when parents, television, films, ads, and computer games perpetuate adversarial models and messages — it is no wonder when children and teens fail to develop any deep identity at all, just a set of fearful, dark reactions. It is no wonder that they cannot find peace or the light within. Too much surface noise.

Adam is fond of computer games, including ones in which the first-person shooter blows away as many enemies as possible in order to save his own skin. I monitor what he plays and for how long, and I especially monitor the attitude he conveys, but I don't forbid the games. In part, I believe boys his age manage fear and aggression by playing these computer games and by chasing each other through the woods with their Nerf guns. That is, healthy boys do this, and boys are healthy when they respect others, when they have adults teaching them that true violence is altogether a different and unacceptable thing from games and toys — but that we all sometimes have violent feelings we must learn to manage. Adam can tell the difference between real and on-screen violence. In fact, when he was ten and put his arm through a window and had to have surgery to repair a tendon, he said, even while he was still shocky, "If this is what real violence does to people, it's horrible."

I have read that the military uses computer games to desensitize soldiers. I know films and television, with their diabolically realistic special effects, can numb those who watch them. But I don't believe the numbing comes directly from these media. I think the numbing — and in turn the media that increasingly manifest and foster it — comes originally through a filter of teaching and life experience. I trust completely that Adam is incapable of real violence, and I trust that because of the way he is with his friends, the way he feels about himself, the humor and intelligence he displays, the way he is learning to deflect teasing or nastiness from others, and his general lack of any urgent concern with what is "cool."

Adam believes hunting desensitizes people to violence even more than computer games and movies do. I point out that that depends on the hunter, that many who hunt are deeply knowledgeable about the natural world and passionate about protecting it, that they hunt for the meat and the hides, that they do not waste or disrespect their prey. He nods, considering, but he is not convinced. To him, hunting remains an enterprise in which innocent creatures are killed for no good-enough reason.

I probe Adam about the catastrophe at Columbine High. Would he come to me if he were feeling alone, angry, fearful, depressed? He says yes. I say promise? He says yes. But neither of us knows, really. Adolescence is indeed a time when children must test their limits and loosen the ties to parental control. What comes with the territory is a lack of any mature judgment about when to stay close and when to range farther away than ever. I try to give Adam the latitude he shows me he can handle, but I don't always know what that is.

I tell Adam I am not asking him to come to me, or to some other adult he trusts, because I think he could ever hurt anyone else. I am asking because I don't want *him* to hurt. I want him to know he is loved and can always find help. If I succeed in getting this message across to him, I will protect both Adam and others.

May

Going Gentle

The farmers' market resumed today, perfect proof of spring. I drove to Sarah's, and we walked from her house. It was sunny and warm, people thronged the booths. I bought olive bread to go with chili for dinner and cinnamon buns for tomorrow's breakfast, since Adam has a friend staying over tonight. I bought a few perennial plants — sweet Annie, gayfeather, coreopsis — just what I could carry on the walk back to Sarah's house. It was hard to resist all the other seedlings, baked goods, crafts, bouquets of spring flowers. I remember that last year it was chill and rainy on the first day of the market, when Alan and Adam and I were in Vermont to close on this house. Even so, the celebratory feeling was just as strong.

Sarah was more upbeat than I have seen her since Easter, despite the crises that keep erupting in her parents' lives. The most recent is that her father must quit drinking, because he is endangering others in the retirement community, burning sausage or bacon at all hours. He must attend a rehabilitation program in another facility. He is angry, ashamed, and frightened. So is Sarah. By the time I left her house — after a long sit and a cup of coffee in the sun — she was sad again. She does not want to wish her parents a quick death, but she sees only grief and crisis for them the longer they live. She thinks her father will not stay in the rehabilitation program, even though he has agreed to go. If he does not change his attitude — at eighty-five! — he might not be able to return to the retirement community. Sarah has no idea where he could go instead.

I think one thing that is so hard for Sarah, when she contemplates her parents' deaths, is how much they themselves fear death. I remember when Emma's mother, Helen, died a few years ago. She too was in her mid-eighties. She had been hospitalized for cancer, but she was stabilized and about to be sent home. There, she would be attended by a visiting nurse. She would sleep in a makeshift bedroom on the first floor so that she would not have to climb the stairs. Nothing was going to be the same. Her children gathered round and tried to encourage her to accept her new reality, pointing out that she would feel better once she was home. When Emma tried this line on Helen, Helen gave her a little smile and a wave and said, "Time to go bye-bye." She died twenty minutes before she was to leave the hospital. It seems she was right — it was time to go, and she not only did not resist, she put on her traveling shoes. That made her death far easier for her children to bear than if she had gone struggling and terrified, as Sarah's parents seem likely to do.

Dylan Thomas, the poet who wrote the line "Do not go gentle into that good night," was only in his thirties when he died. Going gentle in old age seems to me an enviable, admirable thing, but one that is possible only after a life in which a person has learned how, and when, to let go.

Amazing Grace

Last night Alan and I went to what was billed as a "town meeting" on the war in Kosovo, a discussion led by Vermont's only congressman, Bernie Sanders, long the only independent in the Washington power structure. Bernie, as he is known to all Vermonters, has always fought for the little guy, urged the reenfranchisement of people who do not vote (the majority), and refused to declare himself a member of either party because he claims both are in business simply to serve those who are already wealthy and powerful. Bernie is a good guy, but his reception last night was not warm. He had voted to continue the bombing, and most in the audience were aghast, especially his longtime supporters.

There was a panel of four speakers, each of whom delivered about ten minutes' worth of comments, representing several perspectives. Then Bernie spoke, limiting himself to the same amount of time. Then audience members who had signed up to speak had their turns at the microphone. There were some calm and persuasive speakers, but more were hot under the collar. I was surprised by how many pacifists were in the audience but also dismayed by how unpacific some were in their speech. There was a lot of rudeness, interruption, shouting, and booing. One man, in his early twenties or so, ended his two minutes at the mike by shouting, "I . . . HATE . . . THE . . . MILITARY!!!" The screaming amplification of his voice made his words sound like bombs whistling down. His energy was precisely the same energy that makes war.

The hardest thing is not to work against something, which draws us in to negative energy, but to work for something, which draws on our creativity and love. This young man was not a maker of peace but a ranter against violence. What a difference!

Still, he was perhaps easier to read than Bernie, who said, "If you think there is a simple solution to this problem, then you don't know very much about this problem." Did he mean to make those of us who want an end to the bombing feel stupid and uninformed? Was that a defense against his own limitations in dealing with a set of ambiguities so appalling in their effect?

There *is* a simple, if profoundly challenging, solution to this and every war, and that is to declare war wrong, the way we declared slavery wrong. Otherwise we will continue to fight evil with evil, just as we did with slavery in this country. We ended that institution with a war — so how shall we end war? With more wars? Perhaps war is the ultimate evil precisely because it is the one with which we attack all the others. It becomes our first resort, precluding any hope of peaceful resolutions. It reinforces fear, preempts love.

Slavery, like war, was a dark thread woven tightly into an intricate social and economic situation, one with international repercussions.

Little by little, though, people came to see that slavery was base and inhumane. Abolitionist groups were active long before changing economies and new technologies made slavery seem less crucial, long before slavery was outlawed anywhere, abroad or in the United States. Some abolitionists were onetime slaveholders who had a change of heart. They looked into their souls. Gradually, by persuasion, change, or force, cultures here and abroad changed, breaking out of moral boxes that had imprisoned their souls as they themselves had imprisoned their slaves.

Nowadays we seem to fear any revelation of our souls, any open search for the light. Anything is possible, though. Consider John Newton, an eighteenth-century contemporary of the abolitionist Quaker John Woolman and the captain of a British slave vessel, who underwent a conversion — a sea change — in the course of his dealings in the Triangle Trade. Newton had been a drinker, a whorer, an atheist, a corrupter of younger seamen, a fervid preacher against soul and God. Eventually, however, even Newton recognized the evil in his enterprise and refused to deal any further in human lives. He wrote the beloved hymn, "Amazing Grace." He was blind, and then he saw.

A simple solution to any longstanding evil is not the same as an easy one. In the matter of war it seems dangerous, nearly impossible. We fear we will be subjected to aggression if we refuse to be aggressors. War depends entirely on traps set by fear and intellect alone: We must prepare to defend ourselves; we must outgun our enemies; only violence of perpetually increasing magnitude can turn away violence. And look where this has brought us. The Cold War may be over, but now we fear rogue states, terrorists with nuclear weapons, biological and chemical warfare, even cyber-terrorism made possible by stealth, anonymity, and sophisticated technology. We wonder, Just where did those missing Soviet "suitcase bombs" go?

Meanwhile, most people feel foolish even talking about the power inherent in nonviolent action performed in solidarity and by great numbers of people. Few mention that in war the majority permit a much smaller number — usually the young, often the poor, the illiterate — to sacrifice themselves in the majority's behalf. Hardly anyone seems to think this is in any way irresponsible. Hardly anyone seems to have faith in how hungry for peace, and the redistribution of resources swallowed by military establishments, the people of the world are. Without the need to prepare for war, there would be fewer reasons for war. Relieved of the crushing burden — which, to a select few, represents highly profitable enterprises — of maintaining a standing army, researching and producing weapons, engaging in espionage, and continuously posturing at geographic and ideological borders, nations could educate, house, clothe, feed, and care for their citizens. Thomas Jefferson once said, "The care of human life and happiness, and not their destruction, is the first and only object of good government." If governments took that to heart, who among their citizens would feel bellicose?

But of course it is not citizens but governments that make war in the first place. And they do it in the name of taking care of their own and other people — defending liberty, acquiring territory, undermining oppressors. This is the burn-a-village-to-save-a-village mentality. Most people see through it; they just don't know how to undermine it. But most people — that is, the citizens — will someday have to be the ones to say, No, not this way. Without the consent and participation of its citizens, no government could carry out a war.

First, citizens will have to undergo a change of heart and soul like John Newton's, two hundred years ago. We will have to see the anguish of war as if we had a choice about it, the way Newton saw the anguish of his brothers and sisters stacked like stovewood in the airless, filthy hold of his vessel. We will have to look at all the costs of war, not only the deaths but the grieving, the damage to whole nations' souls, the stolen futures, the unborn children of those who die, the unrealized dreams, and we will have to ask whether any war has ever saved more than it has lost. No one else will take these issues on, and we ourselves can do it only through love and amazing grace, not through fury and outrage. Fury leads to hatred, the absence of all love, and an absence cannot generate the very thing it lacks. The only natural offspring of hatred is war, in all its cold and hot forms, which can never in turn beget peace, only lulls in violence.

Only love can bring forth the healing and human understanding that allow us all to live together without violence. Love being difficult, however, we have tended to turn reflexively to argument, judgment, hatred, and war. To change this, we will need to develop the disciplines of love, its sharp-eyed qualities, its necessary toughness, its commitment to discerning and telling hard truths like those in Kosovo, like those of John Newton or John Woolman. Speaking truth to power is not just a slogan but an urgent, strenuous necessity.

Now that Alan has finished digging twenty-four holes, has filled them all with cement — a substance he loathes — and has framed the floors of the new living room and furnace room, he is rewarded by getting to build a twenty-eight-foot chimney for said furnace. This is something he is learning, and cursing, as he goes.

We have ordered a Sam Daniels furnace from a century-old Vermont company headquartered nearby. A human Daniels of recent vintage, named Jim, came out and drew up the specs for us. This furnace will have two units, one for burning wood, the other for oil. The chimney therefore needs two flues, one for each kind of exhaust. Alan has hauled home tons and tons of large cement blocks and orange clay liners. He stacks the blocks two by two and slides the liners into them. He has laboriously cut neat round holes in the liners where the pipes will feed into the chimney. He mortars it all together and then stands back and calls it crooked. Never mind that the whole ugly structure will be housed inside walls or siding; Alan will remember every single place where it is off by half an inch.

The cardboard modeling we did was not for nothing, but it doesn't have all the detail we need. Alan is still perplexed by the bit of roof that will cover a wedge-shaped breezeway in which there will be a set of stairs leading from the existing living room — soon to be dining room — down into the new one. This roof will have to link the dining room's peaked roof, which juts out from a corner of the main rectangle of the house at a forty-five-degree angle, with the new living room's shed roof, which will slope away from the house at roughly a seventy-five-degree decline. As hard as this is to describe, it will be a thousand times harder to execute. Alan won't know how to configure this linking roof until everything else is fully framed.

He has also decided, given the steep drop right near where he will be constructing the living room, that he will build our deck sooner rather than later. It's either that or build a temporary scaffolding from which to work, and why do that when we plan a deck in any case? But that will require fourteen more holes filled with cement.

This, I now see, is what Alan meant when he said a house should grow like a sculpture. There are so many odd angles and topographical variations to deal with that those alone can make an accurate plan impossible. Then, of course, there are the bits of view that we want to emphasize, the two little hemlocks on a small ledge that we want to save, and all our efforts to predict how we will actually use these many odd spaces we are designing together.

Alan groans and mutters, measures and shakes his head. But I love this process. It just unfolds, like the rest of our life.

Joints and Bones

I sent a draft of my most recent assignment in to the Department of Education commissioners on Monday, expecting to revise during the course of the week for a deadline tomorrow. But the department is in turmoil. The commissioner is resigning for health reasons, and the deputy has been out of town because of an illness in her family. No one has looked at my article, so, although I need the money and worry about having no work for several days, I am free to work outdoors some more.

Today, I have continued raking and clearing debris. I've had a recurring sore shoulder, so I take one of Alan's painkillers before I go out. We both have arthritis, and Alan has been told it is worse here, where barometric changes are more rapid, big, and frequent than in Oregon. Alan has suffered for years and is in the habit of masking the pain in order to work. He says that once he is finished for the day, the pain is no worse than when he started, so he sees no reason not to keep pushing. I worry more than he does. We are both taking glucosamine, which supposedly helps rebuild worn cartilage. We have learned we are supposed to avoid tomatoes, eggplant, peppers, mushrooms — our favorite foods! Soon, between the demands of our joints and our cardiovascular systems, we will be able to eat nothing but twigs and berries. I could actually manage something close to that, but not Alan. A whole-wheat cracker, to Alan, is about as appealing as a slice of Presto-Log.

This afternoon, I went in to Bear Pond Books in Montpelier with Adam and saw a book on qigong (pronounced "chee-GUNG") lying on a chair. Qigong is a Chinese approach to righting the flow of life energy in the body. I looked through the book and then bought it, hoping for anything at all that can restore a degree of suppleness and strength to our aching bodies. Alan, in a similar quest, has ordered us yet another bed. We've slept on a waterbed, a standard, high-quality inner-spring mattress with a pillow top, and a Tempur-pedic bed that molded itself to our individual contours after absorbing our body heat. Not one has permitted a full night's sleep, especially for Alan. Now we are going to try an air bed. He is desperate to sleep past 3 A.M., when pain usually wakes him up. So far, since our move to Vermont, his best sleep has been on the air mattress in the loft at Christmas. So, here we go.

We are too young to be so crippled. Much of Alan's pain comes from having broken his back so long ago. I don't know where mine comes from. My mother had arthritis, mainly in her hands. I have it in my neck, shoulders, hands, wrists, elbows, and lower back — or at least I have pain and stiffness in all those places. I suspect the cause is years of emotional stress at home and at work. But that is finished, now, and so I am counting on qigong, not only because it involves no drugs but also because it harmonizes with spirit, drawing upon a life force that is surely related to that of God.

I refuse not to work in the garden, so I need to find a way to keep doing it. I did not step into this simple life just to be prevented from living it.

Green Fire

I made a great discovery at this morning's farmers' market, which is that lavender survives as a perennial here. I had read otherwise, but a woman from Morrisville, fifteen or twenty miles north of us, was selling healthy, just-dug plants in six-inch pots. She assured me that good drainage and winter mulch are the only secrets. I bought two plants, each with lots of fresh green among last year's dried gray stems and foliage. I can put these in the ground right away, since they just came out of hers and are nicely hardened off. Next week, I plan to look for more perennials, shrubs, and trees. There's a nursery a dozen miles north that's noted for their winter-hardy stock. Tomorrow, if the rain holds off, I will yank more wild blackberry and rake more spaces clear for planting. My blood responds to this prospect like maple sap to spring.

Meanwhile, in just the past four or five days, the trees in our woods have burst into a green so incandescent it seems like flame. The woods seems to have edged closer to the house than when the trees were naked. The haze of red over the hills nearby, formed by the flowers on the maples, has given way to a light cover in many shades of green. The world beyond my window seat seems more secret, the birds harder to see, the distant sounds more muffled. I can still picture these woods bare and deep in snow, and the new green, superimposed on that image, is as tender and surprising as if there had been no transition at all — no thaw, no mud season, no buds, just instant spring.

Sticky Buns

Adam had his dates wrong. He thought this commercial, guilt-inducing Mother's Day holiday was next week. Much as I dislike its money-mongering agenda, I still want Adam to develop habits of remembering and acknowledging the important people in his life — so I guilt-tripped him, just a little. That was yesterday. I told him it was no longer his father's job to remind him about my birthday or Mother's Day, and it had never been Alan's job to do so. It was too late for Adam to run out and buy some last-minute trinket that probably would have shown more urgency than thought in any case. So my sweet son decided to make sticky buns for breakfast.

Baking is a new skill and a new interest. Adam is taking "Living Arts" in school, and last week they made cinnamon rolls. He decided to up-grade to sticky buns in my honor, and he found a recipe in the new *Joy of Cooking*. Last night, he mixed the dough and set it to rise overnight in the fridge. This morning, he was up before I was, rolling the dough, sprin-kling on the cinnamon and sugar, forming the rolls, making the sticky syrup, putting everything in loaf pans to rise once more. Then he baked them. They rose a good four inches over the tops of the pans — Adam's eyes were huge. He unmolded the buns onto a plate and surveyed the glazed creation as if he himself had invented yeast, flour, butter, sugar, nuts. He beamed at us and served us with a genuine joy of cooking in his eyes.

Those buns were the best thing I ever ate. They tasted of love and pride. Adam took the second pan next door, to Carter's family, to thank them for the Friday night routines involving dinner and a video and acceptance into a second family. He was beside himself waiting for our neighbors to eat their sticky buns.

Now he has decided he wants to cook dinner for us some night. He will search our cookbooks, choose a recipe, and make a grocery list. I will get the ingredients.

I have tried to interest Adam in cooking from time to time, but my effort never took. I taught him grilled cheese sandwiches and quesadil-las, variations on a theme. That was that. But now the time is right. He's learning with his peers, and it's cool for guys to cook (I guess Adam is not totally insensible to coolness after all). The next scheduled dish at school is pizza, another excuse to make a yeast dough. Adam would never admit it, but I suspect he gets a pleasure like my own from the miracle of yeast, the fragrant way it takes a lumpen mass and makes it breathe.

Nurseries

Yesterday I taxed my body to its limits, pulling blackberry and bindweed from the smaller of my two rocky hillsides. Last year at this time, the hill was wooded and thick with underbrush and ferns. Alan felled a dozen trees and some saplings, and together we moved the brush and logs. Now, I envision gardens. This is where I built that small stone wall a week or two ago. Yesterday, I lengthened it, studying the flow of water into the drainage ditch and trying to prevent any further loss of soil. I opened up the drainage ditch, too, at places where it was clogged with grass and weeds. I found perennials everywhere, which Sandra planted and which were hidden by less desirable plants, so I moved those around. There are hostas, sedum, pulmonaria, coral bells, anemones, ajuga, lady's mantle.

Last night, Alan and I slept for the first time on the air bed we just bought and assembled. I do believe we have found relief there, which, lacking a cure, will do for now. We both arose with fewer aches than accompanied us to bed.

This morning, still stiff in my muscles but better off in my joints, I went out in search of more perennials and some blueberry bushes and shrubs. I started with the funky, small nursery a few miles north that claims it has fruit trees, berry bushes, and flowering shrubs "for the coldest hillsides in Vermont." I called first, to see what time they opened and got a recorded message saying their hours are ten to five-thirty. I got there at ten-thirty, and not a soul was around. I wandered the grounds, looked at the stock, waited, called out, tooted my car horn. No one. The UPS truck came up the mile-long dirt road to the nursery, and the driver unloaded some packages. I asked her if she knew where I could find someone to sell me some plants, and she said, "I almost never see anyone here; they just tell me where to leave deliveries."

Finally, I left, still longing for the low-growing blueberries I had seen, all covered with blooms and promising to fruit heavily. I, or anyone who came along, could have made off with a carful of stock — but this is Vermont. Hardly anyone here even locks doors. Trust in your neighbor runs deep in this culture.

I ended up at Agway, not for blueberries but for perennials and shrubs. Two hundred dollars later, I drove home with campanula, asters, platycodon, peonies, hardy boxwood, phlox, echinacea, spurge, scabiosa, veronica, artemisia, and more coral bells — and began digging. Now, almost everything is in the ground.

More will come. I've just discovered a good nursery, only a half mile to the right at the end of our road. You go up a long dirt driveway, and the front yard of the owners' house is crowded with greenhouse, shaded tables, and ranks of the usual annuals and perennials but a preponderance of rock garden plants. Just what I need! Now I see creeping thyme and phlox and sedum ornamenting the weedy rock ledge at the base of the area I'm cultivating. Dwarf asters appeal to me, along with low-growing varieties of veronica, campanula, geranium.

What I have cultivated so far is about one third of the area I want to plant this year. Next year, I will remove the plastic shroud from my other steep slope and tackle that ground, which is fully the size of my whole lot in Pittsburgh. Slowly, I cultivate right up to the edge of the wilderness, which seems all the more clamorous in close proximity to my careful, if loose, designs.

Love in Hiding

I have been thinking about former loves. The other night, as I lay curled up next to Alan in bed and idly stroked his arm, I thought about other men I have loved and wondered why love feels so different now — so commodious, and sure. I know that those I loved before, I genuinely loved. Even when I was young and deluded, I knew what love felt like. Each time, it taught me lessons — it showed me my fears, my anger, the boundaries around my ability to give and to balance self and other. I think I have grown into the love I experience with Alan. It feels right because it keeps me growing. It does not deny me, it expects me to meet it at eye level and to see into its soul. This time of life is the right time for spiritual discoveries, and I know Alan is the perfect partner for me in such explorations.

I have always imagined that love does not die but just shape-shifts or goes underground. Once we love someone, something indelibly marks our soul. Sometimes I resist this idea, but I think we never stop loving. Even the most disastrous loves persist like a dormant virus. We don't need to see or even like those who stubbornly remain love's object. In fact, they can drive us crazy once love has stopped letting us grow in their company. We can be outraged, wounded, bitter, and resentful about people we once loved easily and without reservation. We don't like to think we could be so stupid as to keep loving someone who has proved unworthy, who has demeaned or impeded us. But those judgments have nothing to do with spirit, which keeps loving whether we want it to or not.

This is a good thing. If we let it be, it can cure us of the resentments and bind up the wounds of love gone awry. If we don't fear love, love will drive away fear. It is a benevolent cycle, which reverses the vicious kind. It is enough, for me, just to know I still love everyone I have ever loved. I may not be big enough to act on that, or show it in the company of those past loves, but it is good for my soul to acknowledge it.

The Real Thing

Last night we went to the third music concert at Adam's school, featuring the seventh- and eighth-grade choruses, bands, guitar players, and after-school jazz ensemble. The auditorium was packed and airless. The whole school is too small, and during the summer new construction will get under way to correct the problems of space, ventilation, and traffic flow. A bond issue was passed last November, and in two years the school's long overdue expansion will be finished.

Alan and I sat high up near the back of the auditorium, because Adam is always at the rear of the stage, in the percussion section. We wanted a good view of him, and we also got a panoramic view of the audience. Parents, grandparents, and siblings of the performers filled every seat and most of the stairs and aisles. They all greeted each other before the show began, talking of gardens, weather, kids, and communities. When the performance got under way, they cheered their own and all the other children.

All the while, at least some of them had to be thinking, as I was, that just that morning another shooting had taken place at another school, this time in Georgia. This time, there were no fatalities — this time, there was only one shooter. But that school and the schools in Littleton, Paducah, Springfield, and Jonesboro had to resemble the one in which we all sat last night. Those other children and parents would once — before the anguish and terror — have looked just like the ones here. They would have looked easy and proud.

When we got home last night we turned on the news. We saw scenes of carnage from the Balkans. We saw stories about school murders of the past and bloody destruction from other wars. In one shot, a lake of blood seeped into littered ground amid shoes and rubble. Adam, recalling a recent conversation about violent computer games and movies, shuddered and said, "What makes anyone think the real thing doesn't desensitize people to violence?"

Keeping Track

Adam made pizza for dinner Saturday night — mixed the dough, set it to rise, rolled it out into two good-sized rounds and covered them with diced tomatoes, fresh basil, three cheeses (mozzarella, parmesan, provolone) and, on one, crimini mushrooms. The pizzas were wonderful, Adam was proud, and I didn't have to cook dinner. This boy has a fine touch with food. If he were a less picky eater, as he might be, one day, he would have real chef potential. Already, he is asking when he can cook again, and what he should attempt.

Yesterday was my turn to get out the flour and yeast. I made two loaves of focaccia to take to a potluck picnic put on by Keeping Track for people interested in taking their training in tracking and recording the movements of wild animals. The project is getting under way as all group endeavors do — slowly and with much to accomplish before the main event.

The picnic was held at a house near the entrance onto our road from Route 12. The owner, Kimberly, is finishing a postgraduate degree in biology and apparently hoping for a formal role in wildlife research or preservation. Seven other people attended the picnic, six women and one man. Before the first day-long training session is held in the fall, we need money and more participants. The costs must cover six full days of in-the-woods instruction for as many as twenty people — a total of about $3,200. We will approach at least one small foundation and several local businesses. We may have to fork some over ourselves, though we have agreed no one will be excluded for lack of cash.

We have all taken the names of people to call, those who signed up at the presentation several weeks ago to express their interest in the project. Most are from the town next door to mine, but we hope to get at least a few from my own village, enough to warrant a true joint effort to monitor part of the range of mountains that straddles both towns. The neighboring town already has a conservation commission, whereas mine would need to form one. Our group of ten to twenty volunteers will report to these conservation commissions, which in turn will consult with each town's planning commission to evaluate the impact of any proposed development on wild habitats.

Once we have the necessary funds and folks, we'll schedule the six training sessions over the course of the next year. Afterward, we'll specify the area for study and then go out as a team four times a year to write down and photograph all the evidence we can collect of bear, moose, deer, fishers, coyotes, bobcats, otters, and other denizens of woods, meadows, and marshes.

Chill

We had fierce winds last night, for the first time in months. They tossed my sleep around, woke up my bats, sent me spinning into panic. There is so much to do here, and Alan sometimes seems beset by it all. We are at an age to be enjoying the fruits of our labor, not planting the orchard. This morning, we were edgy with each other. I tried to express my concern about Alan's mood, his aches and pains, his difficulty sleeping because of his stressed-out back and joints. He said my reminding him was no help — it made matters worse.

I was stung for a moment, but then realized that I focus on Alan because I feel I am not doing enough myself, not bringing in enough money, not getting enough done outside. We talked. I admitted that I don't really know what's ailing me today — and then I began to see that this anxious malaise comes mainly from my work for the Education Department. No one there is available lately; they are all under stress. I am working blind, and my motivation suffers. I don't get in enough hours, so I feel guilty. Alan listened well. He harbors no resentment. Suddenly the pressure is off, for both of us.

I am better at this sort of thing than I used to be. I stop and think, I weigh my words, but I don't deny what I feel. I hold Alan up before me and try to see him clearly, try to balance us and protect us, even as I voice confusion or show that I am upset. He always comes through, even if I have made him defensive or touched a raw nerve. In other times and relationships, the pressure of anxiety would have drawn me full-tilt into a scene, would have generated any old explanation for my discomfort, just to dissipate it. Now, something restrains me, some inner voice that just says, chill. I do. I cool down and say what's what, but carefully. And it works. This is something I probably should have learned a decade or two ago — but I think I was waiting for Alan.

Something True

Realizing how differently I behave with Alan than I ever did with other men strengthens my conviction that all the patterned phases of my life have been necessary to some purpose of my soul. I don't know what that purpose is, not fully, but I am sure of this much: There had to be that time when I was a fearful, overly responsible child, because those qualities arose from something true in me, the way children are true. They arose from innate tenderness and decency that became fear and self-denial because I worried that if I did not please my parents I would lose their inept, uncommunicative love — which ineptness, and which love, rose from something true in them, too. My childhood aims and disappointments reflected real promptings from my particular, identifying nature.

Given that, there had to be the time that came next, when I went out on my own without confidence or any bone-deep belief in my own reality or will. In those years, in college and beyond, I failed repeatedly to honor what others said were my gifts, and so I saw them diminish without knowing what I was witnessing. Almost inevitably, I married too soon and chose a troubled, troubling mate. I thought all our problems were mine. I believed Ned's bitter assessments of my character as thoroughly as I rejected anyone else's praise of my gifts. For years, I lived with little mind, too much emotion, and no sense of soul.

In turn, once free of my first marriage and its denigrations, there had to come the eight-year stretch when I fled to the opposite coast, when I defended myself against intimacy using mean wit and condescending judgments, when I stuck with nothing and no one but followed my restless urges where they led me. It was before and during those California years, which lasted until my early thirties, that I ricocheted without plan or reflection between coasts, jobs, apartments, and lovers, none of which or whom did I take seriously.

At last, because I never confronted the self I had no faith in, there had to come that longest time of all, my second marriage, when all the bats I'd tried to scatter or deny came home to roost in my soul. There they were again — the urge to care for (and also to change and control) another instead of facing myself, the inevitable power struggles, persistent bitterness, neglect on both sides, refusals to give or accept any love or any quarter. But with the bats came brighter creatures, wrapped at first in a chrysalis of sadness, joy, and change. These came out of the loss of my first baby, the birth of Adam, the death of my mother. Adam arrived bearing gifts, and my mother left many of hers behind when she died. Their gifts — experiences of love in wholly new dimensions — eventually rescued me, showing me places in myself I had never suspected, subterranean wells of commitment, strength, competence, clarity.

Sometime during those years between marriages, when I was entirely adrift, I had a dream about a great bird held upside down by its legs. It beat its broad wings and tried to right itself and fly, but it couldn't escape the muscular grip that bound it. It opened its mouth and tried to sing, but all that issued forth were bits of colored stones that fell to the ground and formed a mosaic of a bird in flight. I knew even then that I was that bird, beating the air into eddies, trying for a liberation I could not achieve.

Now I feel free, after all those necessary struggles. I don't know what's next in my life, except that I will age, face further struggles, suffer losses, experience joy, waver in my faith and find it again. But that thing, whatever it was, that rose from my center and made me the child I was — that true thing is still with me. I expect to discover more of its content and lessons, and I know Alan will help me do this, as I will help him. Our truths will out.

"... Queerer Than We Can Suppose"

I recently bought a copy of *Expecting Adam* by Martha Beck, which was reviewed in the Sunday *New York Times* ten days ago. I read it straight through. It's the story of Beck's second pregnancy, conceived during the heavy intellectual stress of graduate school at Harvard. This pregnancy called into question every choice and rational assumption on which she and her husband had so far based their lives. Even before she learned she was carrying a child with Down syndrome, Beck started sensing bigger influences than she had ever believed in. Eventually, she heard, saw, and felt the presence of beings from some plane beyond the one our senses usually perceive. Eventually, in choosing to continue the pregnancy and raise their child, Beck and her husband abandoned altogether their high-powered lives and associates. She tells her story of angels and celestial guidance with a blend of embarrassment, wit, and celebration.

Reading Beck's book, I began wondering whether pregnant women have readier access than others to what lies beyond our five senses. Perhaps our spiking hormones poke holes into that larger realm, giving us glimpses not normally open to us. Perhaps our babies, wrapped in their clouds of glory like lanugo as they swim in their warm, amniotic sea, send us messages, as Beck's son, Adam, did. In any case, I can recall knowledge that came from dreams and voices during my own two pregnancies. In the first one, when so many dire things were wrong with my tiny daughter, I twice woke up sobbing in the night, the only two times in my life that has ever happened. The first time, I dreamed specifically that something was wrong with my baby. The second time, I dreamed that Sarah had died. In those days, she had long been steeped in motherhood, so I think the dream was telling me that my maternal hopes were doomed.

In my second pregnancy, when I carried my own Adam, I had a dream of a different kind, one in which I saw my child's face and he had blue-sky eyes with clouds — of glory, no doubt — sailing through them. This dream reassured me for reasons I could never explain. I welcomed it especially because the early months of that pregnancy were so filled with the terror of another genetic catastrophe. This deepened the tensions in my marriage. One day, after an anguished shouting match with my husband, I stormed up to my third-floor office, shut the door, closed my eyes, and wrapped my arms around my rib cage. As I held onto myself, and the child inside me, I "heard" a voice say, with absolute clarity and unimpeachable authority, "This baby is just fine." For the space of several moments I believed the voice without reservation. Then, after my usual fashion at the time, I explained it to myself as a product of my overanxious imagination.

Now I think I would accept the voice as bearing a true message from beyond my imagination. I would recognize the voice and my dreams as accurate bulletins about the condition of my two babies, ways of preparing me for what I would confront. I might have to keep reminding myself of the miracles in my life and their evidence of celestial intent, but I would do that rather than dismiss the content of my deepest intuitions.

I realize I have lost my nervous skepticism in the course of writing this journal. When I look back now and see that I once feared the derision of doubters and strict intellectuals, I am surprised to find that the fear is gone. There is nothing like experience — one's own and that of others with trustworthy voices — to do away with abstract ideas and defensive rationalizations.

Black Widow

We have furnace ducts now. Jim Daniels, company scion, arrived with another worker at eight yesterday morning, and the two men spent until two-thirty crawling under the house and into the tiny basement that is reachable only through a trap door in the bathroom. They cut vent holes in walls and floors and connected them all with galvanized, insulated pipe about ten inches in diameter. The morning was raw and wet, the afternoon sunny. The men got filthy. They worried about tracking in mud and shedding cobwebs through the house, but they might as well have worried about sunrise and nightfall instead, those being easier to control. I have decided not to give a damn about floors or dust until this summer's work is finished. That will give me more time for gardens.

Jim made an unwelcome discovery while he was supine under the cottage room. He emerged as I was off on an errand, brushed himself off, and said, "Did you know you have some good-sized spiders under there?" I was about to say, "Uh-huh, brownish-gray suckers with stripy legs," when he went on to describe something altogether different. "Saw one about an inch long, had a big black stomach with a red mark on it." I stopped halfway to the car. "That sounds like a black widow," I said, glad he had not been bitten but not liking this conversational turn one bit. "It's okay," he assured me. "I squished it."

Well, fine, Jim, but surely it has relatives under there — children if no husband. That's where the dogs take shelter. That's right below our desks, which are near the brand-new heating vents in the floor. That's where Alan will have to go to replace insulation that the dogs have yanked out.

We live so much closer to wildlife now, both because we are in the woods and because summer is approaching fast. Not all of the wildlife is friendly, or even very tolerant — though some creatures are full of surprises. Just the other day, Kathy was riding her bike on a road across town, and a black bear crossed right in front of her. She stopped, he stopped. They stared at each other and then he lumbered off into the woods, his coat shining and riffling like thick, dark grass in the wind. Kathy wasn't even afraid. I would have shaken hard enough to rattle bike and bones to dust.

I look forward to the Keeping Track training in part because I expect to learn just how to behave if I encounter a bear, a coyote (or six-pack of coyotes), a rutting moose, or a mean-eyed fisher. Not that we'll be likely to do so in our training or monitoring groups — too many of us for that. But I plan to ask for this information because I want to be in the woods on my own and not end up mauled, clawed, or trampled.

As for the black widows, they like to be left alone, and we will be happy to oblige. They like woodpiles, eaves, crawl spaces, and other dark, undisturbed spots. We'll wear gloves while doing wood and keep a lookout in other situations that could bring us eyeball to hourglass with those fierce mamas. I'm told there aren't many of them in Vermont anyway. Maybe Jim squished the matriarch.

A Leap of Faith

June, with its rare days, doesn't arrive until tomorrow, but today was perfect. Alan, Adam, and I drove to Burlington late this morning and met Ann as she stepped off the ferry from New York. We had lunch, wandered through shops, bought books, and sat in the Borders coffee shop and watched the people stroll by. It was hot and sunny, the sky a summer blue with a few high clouds. This was the first meeting for the three A's — Ann, Alan, Adam. They liked each other a lot, they were easy in each other's company. We dawdled the afternoon away until Ann's return ferry at three-thirty, and as we waited for it I gazed across Lake Champlain and remembered that today is an important anniversary for Alan and me.

Two years ago on May 30, at about ten in morning, I sat on the porch swing of the Pittsburgh house with a cup of coffee and watched Alan's red truck approach, right at the estimated hour, all the way from Cave Junction, Oregon, and through the vast American landscape of late spring. I got up and walked a very short distance indeed, down the stairs to the curb. I set my cup down shakily on a step near the front walk. When Alan opened his driver's-side door, I was right there. He stepped out, we saw each other's face for the first time, and then all the space-between became space around us, embracing us as we embraced each other. That was a sunny day, too, but we spent it inside with the blinds drawn. Had my skeptical friends but known!

Alan stayed for ten days with Adam and me. He went to Meeting with me, helped me yank out a ratty hedge and replace it with boxwood, sat on the porch swing with me, silently toured the prints and drawings in my house and said, about the ones I had done myself, "You should do more of this." We played our favorite music for each other. We got e-mail from Edie, asking how this meeting of souls was going. Alan even wrote down his net worth for me — the value of properties and assets he owned and his monthly income from two or three sources.

About eight days into the visit, we talked about "plans." I don't remember who brought it up, but I remember my surprise when Alan said he wanted us to be together and thought he should go home, finish his house renovation, sell the place, drive back to Pittsburgh with Lucy, and move in with Adam and me. I was speechless at first. I had pictured something more gradual — one or two more cross-country visits, then separate dwellings for at least a while, then perhaps a move into shared space. That picture faded, though, and soon it was gone, except for Adam's image.

I worried about Adam at first. What would he think about my living with Alan, and Alan's living with us? Would that set a bad example? Then I realized my anxieties had nothing to do with what I really believed, which was that Alan and I had somehow been led to each other by divine intervention and divine intervention didn't give a damn whether the Commonwealth of Pennsylvania blessed our union or not.

Adam had already seen many examples of blended, expanded, or happenstance families and households. He understood, for instance, the nature of the homosexual unions formed under the care of our Meeting. He knew those couples could not legally marry but loved each other no less for their outlaw state. Alan's arrival in Adam's life would represent another big change in a rapid-fire series, but Adam would have the close attention and loving support of several adults, including a counselor. Life is change. Adam was about to get another dose of life.

Perhaps this sounds unwise. I can understand why Emma thought it was rash. But it has all turned out fine. I cannot fully explain how I knew it would, even before Alan's visit, but I had it on an authority as compelling as the voice that once told me my unborn son was going to be healthy.

My counselor at that time, an insightful, mild-mannered Orthodox Jew with seven children and a soul mate of his own, warned me not to try to explain the connection that Alan and I felt. Dr. Lebovits said no one would know what I was talking about unless they had experienced this mysterious kind of certainty themselves, in which case, no explanation would be necessary. Of course, I ignored his warning and set about explaining, to Emma and Ellen among others. They grew concerned, then indignant. Perhaps if I had followed Dr. Lebovits's advice and had been more patient with their concerns, we would not feel so at odds with each other now.

Alan left on the morning of June 9 as I was heading back to work after a week off. He thought it would take him two or three months to finish the work on his house, settle his business, and turn his keys over to a realtor. But all the way across the country he envisioned "happy buyers" who would want the house just as it was, with nothing further done to it.

Within two days of his return to Cave Junction, in an area — the southwest corner of Oregon — where houses generally sat on the market for eighteen months or so before selling, those happy buyers showed up and made an offer. They loved what Alan had already done to the house, but they said they wouldn't be able to afford it if he put in another nail. They would do the rest themselves.

Within three weeks, not three months, Alan had closed the deal, held a yard sale, packed the truck, hefted Lucy into the passenger's seat, and driven back to Pittsburgh. He arrived on June 30, 1997.

The same good luck worked for the two of us when we found this place. We drove up to Vermont for a weekend of "exploring" in mid-March 1998, nine months after Alan's move to Pittsburgh. We bounced over rutted back roads for two days, discouraged by junky properties with inflated price tags. Then Alan spotted a tiny ad in the Montpelier *Times-Argus*. "Sunny, two-bedroom, cedar-sided home on ten acres," it said. We called, we came, we saw, we bought. Alan was giving me the thumbs-up before we ever walked inside this house.

We handed over some cash to secure the deal and drove back to Pittsburgh in a daze. Then we put our house on the market, and the real estate gods beamed down on us again. We sold the house in ten days, *sans* realtor, to a young couple expecting their first child. Alan's work on the kitchen — not to mention the deck he built in back and the guest room and tiny bathroom he built in the basement — clinched that deal and brought in $20,000 more than I had paid two years earlier. It was just enough to break even. It covered building materials but none of Alan's labor. The price we paid Sandra and Harriet did the same for them.

What Sarah calls our "real estate karma," which later persisted through our purchase of the house in town, which we now rent to the world's best tenants, is naturally just one more reason for us to believe we have been guided to each other and our proper home. We still wonder what will unfold here, once the heaviest work is done and we have time to look about us for our proper tasks in the community at large. We think we might work for universal health coverage in Vermont and beyond.

When I told our story to Ann, she said, "You must be supposed to do something together." I agreed with her. We feel the same way. Then she considered a moment longer and added, "Or maybe you're just supposed to enjoy yourselves."

June

Birds

It has been unseasonably hot and close for the past few days, but this afternoon we had thunderstorms that have helped, at least for a while. I sat in the living room, with the current draft of Ann's new novel in my lap, and I looked up from time to time to watch the birds at the feeder. We know from a science project by one of Adam's classmates that birds feed more heavily when the barometer falls, and today they were gorging. Goldfinches, purple finches, and chickadees occupied the feeder at once, a rare thing. The purple finches warbled, the goldfinches chipped. The birds took turns grasping the wires from which the feeder is suspended, holding on sideways and pushing their heads out to catch the rain dropping like a beaded curtain from the eaves. They were taking showers, and loving it.

Lately, I have seen hummingbirds hover near our windows, so I have bought a feeder for them, too. Hummingbirds are engineered like some sci-fi spacecraft. They move as if going into hyperdrive, the way they hang suspended and then shoot like bullets through the air, their wings a blur. Speedy Gonzales, airborne — *"Andale, andale!"*

The woman who runs the nursery nearby, the one that specializes in rock garden plants, said hummingbirds need to eat every ten minutes or so, they use up so much energy. One recently got trapped inside her greenhouse, high in a corner, beating his wings to exhaustion trying to get out through the transparent panes. When he finally collapsed, she took him outside to a fuchsia loaded with blossoms. He was too done in to eat for another several minutes. He just perched on her finger, his engine idling high, while her husband ran for the camera. At last, having sat for his portrait, the bird caught his breath, sipped some nectar, and shot away.

Sometimes I look at birds the way I would look at a camel if I didn't know what it was. What's that bizarre humpbacked thing with the long legs and supercilious upper lip? And what are those, over there? Winged creatures! Flying things? Wow.

I wonder what it would feel like to be an early human, with no suspicion that my future kin would one day fly nonchalantly from coast to coast (what's a coast?) in machines (what's a machine?). I imagine my ancient eye following a raven, say, as it crosses a meadow and disappears into the woods, pursuing some unknown purpose. I see it bearing mystery on its back and I feel my spirit follow that mystery as my eye follows its flight. I apprehend the mystery in midair and with it the raven's solemn joy. I am anything but nonchalant.

Stepfamily

Adam and Alan need to talk. Given Alan's native reticence and Adam's adolescent leanings into silence, that will be a challenge.

It isn't that Adam is naturally taciturn. In fact, he is loquacious about his interests, his online activities, his reasons for wanting what he wants when he wants it, and his arguments for doing his first things (homework, chores) last. When it comes to serious conversation with adults about emotional or interpersonal stuff, though, he is beginning to clam up. You have to catch him at the right moment, circle the issue in question, and then open it gently if you want him to engage with you.

Lately, Alan has been increasingly annoyed with Adam's thirteen-year-old's self-centeredness, his lack of consideration for others, his headstrong opinions, his computer compulsions, his spaciness. "You're talking to the piano," Alan said to me yesterday, when I thought I was talking to Adam. He was right. My boy was gone, his eyes glassed over.

Last night Alan erupted, as much as Alan ever erupts, which is to say he threw his hands up and left the room when Adam asked to join the Scrabble game we had just set up. There wouldn't have been a thing wrong with his request if he hadn't all day been pushing hot buttons that Alan never before knew he had. Adam and Alan have been tense with each other over chores and expectations — typical adult-child issues in any family, made touchier in a stepfamily. Alan wanted neither a direct confrontation nor Adam's company. The straws had been piling up on his back one by one by one. I reminded Adam about some of those straws, and he said he guessed Alan's exasperation was legit.

Later, I suggested to Alan that he deal directly with Adam so I wouldn't feel in the middle. What goes on between them is between them, but I am unduly affected, being gaga over them both. Alan agreed to talk to Adam after he's cooled down.

This morning, I asked whether he had cooled down yet. He assured me he will approach Adam when he has figured out what to say. I won't feel the need to bring this up again. Either the talk will happen or the need for it will subside until the next time. One of these days, Alan will speak directly to Adam about his own concerns, and that could open a whole new household era.

House

When I was in my twenties I used to dream occasionally that I lived in a treehouse. The rooms were all on different levels, balanced among ascending branches. The furniture was hammocks, swings, and big, richly colored cushions. I would wake up and think: Some dream house — how likely is *that*?

Now Alan is building something surprisingly close. The new living room and the deck surrounding it hover at mid–tree height, right next to a ledge that drops off into the woods. The deck, which was going to have to wait until next year or later, became necessary as a staging area from which to work on the living room. Now the deck is nearly finished. It is eight feet wide around the living room's two exposed sides, and then it broadens to twelve feet the rest of the way, alongside the breezeway and the dining room. Altogether, it covers about eight hundred square feet, and most of its perimeter butts right up to the trunks and branches of beeches, hemlocks, yellow birches, and maples.

The view at eye level leads straight and high into the dense woods. The sun rounds the corner of the house in the early afternoon and stays on the front end of the deck until three or four o'clock, when it starts down behind the topmost branches of the trees. From then until it drops below the Worcester Range, it backlights the leaves, giving a neon-green glow to the woods. This will make the new living room the coolest, most serene place in our multilevel house — this house shaped in my dreams, by Alan's hands, in which nearly every room occupies its own elevation. Once the living room is finished, with its wall of glass looking out across the deck and into the trees, I will resist the urge to fill it entirely with swings and cushions. But I do think one or two of those hammock-like chairs I've seen in catalogues will look great suspended from a beam.

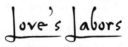

Love's Labors

Yesterday, Emma forwarded an e-mail to me from someone inquiring about a project she and I worked on together several years ago. She wanted my input, which I sent. Her tone was businesslike but friendly, and mine was the same. I think this is where our connection will live now. It is the same neighborhood in which my friendship with Ellen resides — an area of neat but blank facades with who-knows-what furnishing the rooms inside, filling the closets, moving about, or growing rampant in the backyards hidden from view. It is a neighborhood without bridges.

That's all right. The neighborhood is civilized and safe. Its streets might even lead eventually to wide-open spaces. I think of Ellen and Emma now the way I think of former husbands and lovers. Our love has done that shape-shifting thing; it has made itself small and gone into hiding — but it still exists. It has permanently etched my soul, though I think about it less often now, and feel no heart-lurch when e-mail comes in.

Meanwhile, I have finished reading Ann's new novel, *The Whelming Flood*, which illustrates why I so enjoy this renewed friendship. Ann has a richly sympathetic imagination. She has taken a subject that fairly pleads for comic treatment — a thirty-foot wall of molasses-in-January, released by a burst holding tank, that moved at surprising speed through the streets of Boston's North End in 1919, grasping houses, horses, people, cobblestones, streetlamps, and trees in its cloying brown embrace. But Ann, though she understands the temptation of outsiders to laugh and invests her language and imagery with great good humor, sees even more clearly the horrific experience of those whose lives stood in the way of the sticky tide.

The residents of the North End — Italian, Irish, and Jewish families of modest means at best — were already exhausted by two world catastrophes, the influenza epidemic and the war to end all wars. They had just recovered from the former and still rejoiced over the end of the latter. They had lost countless loved ones, and their surviving soldiers had not yet come home. The holiday season, wild with celebration but poignant with loss, had just given way to its bleak winter aftermath. And then the holding tank popped its rivets and tore the world of Ann's ten-year-old protagonist in two, ripping the "before," which had been bright despite the far-off war and the flu, forever away from the "after," which would never be innocent again.

Ann has described to me how her characters assert themselves, surprising her with what they become, what they choose, what they refuse to submit to. She has as much compassion for them as if they were flesh and blood. She is also, remember, the person who set about building a life full of people while living alone. She has deep affection for her friends and students while also surrounding herself with a solitude that must be as nurturing as rain. She has been awarded honors for her distinguished teaching, has written three novels and a book of nonfiction, and seems very happy to have walked into the vision that she laid out to me thirty years ago.

Ann's writing life, and the spirit she invests in it, seem to me to be without the competitive edge so common among writers, academics, artists. She has read my writing, which she praises readily and criticizes without sharpness or self-satisfaction. She sees what she sees. She takes my comments about her work with cheerful thanks and acts on what she agrees with, shelving what she doesn't.

Some people have a certainty about them. It is as if their egos sit contented in a corner, like children engrossed in play, and let them get on with their work — no whining, no sleeve-tugging, no gimme. The egos know their time will come when the day's work is finished.

Both Ann and Alan have this quality. They don't stand back every ten minutes and point to what they've done and look over their shoulders to see who's looking, who's done what else in the meantime, how their efforts stack up in comparison. They stay focused. They do what's in front of them, they finish. Then they assess. Adjust. Nod. Fold their arms and smile and finally pat ego on the head.

I feel this coming to me slowly. Now and then my own ego sets up a clamor from its spot in the corner, impatient for satisfaction but restless or unsure about the work. Little by little, it absorbs a certain discipline and keeps its distance, giving me ever longer stretches of quiet. The work that is most free of ego, for me, is the work of my soul, the work about which I am passionate. That's not the work that pays anything. It is the work that connects to my life and all that I love and believe. Both Ann and Alan have long since fused work and soul, one by choosing a life within the so-called "real world," the other by largely escaping that world. Ann has said her career is what allows her to hang out with her friends. Alan has created a life in which his labor serves what is dearest to him. I am straddling, still — I have one foot in the wage-slave world and the other in the world of my soul, where one day, by means I can't yet name, I will join the privileged company of Alan and Ann.

This is no less than we all deserve. Life should be about the cultivation of soul through work that tills the ground of our passion. I tend to think that ego, at least in its insistent, wheedling form, is what erupts when we can't join our labor and our love under the same yoke. Forced apart, each weakens, becomes unsatisfying, makes the ego insecure and impatient. I lived this way for years. Time to give it up.

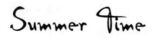

Summer Time

This is Adam's last full week of school. At the end of the month, after some time to do as he pleases, he'll be off to Pittsburgh for three weeks with his father, some of which time they will spend at a family reunion. As soon as Adam returns, Steve, Rita, and Stephen will arrive for the last week in July. I can't wait for them to come, yet I know from ever-longer experience that the time before their visit will fly and their days here will pass like the cars on a high-speed train.

It is true that time accelerates with age. I don't know why that is, but I think it has to do with the increasing number of things that fill it up. I remember a character named Dunbar in *Catch–22*, who deliberately sought idleness or tedium, explaining that if you do nothing all day long the time creeps by, but if you're busy it goes in a blink. He preferred stretching it out, boredom and all, I presume. But I have noticed that when you look back on time that has flown rapidly, it looks long, not short—probably because it has been packed full. Idle, empty time, though it feels endless as we endure it, seems short once it has passed. Perhaps that is why, when I look back at eighteen years with Adam's father, it doesn't seem as long as it was. The marriage itself was for many years as empty as a desert, and perspective shrinks it, fools the eye with its sameness, its featureless expanse. Those same years, considered in the light of other goings-on with Adam, writing, friends, and work, seem cluttered as a cityscape, and my backward-looking eye is stunned by how much has filled that span. It looks big and wide because it has had to contain so many people and enterprises.

Ten or twenty years from now, when I am old or getting there, I imagine looking at the Vermont years and finding them long and full in proportion to how rapidly they will pass. Already, I look at the pages of this journal and realize how dense they are with events, accomplishment, surprises. This page I write just now, on the computer, is number 255. I began writing this journal 259 calendar days ago, with backtracks over a couple of years and more — a lifetime. The threads of this narrative are many, their colors and textures diverse, and they weave a pattern that pleases me, a pattern of love, loss, joy, work, friendship, family, God, nature, home, and community, past and present. These are the elements of life. Our life goes on, it follows its rhythms.

Increasingly, the rhythms in my life here with Alan are those of the seasons: great bustle in warm weather; sedentary, half-hibernating pastimes in the cold; a sense of kinship with nature around us; a sense of needing less than before from the outside world, just visits from loved ones, time with friends, the prospect of new acquaintances, the convenience of utilities, groceries, and a movie or play or meal out now and then.

I suppose I am reflecting on the character of time because summer is here, well in advance of the solstice. The weather is sultry, the vegetation lush, the school year at an end even though it plods on, its serious business finished and only field trips and diversions remaining. I remember the summers of my childhood, how endless they looked in June, how short in August.

Adam has never yet experienced an open, lazy expanse of time. Until this year, every summer has been structured by day camp or overnight camp so that the adults in his life could get on with their work. This year, with both Alan and me home all day, I hope he will hear echoes of what summer used to be for kids. I hope he will balance ease and idleness with just enough effort and intention to keep boredom at bay. I hope he will find friends with the same luxury of choice and haunt the woods with them at least as often as he haunts cyberspace. I hope he will read, think, and pace his days and ride them into fall with that same start-over sense of purpose and possibility that I remember so well. Then I hope he will look back on a summer that felt short in its passing but stays forever broad and full in memory.

Connections

We took Topper to the vet about a month ago because his breath was awful and one tooth looked gray and possibly abscessed. The tooth was not the problem — he had a cauliflower-like growth on the tissue behind his bottom teeth. The vet removed it, but now it seems to be coming back. I fear it is malignant. This cat is only five, and he acts healthy — his coat shines, his appetite is good, he seeks affection, he purrs. The thought that we could lose him brings tears to my eyes.

When I think about more grievous losses, I get a vertiginous feeling below my stomach. Every parent has these fears, everyone who loves another is subject to them. We are all hostages to the welfare of our loved ones. I try to keep in mind what my aunt said to me last summer, when I asked where she found her high energy and positive attitude after the death of my uncle in March. She told me she had long ago promised herself that she would not sink into mournfulness when the time came but would celebrate my uncle's life and their long, happy marriage. She is of Vermont stock, and she has just that toughness and appreciation. She prepared herself for his death long before he even became ill. I do not find this morbid. I find it wise. I wish to do likewise, to anticipate rather than fear the inevitable losses that accompany age — losses of capacity and companionship, of acuity and action. I would like this to make me better at loving, right this minute, in the sinewy Yankee way of my aunt, with humor, tartness, truth telling, and wit.

I will grieve my losses, even though I don't believe grief is warranted in the cosmic scheme of things, and I will do so because this world is where I live — the cosmos is not, yet. I will fight loneliness though I love solitude. I will hate death though I am sure it is an illusion. I will be what I am, which is a frightened human inside a dying body, yet I will cling to the bedrock of love, the single truth in the universe, the real pathway out of this dying body and this world's illusions.

In *Expecting Adam,* when Martha Beck talks about the overwhelming love she felt in the company of otherworldly beings, she admits she began longing for her own death as the gateway to that love. But we can't let ourselves do that, and above all we can't hasten our own ends, because there is purpose in everything we experience in this life. While we are here, we need to live fully in our earthly bodies and experience the limitations and mortality they impose on us. Like my own Adam, and most of the world's people, I think reincarnation makes sense. But whether the karmic cycle is real or not, our souls have business to conduct on earth, and that is why we are here.

We can sense that fear and death are not real. We can glimpse the tapestry of existence from time to time, either dramatically, as Beck did, or dimly, from the corner of our eye. But we are of the earth, and our earthbound experience of fear and death generates compassion. Here, with our limited perceptions, we must go through the fear to get to the love. We must live our bounded life in order to sense the limitlessness of God.

Sometimes, especially as I read over these pages I have written and see how serious they tend to be, I wonder whether life would just be too boring without our sins, illusions, black humor, greed, even violence. For some it might. But the more I offload my skittishness about faith and my need for worldly excitements, the richer my days become and the more I enjoy this life, this world. Nevertheless, I realize how powerfully alluring the surface matters are — the appearances of power, beauty, success, wealth, high living. It's no wonder that those who are most enmeshed in the striving are by and large the ones who end up controlling economies, governments, institutions, corporations. Deeper and more strenuous realities like faith and love are scoffed at as the concerns of church ladies, scam artists, TV evangelists, sentimental fools, goodygoodies, the weak, the needy, the mush-for-brains.

What amazes me is that anybody on this plane sees or senses what lies beyond it. Those who are most attached to earth and their own five senses say that glimpses of the infinite are "only" imagination. But I see no difference between imagination and the inner light. The power to generate images in the mind, especially images beyond our experience, is the power of God. It is love's wellspring. We love what we envision and create. Yes, we can use our power to see nightmares or pursue destructive ends, because we are not-God as much as we are God, we are made of at least as much heavy clay as light. We get confused, and that is why we need to be deliberate about our choices.

George Fox instructed his followers, the early Quakers, to "walk cheerfully over the earth, answering that of God in every person." He was asking them, and us, not only to choose but to be glad about it. Why glad, why cheerful? Because "that of God" truly does exist in all people; therefore we will find what we seek, and in "answering" it we will enlarge our own spirits and the opportunities for spirit in the world.

When we look for that of God in others, we begin to see that the highest function of the imagination is to make other people as real as oneself —literally, to create others, using our imagination, our very God-like power. I once had a professor who said that the purest morality lies in never thinking oneself better than anyone else. And I think it was the Quaker author Jessamyn West who said that the primary purpose of the imagination is to connect dissimilar things, the way bridges do. The imagination is a bridge among people, and it is built of love as strong as stone. This is why my image of faith is a bridge. It equalizes, connects, provides access.

A Weed Is a Weed Is a Flower

Two or three days ago, Alan walked in through the mudroom and handed me an indigo-blue flower he had picked near his shop. "What's this?" he asked. I had seen the same flower in white, growing down near the cabin, and I had been wracking my brain for its name. It has a long stem, from which, at spiraled intervals, grow single bladelike, bending leaves, each embracing a cluster of buds near its base. The top bud had opened on the one Alan gave me, and the blue flower had three flat, wide, overlapping petals and a half-dozen bright yellow anthers in the center. What *was* this plant?

I stood in the kitchen yesterday, my mind on other things, and suddenly memory did one of its favorite tricks. "Tradescantia," it said, loud and clear inside my head. "Spiderwort," it added, showing off. I went to the Internet to test memory, but it was right, of course. I knew it would be.

Tradescantia may grow wild here. I'm not sure. But it is also sold through gardening catalogs for as much as $6.95 a plant. I don't know which variety we have, something native or a cultivated cousin, because so many of Sandra's deliberate plantings have now been overtaken by weeds and wildflowers, and many of these, too, are the wild species of favorite garden plants. We have wild yarrow, phlox, asters, daisies, thistle, and lupine, among others. Some are just as fine as the cultivated varieties, while others have leggier stems, thinner blossoms, or looser habits (well, they are wild, remember, and profligate). As the season wears on, I will see other plants that do not appear in perennial beds, like Joe Pye weed or Queen Anne's lace; yet these are really lovely flowers, especially massed together.

So what does make a weed a weed? Invasiveness is one thing — the tendency to take over and choke other things out. But some invasive plants, like echinacea, certain artemisias, mallows, and lots of ground-covers, are sought after by gardeners, at least by those with plenty of space. Ugliness and nondescriptness make a weed, of course, but these are a matter of taste. Personally, I like the prolific yellow dots of dande-lions on broad lawns and meadows in the spring. Young dandelion greens are tasty, too. And Wilfrid Blount, a British botanical illustrator, has written, "If dandelions happened to cost a guinea a root, and had to be cosseted the winter through, they would find a place in every rich man's greenhouse." Cosseting, of course, automatically means a plant is not a weed. Or does it? A thick, vining nuisance in the tropics can become a prized, pampered annual in a colder zone.

Why is a wildflower not a weed? What's that distinction? I suppose if a plant is pretty, compact, and polite, but hard to cultivate in a garden, it is a wildflower. In recent years, I have seen trillium offered in catalogues — with eloquent prose about how difficult it is to propagate and grow and ship — for as much as $75 a plant! We have it everywhere in the spring, in its red, white, and "painted" versions (the red is called wake-robin), and it costs us nothing. Is it on its way to being like yarrow and phlox, a family broken up into country cousins and expensive, sophisticated, hybridized garden dwellers? It is amazing what people will pay for nature, while not wanting to live in it or know much about its wild state. Most people prefer it hybridized and contained.

My own plan for controlling nature — that is, coaxing it into a design of my choosing instead of letting it have its rampant way — is to assert my will close to the house but permit increasing wildness closer to the edges of our clearing. I picture those edges holding back the thronging weeds and brush like a police cordon holding back gawkers or a riot. But instead of yellow tape and batons, my tool will be the lawnmower. Over these next two or three years, I will till and plant with grass as many flat or gently sloping areas as possible, until finally I can start in early spring and keep mowing down the upstarts or invaders. Soon, our clearing will look like all those other properties in Vermont, about which Alan used to ask, "What's with these enormous lawns everybody has around here?" They're the only way to put nature in her place — or, rather, ours.

First Ex

Last week, I received a phone call from Ned, my first ex-husband, who lives in Maine. He said he would be in Vermont all this week for a conference near Burlington, and he wanted to take Sarah, Ann, and me to dinner. He did not ask whether Alan would like to come. I did ask Alan, after we hung up, but he said no. I was surprised to see his expression stony. Misery and anger moved the air around him in tight little spinning waves. He told me he had no interest in meeting someone who had hurt me the way Ned had. Apparently, "bless and release" works better for him in regard to his own injuries than mine. He was mystified as to why I would have anything to do with Ned. But he told me I should go if I wanted to, and I knew he meant that.

At first I thought I would. I was curious about Ned, whom I left in

1970 and last saw at a barn dance in North Carolina in 1977. After years of ignoring his Christmas cards and notes, and then responding to them with ambivalence, I finally, not so long ago, began finding it possible to be in touch with him without rancor or edginess. I thought going to dinner, with Ann and Sarah as buffers, would test my sense that the wounds Ned inflicted have long since healed. I also wondered about Ned's own recovery, from alcoholism, childhood traumas, and a big, insistent ego. I knew he had pretty much beaten the first two but figured he was still nose to nose with the third. In our infrequent phone conversations, I could still hear the resonant me-me-me in his voice. I could still hear some annunciatory quality: "I've gotten really interested in birds!" he might say, as if he had invented birding and wanted applause.

After Ned's call, everything got rocky for a while. Alan and I spent two days trying to straighten out the most painful emotional tangle we had ever gotten into. I did not understand why Ned's long-ago scorn and meanness were a problem for Alan when they no longer were for me. He did not understand how I could be casual about it, because he did not know about my long struggle to make peace with that difficult part of my past. For a while, he could not admit how offended he was that Ned could so blithely intrude, asking me to dinner but not acknowledging Alan's existence or possible feelings.

I thought perhaps something old had stirred to life in Alan, some dormant effect of having been disregarded and neglected by those who should have loved him long ago. I understood that he felt disregarded by me, when I accepted Ned's invitation, and I apologized to him for assuming that he would feel fine about it just because I did. Something more was going on, though. He was sadder than our misunderstanding warranted. I sometimes think old icebergs are breaking up in him, cracking his stoicism.

More was going on with me, too. While I was at the razor's edge with Alan, I began to see that my curiosity about Ned was pretty superficial. Ned is and always has been a stranger to me. We married way too young. I meant to build the home I had not had as a child, but having lacked it as a child I was bound to fail in my premature attempt. I have no idea what drove Ned back then. Why would he want to marry, at twenty-three? I never knew a thing about his inner life, nor did he have access to mine. Our childish, thorny relationship became a vicious battleground, and I was the losing army, every time. Ned even told me once that there were only two kinds of people, victims and victimizers. It was clear which one of us was which.

Whatever changes Ned has gone through, whatever else he has become, he was once the person who injured me so that I could not heal for many years. I allowed that to happen, and so, whatever else I have become, I was once the naïve and overly sensitive twenty-year-old who submitted to perpetual derision. More things than love indelibly mark our souls.

Sarah says Ned represents an important part of my past. She likes him and finds him witty and interesting. I can understand why. I can let down my guard — at least partway — and enjoy Ned, too. But the caustic wit that makes him good social company makes him, or made him, a cruel mate. Besides, my "enjoyment" now takes the form of shallow parrying and banter, which in fact I find tiring. The part of my past that Ned represents is not any history I care to relive. Relive it I might, however, if I ever tried to pursue an actual friendship with him. Face to face, I would either have to maintain the strangerhood we have always clung to or find a way to know him and be known. One option is false and thin, and the other risks dredging. I don't want either one, so I choose not to see him — at least not this year, at least not until new insights settle in. What would be the point? The only way to know whether Ned is now trustworthy would be to make bets I am unwilling to lose.

None of this is to say I don't also have a lot of real affection for Ned. It's a weird world.

If it had not been for Alan's suspicions and strong reactions, I would not have examined very closely my initial impulse to see Ned. On my own, I would have gone. Knowing this, Alan resisted my decision not to go. He does not try to control what I do. I tried to explain to him that my choice was entirely my own, even if it was also a response to what he was experiencing. This Alphonse-and-Gaston situation is one of the conundrums of caring for each other. With Alan, I have discovered in myself an unprecedented ability to respect another's feelings as much as my own. I trust his emotions even when I don't understand them, and I have learned that they can lead me to more knowledge of myself. If I ever needed proof of my recovery from old wounds, this is it, right before my eyes. With Alan, I have the home I was too young to build with Ned. When our recent two-day wrangles were over, I leaned against him, inside his arms, and felt weary, grateful, and full of peace. Because I am finally home, and have some understanding that everything on my path to this place has been a necessary preparation, I can no longer bear any serious grudge against Ned or anyone else who has hurt me. Neither do I wish to invite into my safe haven the sorrows that brought me here. They may sometimes drop in unannounced, but they can't live here.

On the other hand—I went to see Ann in Plattsburgh yesterday. She offered a while ago to go over this book with me and discuss her observations page by page and in person. I eagerly took her up on that. We spent a fine editorial day together, breaking it up with lunch, errands, and talk about other matters. Before we even got down to work, Ann told me about her dinner with Ned on Monday night, a date they arranged after I had bailed out.

I think Ann and Ned had not seen each other since graduate school in Toronto, though they have stayed sporadically in touch. Ann confirmed my impression that Ned is still in thrall to his ego but is also an entertaining and funny companion. She said, "Everything is still all about Ned, but a much improved Ned." She thought he was "bemused and perhaps a little hurt"—but not offended—that I had canceled out of dinner. I found it odd that I should regret causing Ned any pain, given the amount he once caused me.

When I told Ann I could see little reason to confront Ned in person, she said, referring to the image I have used so often, "To keep the tapestry whole." I took her to mean that I should not drop any threads, and that there is a thread for every bright or black mark scratched into my soul.

The past is remarkably powerful. It is not a thing to be repudiated.

My own past has been circling around recently, reentering my life through Sarah, Nora, Ann, Ned, and my love of New England. It greets my future, which enfolds Alan, Adam, this house, and the light, and in doing so it not only keeps the tapestry whole but lets me trace in it the threads that are my own. It shows me pattern and purpose in my life. My past, picked out in its light and dark colors and their interlocking design, allows me to understand where I am and how I got here. It shows me that I have always been the same person—or cast of characters—but I have had to uncover and grow into my many-sided identity instead of denying, rejecting, or belittling it and allowing others to do likewise. If I feel sorry to inflict any hurt on Ned, it is because I have always had little aptitude for vengeance. I really am a fairly benign fish, not toothed or venomous—but not in a barrel anymore, either. My job has been to dodge the bullets and find the sea.

Summer Solstice

I began setting this story down at the autumn equinox, a moment of precarious balance between the light and the dark. I was still hedging my spiritual bets, fearing the derision of the hard-nosed, not quite coming out about the faith that brought me here. It now seems fitting to end exactly a year after arriving in Vermont, at the summer solstice, the moment of maximum light.

The more I experience faith and sense its power, the more peculiar a person I begin to seem, even to myself. The things I believe appear very odd sometimes—at the least, they are contrary to most accepted wisdom. But this is who I really am, this spiritual maverick, this Quaker, this seeker of the light who keeps being surprised by insistent and unusual leadings, who thinks our eternal selves may choose our parents before we are born, may live in more than one body (at a time, even), may traverse the universe with unseen companions before coming home at last to the God who has all along lived inside us, and abided with us.

When I was more conventional, it was because I was more afraid.

Now, though fear still attaches to my earthbound self like my skin, I sometimes have a liberating, out-of-fear experience, seeing myself as if from a height. I believe fear is an old habit, which I might largely shed in time, as I pursue and persist in faith. I believe, as I have said throughout these pages, that love casts out fear, however long that takes. I see now that we can hasten the pace of the exorcism through reflection and choice. We can ask ourselves whether our actions are prompted by love or fear. If the answer is fear, we can stop, consult the inner light, and ask for the strength to love. The more we love, the less we fear. The less we fear, the more perfect our freedom becomes, and the more we can extend that freedom to others.

Right now, in the temporary brilliance of the summer solstice, I feel sure that Alan and I can withstand any dark, cold seasons that will come. We have extended to each other our growing freedom from fear; we have learned to trust. We have blessed and released past sorrows. From our stone bridge, here in the northwoods, we have perspective on our human transience, our souls' immortality, and our great good fortune in having found each other, finally, at just the moment when we were ready to. That moment could not have arrived without every instant that came before. Even the dark instants carried a light within.

> *It is through story that we embrace the great breadth of memory,*
> *that we can distinguish what is true, and that we may glimpse, at*
> *least occasionally, how to live without despair in the midst of the*
> *horror that dogs and unhinges us.*
>
> Barry Lopez, *About This Life*

> *Immunity to murderous loudspoken storytelling is*
> *Storytelling, isn't that so?*
>
> E.L Doctorow, *City of God*

Epilogue

Here and there in the Vermont woods, a hiker or tracker may come upon a "witness tree," a massive specimen of beech, maple, or other long-lived species standing among the spindlier upstarts of only the past fifty to one hundred years. Most of these majestic old trees have been left alone during at least two centuries of clear-cutting and gradual reforestation because they once marked a property line. They have served thus as legal witnesses, but also, in my mind, as witnesses to change in the landscape, wildlife, and human populations over the long years. Their size and beneficent presence can make a person feel the weight of history and the significance of any living thing that has survived centuries of storms and trials, especially anything that has been spared the ax. Whatever damage these trees have witnessed or sustained, they also tell a story of restraint.

Recently, on a work-related trip to Vietnam, Alan and I saw witness trees of another kind — coconut palms growing outside a memorial museum at My Lai, where on March 16, 1968, American GIs slaughtered more than five hundred South Vietnamese villagers, including grandparents, mothers, children, and babies. The soldiers had been told that Viet Cong rebels — guerrilla fighters living in the south but siding with the North Vietnamese Communists — were hiding in the area. They had been warned that the villagers might be Viet Cong sympathizers. Even the women and children could not be trusted, and so the GIs were ordered to kill anything that moved. As it happened, no one returned a single shot fired by the Americans. Only the innocent were killed. The coconut palms remain today, riddled with neat rows of bullet holes, mute witnesses to a story of mayhem.

In my lifetime so far, mayhem seems to have grown steadily more common and more murderous, and it seems always to arise from a quest for supremacy, wealth, or control. Those who succeed remarkably in this quest overmatch the rest of us. We greatly outnumber them, and yet we often feel helpless to assert our own hopes and desires. It is difficult to believe that a single vote or voice makes any difference at all when deep pockets can buy elections, when many who hold power reward only the powerful, and when the gap between rich and poor — whether people or nations — is now so broad that neither side can see the other.

Although a courageous few in politics, education, and other public arenas keep struggling to clear an uphill path, they face enormous resistance. There is so *much* evidence, everywhere, that the ancient sea of human knowledge and wisdom goes largely unfathomed. It seems to keep afloat mainly the privileged and powerful, who are generally concerned only with their own buoyancy upon its surface. There is in high places a terrifying lack of depth. There is in our popular culture a tragic dearth of the values and hunger that the arts and humanities once instilled. Where is our love of knowledge, our celebration of beauty, our search for wisdom, or our gradual, artful weaving together of a code by which to live?

We are in a great darkness, and the only way out is through the light in each of us. This is no easy path. Embarking on it can feel foolish; it can open a person to accusations of naïveté or stupidity. And yet each of us ordinary persons has more influence than we think. Each of us has an important story, a long, intensely personal account of ourselves that we compile gradually with our every act and word. Our stories become witness trees. We grow them, and then they outlive us, sometimes by centuries. For as long as they survive, they are our testimonies. They will flow through the minds of generations we will never know, just as our genes will flow through the blood of our most distant descendants. Even our smallest word or gesture can reach people still unborn when we die.

We live with eons before us and eons yet to come. We are sequels to what has gone before, prologues to what follows us, and either the careful authors of our lives or blind players, improvising. Everything—literally everything in the world—rests on whether we choose mindful reflection or a life of reaction. Each has power. What we pass on, someone else will carry on.

Having learned something about this through my experiences, I try now to explore the depths in difficulties and misunderstandings, to understand where and why the light in me or someone else has dimmed.

I have always been helped in this struggle by other people whose words or examples tune my jarring notes. Whatever care I now exercise in my life, I have first seen others practice. I have learned restraint and deliberation from friends, family members, artists, writers, strangers, and even a few public figures. I once asked a woman I admire how she had managed to overcome a devastating betrayal with grace and generosity. She said, "I decided what kind of person I wanted to be. And I just kept trying to act the way that person would act."

In similar efforts to craft my own character, I gain patience and courage from this woman's story and many others. I try to remember that it will take my entire lifetime to grow into myself and a longer time than that for my influence to play out. I think often about John Woolman, the colonial Quaker who spent most of his life speaking out against slavery when slavery was a cornerstone of his new country's economy. He never saw the cracks he made in the cornerstone, and he died a century before slavery was ever outlawed, but he never quit. He saw a grievous wrong, and he pointed it out again and again *because* it was wrong.

Woolman speaks to me across the centuries since his death. He is in my heart and soul, and he affects the way I live my life. His story is now as old as many witness trees in the nearby woods, and it is still strong, not because he reached a particular goal but because he worked on behalf of the light in every person and trusted that light to prevail.

Not one of us will live long enough to see a fraction of the difference we make, but it is essential that we pursue our ideals anyway. Many of the first Quakers never saw freedom of religion come to England. Most of the original suffragists never got to vote. The murdered civil rights workers did not get to see racial tensions ease. Few idealists live long enough to see their dreams made real, and yet their influence lives after them, and their dreams do, sometimes, come true for others. Idealism at its best is not naïve but deliberately and knowingly innocent, despite the odds and evidence against it, despite the pressures of cynicism and expedience. It is forever having to renew its innocence. Woolman knew this and struggled with it every day of his life, yet he drew the deepest kind of joy from his effort, the kind of joy that announces the presence of God.

Writing this book has drawn my attention to important passages in the story of my life. It has taught me the power that lies in composing oneself — that is, in stopping, thinking, and consulting the light that lies beneath easy assumptions or quick reactions. That power reflects God's creativity and love and makes it possible to hope. Without high and joyous ideals, without the connection they give us to the immense ground of our being, we are not only powerless but bereft. Upheld by ideals, we can shape our lives into testimonies that shed light now and for long years to come.

Acknowledgments

Among the many people whose love and generosity have helped this book into being, I especially thank Steve Maloy, Rita Maloy, Ann Tracy, Rebecca Sheppard, Patricia Stanton, Shari Kubitz, Victoria Tepe, Evelyn MacKay, Edie and Sam Cattle, Carl Williams, Kitty Bammer, Preston Covey, Juana Olga Barrios, Rosemary Holland, and Jean Melusky.

I am indebted as well to the people of Counterpoint Press who have honed and helped my work: Jack Shoemaker for believing in books like this one; Jane Vandenburgh for gracious and savvy editorial counsel; Kate Scott for meticulous copyediting; David Bullen for elegant design; and everyone else at Counterpoint, including Trish Hoard, Keltie Hawkins, John McLeod, and Heather McLeod, for exemplary work and unwavering support.

Most of all, day in and day out, I am grateful to my husband, Alan, and my son, Adam, for gifts beyond telling. I am grateful as well for the joyous life that the three of us embarked upon in 1998. That life changed on September 11, 2001, along with lives throughout the world, and yet the truths that emerged as I wrote this book have remained constant for me. In their light I can see no enemies. I can seek no violent return for the violence that has sown such pain. I can only pray for peace upon us all and the courage to live my faith and keep rejoicing.